SOCIAL INSTITUTIONS
AND ECONOMIC
PERFORMANCE

SOCIAL INSTITUTIONS AND ECONOMIC PERFORMANCE

Studies of Industrial Relations in Advanced Capitalist Economies

Wolfgang Streeck

SAGE Publications
London • Newbury Park • New Delhi

SAGE Publications Ltd
6 Bonhill Street
London EC2A 4PU

SAGE Publications Inc
2455 Teller Road
Newbury Park, California 91320

SAGE Publications India Pvt Ltd
32, M-Block Market
Greater Kailash – I
New Delhi 110 048

British Library Cataloguing in Publication data

Streeck, Wolfgang
  Social Institutions and Economic
  Performance: Industrial Relations in
  Advanced Capitalist Economies
  I. Title
  331

  ISBN 0–8039–8475–8
  ISBN 0–8039–8775–7 (pbk)

Library of Congress catalog card number 92–050449

Typeset by Photoprint, Torquay, Devon
Printed in Great Britain by Biddles Ltd, Guildford, Surrey

Contents

Preface

The essays assembled in this volume were written between 1982 and 1989 and were published in widely dispersed places. Originating from a variety of research contexts, their common concern is with the political organization and representation of economic interests, of both labor and capital; with the social institutions that regulate the articulation of such interests; and with the effects of these institutions on the performance of advanced capitalist economies.

The general ideas that, I believe, connect the papers included in this book are developed in detail in Chapter 1. While frequently setting out from industrial relations, the book places these in the broader context of a society's social and economic institutions, its polity as well as its economy – thus treating industrial relations as one subject among others of an institutionalist sociology of advanced capitalism. In doing so, the essays in the book take institutional variations between advanced capitalist countries seriously, in particular by relating differences between systems of interest articulation and intermediation to differential economic performance. Unlike in the distributional politics and demand management perspective of much of the 'corporatist debate' of the 1970s, however, the practically most important and theoretically most intriguing effects of institutional arrangements on performance are sought on the 'supply side', that is, in the sphere of production defined in the widest sense.

Ultimately, the essays in this book should be regarded as related attempts to move towards *an institutional theory of the supply side of advanced capitalist economies* that refuses to abide by the self-imposed limitations of neo-liberalism and its theoretically more elevated academic cousin, 'rational choice'. To the extent that such an effort can be successful, it may provide a powerful rationale for positive political intervention in post-socialist capitalist market economies. A non-liberal politics of the supply-side may be based on the insight that markets and rational economic action are embedded in – 'cultural' or 'political', but clearly *not themselves market-generated* – institutional opportunities and constraints, some of which happen to be more conducive to economic performance under given technological and market conditions than others. An approach like this may overcome a view of social institutions, political intervention or, for that matter, industrial relations that conceives of these as no more than exogenous additions to an otherwise autarkic economy – or, more precisely, market economy – from which they are usually regarded as extracting an efficiency price. The alternative, suggested by this book, is to consider social institutions as inherently present in and preceding economic action, and as conditional for it – with conditions and consequences related to each other according to a social and political logic that would typically appear counter-intuitive or paradoxical from a 'pure' economic perspective.

Most of the chapters in this book draw, in one form or other, on material from Germany. For a while I thought that my tendency to rely so heavily on German examples was an unfortunate but, alas, inevitable consequence of having grown up in that country. It was only after I had moved to the United States that I began to see how important a sound comparative understanding of the peculiarities of the German political economy is, not just for the study of Germany, but for any general, and especially institutionalist, theory of modern capitalism. Very much like Japan, the exact reasons for Germany's astonishing economic performance (as reflected, for example, in Chapter 6) are far from clear – and indeed seem to be especially inaccessible to two groups in particular: academic economists and national 'insiders'. The reason, I believe, is that the German just as the Japanese economy is supported and governed by strong social institutions of a non-market character that are both too alien and too exotic for the neo-classical paradigm, and too familiar, trivial and self-evident to those who have grown up with them, to be deemed worthy of systematic study and to be able to inspire theoretical generalizations.[1]

With respect to Germany, this holds for an institution as vastly under-researched as co-determination as much as for a phenomenon as bizarre and, at the same time, instructive as the artisanal (*Handwerk*) sector. As I discovered during the research for the paper included in this book as Chapter 5, there is no postwar German literature on *Handwerk* that would be only nearly aware of its enormous comparative significance, or of its far-reaching implications for economic theory and policy. As a result, given the vast and arcane complexities of the subject, there is not much non-German literature either. The same applies, by and large, to the German vocational training or financial systems. While Japan has moved to the center of worldwide attention, the German case, remarkably enough, has – with a few notable exceptions – remained the domain of country specialists with often little interest in comparative political economy. After unification, that may now come to an end. I maintain that without a full appreciation of the German variant of advanced capitalism, the discourse of political economy will not escape from its present dilemma between the 'fake universalism' of neo-classical economics and the particularistic culturalism of popular Japanology. I have therefore convinced myself that there is nothing wrong with German examples, and indeed have selected Chapters 4, 5 and 6 consciously for elaboration and illustration of general claims made especially in Chapter 1.

The research on Germany that informs the essays in this volume was completed well before 1989, the year of unification. This is bound to raise the question of its continued validity. Fortunately for me, it appears that unification has by and large merely extended the West German institutional system to the rest of the country, without changing it in the process. This applies to co-determination, collective bargaining, industrial unions, employers' associations and chambers, as well as to *Handwerk*, *Hausbanken*, and the 'social market economy' in general. In editing the papers included in this volume, therefore, all I have done to take account of unification was to change, 'West German' to 'German' where reference was made to lasting features of German institutional arrangements. Unless I have overlooked or misjudged individual passages, the geographic modifier is now present only where the text refers to historical events or structures that took place or existed exclusively between the end of the Second World War and 1989 in the Western part of the now united country.

All papers that went into this volume, with the exception of Chapter 7, were edited for the occasion, some more and some less. In part, this was for reasons of space and to eliminate overlap. But I have also freely cut passages with which I felt no longer comfortable – be it that with better information, they now appeared factually incorrect or imprecise; or that I had come to dislike the concepts I had used, or the assumptions I had tacitly made; or that I found myself embarrassed by predictions or speculations that had simply turned out to be wrong. While I did not have the time to update my research, I believe that no sensible purpose would have been served by documenting for the reader the progress of my education. So, conveniently, I allowed myself to exorcize my errors and misjudgments from the record wherever I could do so without jeopardizing the general point I was trying to make.

In writing the essays that now compose this book, I have been inspired and encouraged by a number of colleagues who over the years became close personal friends. Philippe Schmitter, with whom I have collaborated since 1978, is co-author of Chapter 7 and might well have co-authored Chapters 3 and 4 also. With Claus Offe, who had been one of my professors at Frankfurt as far back as 1969, I have continued to debate for, by now, more than two decades; he read most of the included papers at an early stage, often commented on them in detail, and has been urging me for some time to publish a selection of them as a book. Chapter 2, incidentally, was in its original form my *Habilitation* lecture at the University of Bielefeld, where he chaired my committee – controversies like the one documented in Chapter 3 notwithstanding.

Fritz Scharpf, of course, was the director of the labor market research unit at the Wissenschaftszentrum Berlin where I spent almost 12 years doing the research on co-determination and the automobile industry that resulted, among other things, in Chapters 5 and 6. Occupying the office next to mine at that time was Arndt Sorge, whose work in industrial sociology and on the sociology of *Technik* I have always admired and so deeply absorbed that I sometimes forgot that it was his. Chapter 5 I wrote at his instigation for a volume on industrial democracy that he co-edited. Similarly, Chapter 1 was written when I was a visitor at the Wissenschafts-zentrum in the summer of 1989, invited by Egon Matzner who, at the end of his tenure as Fritz Scharpf's successor, had asked me to prepare a paper for a conference summarizing the unit's work. And Chapter 3 was a contribution to a conference organized to honor the 60th birthday of Gerhard Lehmbruch – who, in a then unpublished paper that I came across in early 1977, had first introduced me to the concept of 'liberal corporatism'.

There are innumerable others who, willingly or not, have con-tributed to this book. With some of them I worked closely together at Madison in the last four years. A jointly taught course with Leon Lindberg on 'The Political Economy of 1992' introduced me to the theory of regional integration; much of what I learned then entered into Chapter 7. Rogers Hollingsworth's shared interest in the themes of Chapter 1 has resulted in a research project we organized jointly with Philippe Schmitter, and in a collection of essays, *Comparing Capitalist Economies: Variations in the Governance of Sectors*, due to come out in 1992. Throughout, Joel Rogers' profound inability to suspend his sharp critical judgment when matters as serious as the quality of an argument are at stake has kept me on my toes and made me revise sentences and paragraphs even more often than I would have on my own. Whether this was to any avail is of course a different question, and the usual disclaimers apply as always.

Wolfgang Streeck

Note

1. Among other things, this situation is reflected, again in Japan just as in Germany, in the desperate efforts of local economists to show their American teachers and colleagues that they have dutifully learned to press events and institutions in their respective countries into neo-classical terms, cost what it may.

Bibliographical Notes

Chapter 1: first published in Egon Matzner and Wolfgang Streeck (eds), 1991: *Beyond Keynesianism: the Socio-economics of Production and Employment*. London: Edward Elgar. pp. 21–61. Slightly revised.

Chapter 2: first published as 'Status and Contract as Basic Categories of a Sociological Theory of Industrial Relations', in David Sugarman and Gunther Teubner (eds), 1990: *Regulating Corporate Groups in Europe*. Baden-Baden: Nomos. pp. 105–45. German version: 'Status und Kontrakt als Grundkategorien einer Theorie der industriellen Beziehungen'. Habilitationsvertrag vor der Fakultät für Soziologie der Universität Bielefeld. *Discussion Paper* SP–LMP 1988, Wissenschaftszentrum Berlin. Slightly revised.

Chapter 3: contribution to a Conference on 'Political Institutions and Interest Intermediation', organized by the University of Konstanz on the occasion of Gerhard Lehmbruch's 60th Birthday, 20–1 April 1988. First published in Roland Czada and Adrienne Windhoff-Heretier (eds), 1991: *Political Choice: Institutions, Rules, and the Limits of Rationality*. Frankfurt am Main: Campus, Boulder, Col.: Westview Press. pp. 161–98. Italian translation in *Stato e mercato* 31 (1990): 7–45. Slightly revised.

Chapter 4: first published as 'The Territorial Organization of Interests and the Logics of Associative Action: the Case of Handwerk Organization in West Germany', in William D. Coleman and Henry J. Jacek (eds), 1989: *Regionalism, Business Interests and Public Policy*. London: Sage. pp. 59–94. Spanish translation ('La organizacion territorial de intereses y la logica de la accion asociativa') in Carlota Sole (ed.), 1987: *Corporatismo y diferenciacion regional*. Madrid: Ministero de Trabajo y Seguridad Social. pp. 71–114. Shortened.

Chapter 5: first published in Bernhard Wilpert and Arndt Sorge. (eds), *International Perspectives on Organizational Democracy*. International Yearbook of Organizational Democracy, Vol. II. London: John Wiley & Sons, 1984. pp. 391–422. Slightly revised.

Chapter 6: first published as 'Successful Adjustment to Turbulent Markets: the Automobile Industry', in Peter J. Katzenstein. (ed.),

1989: *Industry and Politics in West Germany: towards the Third Republic*. Ithaca, New York and London: Cornell University Press. pp. 113–56. Shortened and revised.

Chapter 7 (co-authored with Philippe C. Schmitter): paper presented at a conference of the Joint Committee on Political Sociology of the International Sociological Association and the International Political Science Association, on 'The New Europe(s)', Mannheim, 21–23 February 1991. An earlier version, under the same title, was published in *Politics and Society*, 19(2) (1991): 133–64.

1

Productive Constraints: on the Institutional Conditions of Diversified Quality Production

Little attention is paid in the Keynesian theory of full employment to the operation of the *supply side* of the economy and to the social and political *institutions* required for its efficient performance. For Keynes, the mechanisms by which supply was to respond to managed demand, and the process of demand management itself and how it was to be protected from interference by macro-irrational, particularistic political interests were not seen as problematic. It was only in the revisionist literature of the late 1970s, after the eclipse of Keynesian politics, that writers like Skidelsky (1979) pointed to the remarkably orthodox assumptions and requirements underlying Keynesian theory and practice: in particular, those of a 'free' and 'flexible' product and labor market as a necessary precondition of efficient micro-adjustment on the supply side; as well as of state institutions sufficiently shielded from popular pressure to be capable of making technocratic decisions solely on the merits of complex econometric analyses. If the blanks in the Keynesian discourse are taken, as they should be, as indicating agreement with the institutions and orthodoxies of the time, the conclusion appears justified that, for Keynes, the *size of aggregate demand* was to be determined by central bank and treasury technocrats while the *structure of supply* was to be left to the two, as it were, *minimal institutions* of standard economics: *competitive markets* and *managerial hierarchies*.

It seems that it was not least the political and economic traditionalism of its implicit assumptions that rendered Keynesianism so defenseless against the onslaught of supply-side economics in the 1980s. The discovery in the postwar period that the very practice of demand management had changed the 'rational expectations' of market participants and thereby 'distorted' the market (Brittan, 1978); that furthermore the 'flexibility' of markets, particularly for labor, had progressively declined due to institutional growth 'beyond contract' (Fox, 1974); and that macro-managerial decisions had become subject to and entangled in democratic electoral politics – inevitably shook the foundations of a theory of full employment that was for its practice dependent on both classical market economics and traditional codes of political authority and deference. Keynesians, in spite of their 'Keynes-plus' rhetoric, found it hard to object to the call of the new 'supply-siders' for a speedy restoration of state sovereignty, market flexibility and management prerogative. While they had placed their hopes on a different use of sovereignty, they had nothing to hold against their opponents' insistence that in a capitalist society state authority had to be protected from popular-democratic dilution. They also, and more importantly, could not but accept the standard economic wisdom that only if firms are left alone by governments, and managements by their workforces, will they end up in the market segments, produce the range of products, adopt the production technology, develop the organization of work, generate the skills and pay the *wages* that will allow for full employment. Seen from the perspective of the late 1970s, the debate between Keynesianism and supply-side economics never went beyond the question of whether or not it was necessary, useful or possible for the national state in addition to provide for an adequate level of aggregate demand. To the extent that this, for all kinds of contingent reasons, had to be answered more and more in the negative, mainstream Keynesians had little with which to oppose the increasingly self-confident demands of their neo-classical opponents for deregulation of product and labor markets and for a return to the institutional minimalism of market and hierarchy.

Deviating from the Keynesian as well as the neo-classical tradition, in the 1980s a number of social scientists and political economists began to develop a social-institutional perspective on the supply side of modern industrial economies. Just as in neo-classical supply-side economics, they emphasized the importance for full employment of the international competitiveness of a country's pattern of industrial output and industrial organization. They also agreed with the, mostly implicit, claim of both economic camps that such patterns are importantly shaped by the social institutions within which economic action takes place. At the same time, they sharply rejected as simplistic and functionalist two fundamental assumptions that are explicitly or implicitly made by most economists of whatever denomination: that there is, at least in the long run, only one path towards competitive survival – one homogeneous 'best practice' without functional alternatives or equivalents, inside which national or regional differences are essentially insignificant – and that patterns of industrial output and industrial organization ('production patterns', as we will call them from now on) are the more efficient, and therefore the more likely to bring about full employment, the closer the institutions that govern them resemble the neo-classical minimum of unregulated markets and unlimited managerial prerogative, complemented at most by a liberal (in the, European, sense of non-interventionist) and, in questions of property rights, non-majoritarian democratic state. While taking a firm supply-side view of the employment problem and its possible solution, contributors to the emerging new approach shared an unwillingness to accept a conceptual framework under which the only constructive contribution of politics to full employment would appear to be the dismantling of whatever socio-economic institutions exceeded the neo-classical minimum; one that relegates politics to the demand side where its residual function is to extract an equity price from an inherently efficient market economy in exchange for social stability; and that is guided by the pre-conception that a return to full employment requires above all unregulated markets and unlimited private hierarchies.

Central to the new political economy of the 1980s, then, was an attempt systematically to understand what could be called, with a recently fashionable expression, the *social dimension* of the supply side. In various contexts and through alternative approaches, it tried to support claims like the following:

1 that different institutional conditions may give rise to different production patterns that may represent functionally alternative, and sometimes functionally equivalent, responses to common economic challenges;

2 that to the extent that alternative responses are not equivalent in competitive terms, institutionally impoverished economies that rely solely on markets and hierarchies for the governance of economic activities do not necessarily perform better than societies where economic behavior is more socially regulated;

3 that quite to the contrary a repertory of social institutions that exceeds the neo-classical minimum may in specific conditions make a positive contribution to competitive market performance;

4 that in particular certain highly successful production patterns require for their emergence and survival strong non-market institutions that modify and partly suspend individual market rationality and unilateral managerial control and thereby make for higher efficiency;

5 that therefore public and private choices between high wages, stable employment, worker participation and social equity on the one hand, and full employment, monetary stability, competitiveness and efficiency on the other are not nearly as simple as

suggested by standard economics in general and the supply-side economics of the 1980s in particular;

6   and that, given the right kind of institutional regulation and political intervention, an institutionally saturated and politically bargained pattern of production and employment may be possible which may be highly competitive in an open world economy.

This chapter is on the institutional preconditions of an advanced neo-industrial production pattern referred to as *diversified quality production*. Drawing on both empirical research and theoretical reasoning, it tries to specify a set of functional requirements that firms, and the economies in which they operate, have to meet in order for diversified quality production to thrive. The chapter identifies three such requirements: a *congenial organizational ecology*, the presence of *redundant capacities*, and a rich supply of *collective production inputs*. It also tries to show that the functional requirements of diversified quality production can be met only to the extent that the economy in which production takes place *is at the same time a society* – that is, is supported by an institutional substructure that exceeds minimalist prescriptions of standard economics.[1] In essence, the chapter tries to show that societies that want to make use of the opportunities offered by advanced forms of demand need to develop and cultivate a rich institutional structure capable of imposing enforceable social constraints on rational market participants, as well as offering them effective opportunities to restructure towards higher product diversity and quality.

Diversified Quality Production

Beginning in the late 1970s, researchers in many countries were engaged in an attempt to understand the social origins and conditions of emerging 'neo-industrial' (Hirschhorn, 1984) production patterns. These had in common that they seemed to be able to attain superior competitiveness in world markets through sophisticated application of information technology, a diversified product range and non-price-competitive marketing strategies, combining all these with high wages, skilled labor and a flexible, non-Taylorist organization of work. Due to different research experiences, points of access and initial theoretical orientations, the new supply-side institutionalism developed along different trajectories, emanating in partly divergent and partly supplementary lines of work like the 'flexible specialization' tradition (Piore and Sabel, 1984), the 'new production concepts' approach (Kern and Schumann, 1984), and others. The present chapter is informed by the concept of 'diversified quality production' (Sorge and Streeck, 1988) which was proposed in an attempt to reconstruct the property space of the neo-industrialism debate so as to relate it more closely both to certain comparative empirical observations and to possibilities for political intervention.

The immediate origin of the concept of diversified quality production was in the analysis of alternative 'manufacturing policies' (Willman, 1986) associated with the absorption of new, micro-electronic production technology. Three variables were found to be of importance (Sorge and Streeck, 1988): the degree to which products were standardized; the type of competition they tried to meet; and the volume of output. The first two factors appeared to be closely related in that standardized products are generally sold in price-competitive markets whereas customized products tend to be quality-competitive. This suggested a distinction between *standardized price-competitive* and *customized quality-competitive* production on the one hand, and *low-* and *high-volume* production on the other. Crossing the two dimensions generated four alternative products, or manufacturing, strategies, two of which – the *low-volume production of customized quality-competitive goods* ('craft' production) and the *high-volume production of standardized price-competitive goods* ('Fordist' production) – were quite conventional. Indeed, with some simplification one could say that before the advent of micro-electronic technology these would have been the only production patterns possible.

This comparatively simple picture was found to have become considerably more complicated as a result of technical change. For instance, new technology seemed to have lowered the break-even point of mass production, both enabling traditional mass producers to survive with shorter production runs and, perhaps, making it easier for artisanal low-volume producers to achieve economies of scale and enter mass-type markets. At the same time, the capacity of new technology for fast and inexpensive retooling seemed to have made it attractive for small component producers dependent on large assemblers to differentiate their product range and move into an advanced form of craft production, so as to reduce their exposure to price fluctuation and monopsonistic demand.

The most important impact of new technology on manufacturing strategy, however, seemed to be that it created a new option for firms in the form of high-volume production of customized quality-competitive goods. In many manufacturing sectors, micro-electronic circuitry eroded the traditional distinction between mass and specialist production. The high flexibility of micro-electronic equipment and the ease and speed with which it can be reprogrammed enabled firms to introduce a hitherto unknown degree of product variety, as well as product quality. The result was a restructuring of mass production in the mould of customized quality production, with central features of the latter being blended into the former and with small batch production of highly specific goods becoming enveloped in large batch production of basic components or models. This pattern was what came to be called 'diversified quality production'. It can be approached by firms through two different paths of industrial restructuring: by craft producers extending their production volume without sacrificing their high quality standards and customized product design, or by mass producers moving upmarket by upgrading their products' design and quality and by increasing their product variety, in an attempt to escape from the pressures of price competition or from shrinking mass markets.

Two empirical observations in particular made diversified quality production interesting. One was that its presence and absence seemed to covary with certain national and regional differences in economic performance and competitiveness which standard economics appeared unable to account for (Sorge and Warner, 1986). The leading case was the West German economy in the 1973 crisis and after, and inside Germany regions such as Baden-Württemberg where the highest average wages and the lowest level of unemployment in West Germany resulted from an export performance that included a positive trade balance even with Japan (Maier, 1987). Here, superior competitiveness coincided with a pattern of production, in part of long historical standing, at the core of which were customization of products, differentiation of product ranges and high product quality providing shelter from price competition. Restructuring towards this pattern seemed to offer a promising strategy for other regions in Germany – and, by extension, for old industrial, high wage economies in general – that were at the time striving to protect their employment in the face of more volatile and crowded world markets.

Another point that stood out was that Germany in general and Baden-Württemberg in particular are institutionally rich societies where markets are deeply embedded in an array of cooperative, redistributive and regulatory institutions (Sabel et al., 1987). Detailed analyses in various studies gave rise to considerable doubts whether the performance of economies of this kind could, as standard economists would have predicted, be further enhanced by changes towards the institutional minimalism of neo-classical theory.[2] Quite to the contrary, there were numerous indications of a peculiar, complex interaction between diversified quality production and thick institutional structures, with the latter simultaneously being sustained by and sustaining the former. In particular, not only was diversified quality production not obstructed by social institutions, but there was reason to believe that markets and managements on their own would be unlikely and frequently unable to generate that pattern, and that if firms were reduced to their own devices the production pattern and the prosperity it had wrought would be at risk. This, at least, became one of the guiding hypotheses of much of the research on the institutional conditions for the supply of diversified quality production.

The concept of diversified quality production is just one in a number of attempts to make sense of profound transformations in the 1970s and 1980s in the structure and functioning of developed industrial economies. The fact that it took off from comparative studies of political economies like West Germany and, to some extent, Sweden seems to have entailed certain advantages for the understanding of neo-industrial production in general. Work on diversified quality production has always kept its distance from theories of industrial change that rotate around concepts like 'high technology', 'knowledge-based' (Hirschhorn, 1984) or 'post-industrial' (Jaikumar, 1986) manufacturing. While these no doubt point to important properties of neo-industrial production, the conceptual emphasis on product diversity and quality, by comparison, directs attention towards the shopfloor and the institutions and organizational forms that regulate and sustain complex manufacturing work. In this sense, the concept of diversified quality production involves the program of an empirically grounded sociological production theory. It is conceivable that the dominant concern in the study of diversified quality production with the 'low politics' of comparatively glamourless everyday institutions like industrial training systems and industrial relations, and with 'manual' work rather than university-trained engineers, represents a German bias, and indeed this preoccupation is shared by authors like Kern and Schumann (1984). But one might also argue that a production-oriented perspective has the advantage that it draws attention to important institutional conditions of successful quality-competitive performance whose discovery may be obstructed by excessive fascination with 'high technology'.

Differences and similarities between the various approaches to the study of neo-industrial production patterns result partly from different roads of empirical access and partly from different prejudices. Especially important for the analysis of diversified quality production was the rich and influential literature on 'flexible specialization' (Piore and Sabel, 1984). Among other things, research efforts on diversified quality production and on flexible specialization have in common that they are ultimately politically motivated, in that their guiding interest is in the potential of advanced industrial production systems to underwrite an egalitarian society at a high level of welfare, with political democracy rooted in autonomy and participation at the workplace. They also attempt to transcend a merely redistributive definition of politics and political institutions in relation to the economy, trying to leave behind the traditional disjunction between economics looking after efficiency, and political or sociological analysis studying equity. Moreover, both are strongly and even primarily interested in the institutional underpinnings of neo-industrialism, and thus share the broad methodological program of an institutionalist political economy.

But there are also differences that have persistently stood in the way of merging the two concepts or simply taking over the more popular one. To the extent that 'diversified quality production' was set polemically against 'flexible specialization', this was primarily for the following reasons:

First, while Piore and Sabel (1984) locate their 'industrial divide' primarily in time – defining it in terms of a break in the historical continuity of industrial society in general – the study of diversified quality production placed its emphasis on synchronic differences between social systems, national and regional societies in particular. It is true that the 'flexible specialization' tradition recognizes national, or spatial, variation in the degree to which 'Fordism' was historically able to supersede craft production. In the same way, the concept of 'diversified quality production' is compatible with the notion that due to evolutionary changes in the structure of demand, producers of customized quality-competitive products today have even better market chances than they had in the past. Still, the differences in emphasis are important. Obviously they go back to the fact that diversified quality production was 'discovered' in cross-national comparisons, in particular between societies like Germany on the one hand and the United Kingdom or France on the other where the differences in production patterns are of long historical standing.[3]

Secondly, the 'flexible specialization' concept is colored by the study of Italian small-firm communities from an American perspective, whereas 'diversified quality production', as indicated, derives much of its inspiration from the German experience. For the latter, the existence of highly competitive, highly flexible, and highly skilled and technologically sophisticated small firms, which is Piore and Sabel's formative empirical anomaly, is not surprising at all (and indeed is, unfortunately, all too often taken for granted). Thus, work on diversified quality production emphasized the extraordinary potential, compared to other countries, of large firms in Germany for customized, quality-competitive production (without always pointing out how much this is historically and economically owed to the, legally protected, presence of a large number of small artisanal firms). While Piore and Sabel do report 'flexible specialization' in large German companies, they present this more or less as an odd exception, and the observation is neither explained nor systematically theorized – the paradigm case of a 'flexibly specialized' economy remaining the Italian industrial district.[4] By comparison, the concept of diversified quality production decidedly refers not to a specific organization of the production process – for example, flexible recombination of independent small firms or 'mass production' in large factories – but only and exclusively to a type of product, leaving deliberately open for empirical analysis in what kind of industrial organization it is produced.

Thirdly, having grown out of the 'hard' German rather than the 'soft' Italian experience, the concept of diversified quality production has always kept its distance from the communitarian voluntarism that informs the more speculative chapters of Piore and Sabel's book. Diversified quality production is not a new type of society but a – in principle rather old – type of industrial output that today has come to be related to a particular kind of technology use. Unlike Piore and Sabel, who see flexible specialization giving rise to a high-technology version of Jeffersonian 'yeoman democracy', analysis of neo-industrial production patterns under the concept of diversified quality production does not entail utopian expectations of a dissolution of large organizations in horizontal market relations between solidaristic free traders. Diversified quality production, as it exists in the real world, clearly does not require the disappearance of corporate hierarchies, although it may demand their containment and counterbalancing through institutions like, for example, co-determination.

Finally, following from this, the most important difference between the two concepts may be that unlike flexible specialization which often appears to be based primarily in communitarian–cultural–contractual–voluntary bonds, in the generation and operation of diversified quality production organized social conflict and hard and formal institutions like trade unions, employers' associations, the law and the national state continue to play a constitutive part. As will be pointed out below, diversified quality production has been found to thrive on the presence of competing and even incompatible perspectives and interests that may need to be accommodated through overt social conflict. In particular, it requires that the rational-individual pursuit of economic advantage be embedded in, and constrained by, institutionally enacted and enforced social obligations, on the assumption that the free, 'rational' decisions of individuals and organizations are by themselves insufficient for moving an economy-cum-society towards diversified quality production. The implied claim, of course, is that the 'softer', cultural mechanisms on which Piore and Sabel (1984) essentially rely to contain competition and enforce obligations in their industrial districts, will in reality not be able to perform that function, or will at least in the long run fail to ensure the reproduction of advanced neo-industrialism.[5]

The present chapter makes the assertion that today's growing markets for diversified quality products can only imperfectly be served by an economy that is not also a society, that is, one which is not in a particular way regulated and supported by thick, non-economic social institutions. It also argues that among the possible institutional arrangements on the supply side that may sustain diversified quality production are some that are highly compatible with traditional social-democratic objectives like high wages, a low wage spread, workplace participation and full employment. To make its case, the chapter uses examples from different traditions of research on advanced industrialism, in an attempt to draw out, in an ideal-typical way, the institutional implications of a number of functional requirements for quality-competitive and customized production. In doing so, the chapter uses the concept of diversified quality production generically to denote the full range of neo-industrial production patterns – as defined by their attempt to attain competitiveness through product diversity and quality – rather than just a large-firm version of 'flexible specialization' or a set of certain German idiosyncrasies.[6]

Market and Hierarchy Failure

The central claim of this chapter is that a regime of free markets and private hierarchies is not enough to generate and support a pattern of diversified quality production, a favorable product demand environment notwithstanding. This is not to say that individual firms may not come to be diversified quality producers even in institutionally impoverished settings. However, it is argued that they will remain islands ('of excellence') in a sea of more traditional production and lower production competence, and their performance will likely be less good and less stable than if they were part of a general pattern. By implication, in a neo-classical institutional environment part of the existing demand for diversified quality products will remain unsatisfied due to a sluggish supply-side response, and employment opportunities offered by the evolution of product markets and demand structures will remain unexploited.

Diversified quality production is more than an individual firm's commercial strategy. It is conditional on an industrial order (Herrigel, forthcoming), or a social structure, that can only partly, provisionally and precariously exist on a voluntaristic-contractual basis. Where it is fully developed, it is the outcome of a collective, 'cultural' choice (usually long-term, gradual, incremental in character) mediated by and crystallized in a set of social institutions. This is because, as we will argue in the present section, diversified quality producers thrive in an organizational ecology, or community, where other firms engage in the same kind of production; they require investment in redundant capacities that are difficult to build as a matter of interest, and more likely to be created as a matter of obligation; and they depend on factor inputs that, if optimally provided, have significant collective goods properties.[7] Rational individualism of competing firms and unilateral managements is not an ideal decision-making mode for the creation of community, the generation of excess capacity, and the provision and repletion of collective production factors. Unlike the Fordist 'cathedrals in the desert' (Lipietz, 1980), firms in diversified quality production are neither self-sufficient nor can they in their own interest hope to become so; in fact, they perform best, that is, serve their markets most successfully, if, rather than relying on their 'private' organizational endoskeleton, they build on, submit to and invest in a common, 'public' institutional exoskeleton to guide their decisions and facilitate their activities.

An important implication, again distilled from empirical research, is that neither technological change nor the evolution of product markets are by themselves sufficient to move industries into a diversified quality production mode, even if alternative production strategies are economically clearly less attractive. In this respect, the concept of diversified quality production takes on board the expanding literature in management science and organizational analysis on strategic choice, drawing on a realistic image of the firm as revealed by empirical research (such as in, for example, Child, 1988). Far from determining firms' behavior, technical and economic change are seen as having increased the range of, as well as the burden on, 'rational' managerial choices. While new technology and new demand structures create opportunities for firms, regions and national economies for blending specialist into mass production, they do not necessarily provide the rational motivations, irrational predispositions, technical capacities, and economic factor endowments required for this. Indeed, micro-electronic technology has been found to improve firms' survival chances in quite different types of production and product markets, price- as well as quality-competitive. Similarly, while product strategies respond to the market, they are not determined by it. Firms have always had a degree of choice with regard to their own performance standards, and have differed among other things along organizational, sectoral and national lines with respect to the time they are willing and able to wait for investment to become profitable. Moreover, market signals are never conclusive – partly because active marketing may be able to change them, partly because there are always different markets and market segments to select from, and partly because even the best marketing department cannot safely predict where future profits will be found, especially given today's wider range of economic options complementing an increased menu of technical possibilities.

Secondly, for a firm to be able take up diversified quality production as its economically most efficient strategy, certain factor endowments may be required which firms on their own find hard to produce or procure since their provision depends on some form of coordinated collective action. Whether or not such public production factors can be generated may in turn depend on the presence of institutions that resolve prisoners' dilemma-type rationality conflicts between and within the firms involved. As has often been pointed out, individual choice may produce suboptimal results even from an individual perspective if there are no institutions that protect rational motives for cooperative behavior from rational expectations of defection. To the extent that diversified quality production requires collective factor inputs, institutionally unfettered market-rational behavior of the neo-classical type may stand in the way of a full use of product market opportunities for diversified quality production. A neo-classical institutional environment may thus prevent an economically optimal supply-side response to the evolution of demand even if the market opportunities on offer are correctly perceived.

Proceeding from literatures on regional economies (Sabel, 1989), industrial organization (Piore and Sabel, 1984), national differences in work organization and technology use (Sorge and Warner, 1986), and comparative industrial relations (Hotz, 1982; Streeck, 1987a), there seem to be at least three dimensions of market and hierarchy failure with respect to diversified quality production, giving rise to a need for an institutional exoskeleton for rational individual actors not to be constrained by the limits of rational individualism. Each dimension stands for a category of functional requirements for firms trying to increase, in response to new economic opportunities and technological possibilities, their productive flexibility[8] by blending craft into mass production.

1. The Requirement of a Congenial Organizational Ecology

Diversified quality producers seem to prosper in the presence of other, equally competent producers of the same kind. The problem here is one of creating and protecting a polycentric, decentralized pattern of industrial organization that would be unlikely to originate and persist if markets and hierarchies were allowed to operate without interference. Under a competitive market logic, the prosperity of one firm is based on the elimination of other, competing firms; under a hierarchical organization logic, it entails the inclusion of different levels of the production chain in one corporation and their subjection to centralized managerial control. Neither of these seem to be fully functional for diversified quality production where shorter (sub-) batches enveloped in long (sets of) batches, as well as higher quality standards, appear to put a premium on strategic alliances and joint ventures between firms at the same level of the product chain, and on close, privileged and trust-based cooperation between assemblers and suppliers at different levels. The reasons for this include high research and development costs due to more rapid product turnover and more specific product customization, making it difficult for individual firms to maintain sufficient R&D capacities inhouse; as well as higher quality standards and advanced logistical methods requiring suppliers to be both technically competent and closely tuned into the operation of their customers.

High product diversity and quality sometimes seem to go together with an attenuation of the distinction between firms and their competitors, as well as a blurring of the boundaries between firms and their suppliers (Sabel and Kern, 1990). To the extent that diversified quality production is enhanced by a fluid, quasi-consortial pattern of industrial organization – with joint ventures being set up, like building sites, for special projects, to be dismantled after their completion – firms in a given industry are at the same time competitors and potential allies. While competing in some areas, they depend in others on their competitors cooperating with them in good faith, as well as maintaining a level of technical and marketing excellence that matches their own. Firms' interest in the technological strength of their suppliers seems to account for the often described trend from multiple-sourcing from firms that were not allowed to work also for other customers to single-sourcing from firms that are encouraged to improve their technological capacities by working for more than one client. The advantages of this new configuration seem to outweigh the risk of a firm's know-how being transferred to its competitors through a joint supplier, or of suppliers becoming so technologically powerful that they may move into their client's product markets themselves.

Markets and hierarchies are not well equipped to govern the complex mixture of competition and cooperation required for diversified quality production since they do not help firms to act on their self-interest in their competitors' and suppliers' competitiveness and well-being. Where a firm's best interest is no longer in the competitive elimination or hierarchical incorporation of other firms, but rather in being part of a rich, diversified, polycentric economy, forms of governance are necessary that allow for cooperative upgrading of technological capabilities, and that protect the mutual confidence in each other's 'good will' that is central for holding down transaction costs and enabling firms to shift flexibly from competition to cooperation and back. Governance in diversified quality production, in other words, is the better the more it can help increase the number of potential strategic allies. This is particularly important with respect to small firms, which, while they tend to find it comparatively difficult to attain a high degree of technical capability, appear particularly indispensable for productive flexibility.

For a pattern of industrial organization in which large firms are to coexist and productively interact with a large number of technically and economically independent small firms, it is not enough for policy to remove barriers to market access.[9] Indeed in an important sense it may be exactly the opposite that is necessary. Large German firms engaging in diversified quality production today benefit immensely from the presence in their immediate environment of a strong artisanal sector. Still, there can be no doubt that without protective legislation that prevented and prevents large firms from entering artisanal markets, they would, like their British counterparts, long have wiped out their artisanal competition. Similarly, if small and medium-sized firms are to become full participants in diversified quality production, enabling institutional mechanisms are needed that provide for their upskilling through an efficient inter-firm transfer of technology and know-how. Such mechanisms may be implicitly or explicitly built into contracts between large and small firms; however, cooperative cultures and regulatory institutions beyond contract, like corporative associations of small firms under public facilitation (chambers of artisans, or of commerce and industry), or privileged market access for small firms that commit themselves to long-term investment in their technical capabilities, seem to be much more effective. Institutional mechanisms that overcome suspicion among competitors; insure firms against opportunistic defection of partners from implicit contractual understandings; and enable firms to invest not only in their own performance but also in that of other firms in their environment, thereby contributing to the collective good of a dense organizational ecology of potential strategic allies, are a major contributing condition of diversified quality production.

2. The Requirement of Redundant Capacities

Diversified quality production requires not just high investment but also a type of investment that is likely to be under-supplied where economic rationality is not institutionally protected from becoming excessive, that is, from turning into 'economism' or 'hyper-rationality'. Successful diversified quality producers seem to have an investment function, in the widest sense, that contains arguments that cannot easily be included in individual-rational calculations of 'return on investment'. This is because volatile markets and changing technological possibilities reward organizations with a capacity for fast retooling without loss of quality in response to unpredictable new demands. A central precondition for fast retooling is the presence of generalized, unspecified, non-dedicated, 'redundant' capabilities that can be put to many different, previously unknown uses (Sorge, 1985). This applies regardless of the fact that diversified quality producers, as has been pointed out, often prefer to combine and recombine with others for specific projects, rather than produce everything inhouse. Indeed recognizing fast-changing and highly specific market opportunities, identifying potential allies and combining with others in interactive networks requires an organizational intelligence and polyvalence that is in itself a general, unspecific, 'reflexive' organizational resource.

In firms that try to blend craft into mass production, a large share of their investment is only indirectly related to specific production purposes, and the causal chain between investment and return is longer and more difficult to trace. Investment in general capabilities for as yet undefined future purposes is not easy to justify for managements under competitive pressure, and is likely to be challenged by controllers and accountants as excess investment. It therefore runs a greater risk than more dedicated expenditures of coming under attack by higher levels of the managerial hierarchy if cost pressures rise. While large firms may sometimes be rich enough to resist economistic temptations, small firms find it particularly hard to build polyvalent, redundant capacities for production and, even more so, for design and marketing.

Redundant capacities are difficult to build in markets and through, or against, hierarchies, even if investing in them would open up superior market opportunities. To the extent that individually defined rational interests are not sufficiently instructive for investment in redundant capacities, following such interests may be the same as violating them. Examples of conditions of diversified quality production that are redundant capacities and that therefore are more likely to be provided through collective institutional obligations than through individual-rational calculations, are as follows.

(i) *Broad and high skills*. There is widespread agreement that a crucial resource for firms in technologically and economically volatile markets are high skills that are at the same time broad enough to allow for application to a wide range of rapidly changing, as yet unknown tasks. Skills are broad to the extent that they are polyvalent – that is, not functionally dedicated to any specific purpose or activity. The most important polyvalent skill is the general capacity to acquire more skills (referred to in Germany as '*Schlüsselqualifikationen*'), with even less specific ('extra-functional') attitudinal and behavioral skills like diligence, attention to detail, and willingness to accept responsibility in a group running a close second.

The problem with broad and high skills is that, whereas they seem to be best generated in a workplace environment, investment in them is not easy to justify for profit-maximizing firms in competitive markets. The reason lies in a specific, intrinsic and inevitable 'fuzziness' of skill as a productive resource, which is especially in evidence for the kind of broad and flexible skills that are vital in periods of industrial restructuring and in production processes in which change is rapid and uncertainty high. Among other things, this fuzziness is apparent in the fact that both training costs and training returns are extremely difficult to calculate. Workplace training, especially if it is to be effective, inevitably shades into work and production, and its outcomes often and typically dissipate in the organization and are impossible to trace precisely. As a result, where the costs and returns of training have to be explicitly calculated in order for the latter 'rationally' to justify the former, firms' human resource investment decisions are likely to be excessively, and irrationally, conservative. Indeed this may be the most important explanation for the fact that in institutionally 'thin' economies where training decisions are exclusively or primarily driven by market-rational economic motives the supply of skills tends be suboptimal for advanced industrial production purposes.

In diversified quality production, even more than in other production patterns, firms and managements find it hard to determine how much training is 'enough' training. What many of them know is that firms that create only those skills that they need may well end up with less than they need. Cost- and profit-consciousness are more part of the problem than of the solution. When it comes to the creation of redundant capacities, it would appear that profit-maximizing firms may have to be protected by cultural restraints or political regulation from their profit motive becoming overwhelming and depriving them of the capacity to generate profit from diversified quality production. While a culture of training conceived as education that values skills as such and apart from immediately discernible economic benefits would appear to be economically functional, institutions that impose on firms formal obligations to train can in part substitute for culture (for more on this, see below). The design and 'gardening' of such institutions constitute an important function for public intervention in industrial skill formation as part of an affirmative supply-side policy.

(ii) *A polyvalent organizational structure.* Much has been written in recent years on changes in the division of labor in response to new demands on organizations for higher product diversity and quality (for a synthesis see Gustavsen, 1986; as an example of an early, semi-popular treatment, Ouchi 1981). If there is at all a common denominator in this literature – which runs the entire gamut from organizational and industrial sociology to the management press – then it is that for organizations to acquire a capacity for flexible retooling, duplication and overlap in organizational structures are, not a liability, but rather a crucial productive asset. This, at least, became the widely accepted explanation for increasingly frequent observations of empirical anomalies in the 'modern', functional differentiation paradigm of organizational structure, whose main practical application was Taylor's 'science' of industrial engineering.

The emerging orthodoxy in organization analysis today appears to be that organizational units – work roles, departments, organizations themselves – should not be narrowly specialized but should rather be polyvalent: capable, that is, of performing more than one operation, and of switching flexibly between different operations. The consequences of this for skill patterns have just been described. For organizational structures, polyvalence involves a blurring of the functional boundaries between subunits, with the effect that, in the limiting case, subunits become able to substitute for each other by taking over each other's functions – although in most conditions functional overlap will be utilized primarily to facilitate non-routine cooperation. In both cases, the implication is that the organization, in any given operational state, must have at its disposal potentially vast additional capacities that, while they may be employed for some future task, remain unused in the background. These capacities are, for this reason, redundant.

One development for which redundant capacities have been found to be of importance is the erosion of the traditional distinction between direct and indirect labor in the organization of work on the shopfloor (Demes and Jürgens, 1989). In modern manufacturing plants, operation and maintenance of advanced equipment are often in the hands of the same, highly skilled workers. This applies also to the handling of supplies and the feeding of machines on the one hand, and the programing and reprograming of equipment and similar skilled functions on the other. Where new forms of group work are being used, it is often regarded desirable that all team members should be able to perform all tasks assigned to the group, often including formerly managerial functions such as accounting or logistics. Simple 'direct' tasks are then carried out by workers who are far more skilled than would be necessary for such tasks to be satisfactorily executed.

Similarly, there is evidence that organizations engaging in product diversification for quality-competitive markets benefit from close, synergetic cooperation between different functions, or departments, especially sales, product design, production engineering, production management and personnel, as well as between various management functions and the shopfloor. Functional interpenetration complements and even supersedes functional differentiation where tasks cease to be highly routinized and need to be constantly redefined (Sorge, 1985), and where as a consequence the mutual obligations of organizational subunits have to be redefined from project to project. One central condition for this to be done efficiently is that each function understands the tasks and concerns of the others. Where this is the case, the organization's internal structure can be flexibly rearranged to fit changing environments, in the same way as consortia of independent, polyvalent firms can be formed and disbanded in response to fluctuating customer demands.

A polyvalent organization whose subunits are capable of flexibly crossing the boundaries of their assigned functions is expensive, and the return on investment in polyvalence is difficult to establish. This is why the de-Taylorization of work organization, profitable as it undoubtedly is for firms pressed for higher product quality and diversity, seems to proceed faster where there is additional and independent pressure for re-organization of work, for other than economic reasons. In the same way in which institutionally imposed obligations to train improve firms' skill base, legislation or industrial agreements mandating employers to enlarge and enrich job definitions may contribute to operational flexibility. In both cases, competitiveness increases as a result of adjustments individual firms would or could not voluntarily have made. Likewise, small firms that try to move from the position of dependent supplier to that of a diversified quality producer integrated into a network of joint ventures seem to need above all a set of polyvalent marketing, engineering and other capacities that they are often unable to acquire on their own; helping them become polyvalent would thus appear to be a major function of the institutions that support diversified quality production.

(iii) *Decentralized competence.* Another redundant capacity which is related to, but not identical with organizational polyvalence is a decentralized structure of decision-making. In the same way in which investment in polyvalence runs up against market pressures for cost effectiveness, decentralization of competence may interfere with the hierarchical principle of unity of command and may violate vested interests in the integrity of managerial and proprietorial prerogative.

Pressures for decentralization in diversified quality production result from the need to adapt and re-adapt to an unpredictable market on a routinized non-routine basis. This requires lower hierarchical levels to have the competence – that is, the authority as well as the cognitive capacity – to make fast and independent decisions. Recent writings on organizations suggest that high diversity and quality of output are difficult to attain in organizations that are run on a 'need to know' basis, since who 'needs' to know what is hard to establish under high task uncertainty. Similarly, the flexible regrouping of organizational resources in response to changing tasks appears to be facilitated by delegation of decision-making powers to the subunits by which tasks are carried out. This is the principle underlying the widespread interest in a reintegration of management and production, or conception and execution.

Building decentralized competence may appear as excess investment to the extent that it involves the creation of high and broad, general skills. But in addition, managements asked to share information and authority with lower hierarchical levels may be afraid of redundant competence undermining swift acceptance of central decisions and delaying decisions generally. While the influence of quasi-political self-interests in managerial power and control can easily be exaggerated, as it appears to be in the Bravermanian 'labor process' theory, sharing competence with inferior ranks in a hierarchy is difficult. Especially where the costs and returns of decentralized competence are uncertain – as they typically are – there is likely to be a tendency for managements to be restrictive: to do less rather than more and keep to themselves as much as possible of what the German sociologist, Karl Mannheim, has called '*Herrschaftswissen*'. Here, too, perverse incentives to cheat on one's own longer-term interests may easily become overwhelming. Hierarchy failure of this kind may be corrected, as Neuloh (1960) has found long ago when studying the impact of co-determination on German coal and steel companies, by industrial relations procedures obligating managements to communicate their strategic thinking to workers representatives, and thereby to themselves, on a current basis and in advance of action being taken.

(iv) *Social peace*. It has often been pointed out that a 'professional' work motivation and a quality consciousness among workers that do not need to be supported by specific monetary incentives or the possibility of negative sanctions are indispensable resources for what is here called diversified quality production. For this kind of cooperative orientation of workers to become available for a decentralized production process, a degree of mutual trust and loyalty between employer and worker seems to be required that can grow only on the basis of stable social peace. The latter, however, does not come to employers without costs, in both money and managerial prerogative. Moreover, even where the productive contribution of social peace is indisputable, its exact price is as difficult to calculate as are the returns on a firm's investment in social peace. This is why social peace, just as general skills, is fuzzy from a rational accounting perspective, and why rational managements tend to be tempted to invest less than they should invest in their own interest.

For a firm to have a sufficient supply of social peace when it needs it, it must be willing to incur potentially significant costs at times when it apparently does not need them. In this sense, investment in and cultivation of social peace creates a redundant resource which is exposed to the typical hazards of excessive rationality and short-term opportunism. In particular, if firms are free to select their own 'social peace equilibrium', they will often be tempted in competitive markets to exploit a temporary lapse in the market power of their workforce for short-term advantage – not least since firms know that their competitors are under the same temptation. As this, in turn, is unlikely to escape the attention of workers, the long-term result will fall short of the kind of 'high trust' (Fox, 1974) that appears to be such an important input in diversified quality production (Heckscher, 1988).

Being most of the time a redundant resource, social peace is more likely to be created as a matter of obligation than of interest, even though having it may very much be in a firm's interest. A case in point is co-determination in Germany (see Chapter 5, this volume). Since co-determination increases labor costs and interferes substantially with managerial prerogative, its introduction was at every step resisted by employers. While there is little doubt that co-determination has contributed to the superior performance and competitiveness of German manufacturing in the (diversified quality) world market segments for which it produces, it is also obvious that German employers would not have adopted it voluntarily. Regardless of its beneficial economic effects, co-determination had to be imposed on employers by law so as to make it impossible for individual firms to 'cheat' on social peace in order to improve their competitive position. Moreover, the fact that co-determination is precisely not a voluntary arrangement, but is legally enshrined in what the Germans call a works constitution, insures workers that it will not be unilaterally withdrawn in times of economic hardship, and thereby increases their trust in the fairness of the employer.

Social peace and the resulting mutual trust are often based in long-term employment relationships. Indeed even in countries with flexible and easily accessible external labor markets, there are firms, often ambitious diversified quality producers, that commit themselves to stable employment for their workforces in exchange for their cooperation. Like 'unionism without unions', this may sometimes result in an effective pacification of industrial relations. However, as Dore (1988), in particular, has pointed out, voluntary employment guarantees based on a firm's enlightened self-interest that are exceptions from a majoritarian pattern of flexible employment tend on the whole to be less stable and less effective for worker commitment than, culturally or legally, compulsory arrangements that originate from institutionalized obligations and have to conform to a general rule. This is because in a voluntary arrangement, a possibility of defection remains always present in the background. Diversified quality production seems to be more likely to be enhanced if social peace is not generated inside individual firms with their own resources, but externally through a collective institutional exoskeleton. Again, privatized, contractual generation of redundant capacities appears inferior to publicly imposed and enforced behavioral obligations.[10]

3. The Requirement of Collective Production Inputs
Blending craft into mass production seems to increase the dependence of production systems on a range of factor inputs that have

significant collective goods properties. To the extent that diversified quality production requires, as suggested by empirical research, a rich supply of individually non-appropriable production factors, industrial restructuring towards high levels of product diversity and quality is impeded by a neo-classical institutional environment that gives rational-possessive individualism precedence over collective, cooperative and collusive action. A lack of appropriate non-market institutions on the supply side may thus stand in the way of an optimal use of productive resources in response to rising demand for diversified quality production.

In standard economics, non-appropriable production inputs, to the extent that they are allowed for at all, are few in number and their supply is not in principle regarded as problematic. As a result they can essentially be neglected. The production inputs that count are assumed to be easy to appropriate and, therefore, to produce for and acquire through free markets. The few collective factor inputs that are needed can typically be generated through unilateral government provision – the only problem being to limit state supply to the very few resources that cannot be more efficiently provided by the market.

The analysis of diversified quality production casts doubt on these assumptions. First, it indicates an increase, with the evolution of production systems in response to more demanding markets, in the relative dependence of private production and prosperity on collective factor inputs. Secondly, it suggests that at least with some of them, unilateral state provision, as for example through the public educational system or through institutions of basic science and research, is less than ideal, and that behavioral regulation of market participants and the creation of obligations for them may be superior modes of public intervention. This is especially the case where limited appropriability creates prisoners'-dilemma-type problems that require institutions capable of suspending competition and of protecting mutual expectations of bona fide cooperation. In particular, managing the complex mix of competition and cooperation between market participants needed for the provision of important collective factor inputs seems to demand a qualitative rearrangement and enrichment of organizational interfaces in the crucial zone between state and market that seems to be impossible to accommodate in liberal doctrine.

Possessive individualism of rational market participants creates shortages of major production inputs that are typically required for diversified quality production. Examples are as follows.

(i) *Social peace.* Inside firms, as Fox (1974) among others has pointed out, trust cannot be hierarchically owned but has to be reciprocally and equitably shared. There also seem to be significant externalities between firms which make it more likely for any individual firm to achieve long-term peaceful labor relations if these exist also in other, neighboring firms. As conflicts can spread from one firm to another, for example through competitive bargaining, firms cannot safely 'own' *their* social peace, and their investment in it remains at risk. Moreover, firms that know that other firms may choose to cut costs by cutting their expenditure on peaceful labor relations, are involved in a prisoners' dilemma that may make them adopt an irrational strategy for rational reasons, chopping away at crucial conditions of their competitive capacity for diverse production at high quality levels. *Nota bene* the often observed fact that strike rates are much lower in countries where social peace is jointly produced and, as it were, co-owned by employers negotiating at industrial or national level through strong employers' associations.

(ii) *Competence.* In organizations engaged in diversified quality production, attempts to appropriate jobs through possessive job demarcations, for example by craft unions, depress productivity since they stand in the way of flexibility. Job ownership, defined as an individual or collective property right in a given organizational function ('competence'), is incompatible with group work or with functional interpenetration of tasks. Where organizational polyvalence and decentralized competence are desired, institutional arrangements have to be found that motivate investment in knowledge and authority with incentives other than the prospect of individual appropriation.

(iii) *Ecological synergies.* By definition, a firm cannot own the community of firms of which it wants to be a member. The positive interest in the prosperity and technological capability of non-appropriable competitors-cum-allies cannot be acted upon through possessive individualism alone. Especially as industrial structures change to match the demands of diversified quality markets, the institutional embedding that they require seems to grow so complex that it can no longer, not even for pragmatic purposes, be treated as given or negligible. Instead, it turns into a collectively owned production good whose provision is conditional on sophisticated institutional arrangements.

(iv) *Knowledge.* Excessive consciousness of property rights on the part of firms may undermine and prevent potentially productive strategic alliances and cooperative relations. The blurring of inter-firm boundaries, both among competitors-cum-allies and between clients and their privileged single suppliers, inevitably entails a loss of control over intellectual capital. Similarly, technology transfer, conceived as investment in a congenial organizational ecology, directly involves a sharing of knowledge among potential competitors; it is therefore typically impeded by excessive property-consciousness. In terms of internal organizational structures, treating the knowledge vested in a firm as the hierarchical property of management prevents flexible decentralization of competence as well as the creation of high and broad skills. Management concepts geared towards the achievement of high flexibility in response to fluctuating, diverse markets therefore emphasize the need for internal socialization of knowledge, contesting members' and departments' claims to privileged or exclusive access to specific sets of information (see for example Peters and Waterman, 1982).

(v) *Skills*. Where workers may move from one firm to another, and where they do not feel socially obliged to stay with their employer for all their working lives, firms will always have to be concerned that their investment in training may not pay for them since the worker may leave before it has amortized. Unlike in Japan, returns on training investment in Western firms can never be safely internalized as the skills imparted on a worker cannot be appropriated by the employer: if at all, they become the property of the worker. In effect, the fundamental uncertainty for employers recovering their training expenses in an open, contractual labor market turns skills, from the viewpoint of individual employers, into a collective good. By providing training, employers add to a common pool of skilled labor which is in principle accessible to all other employers in the industry or the locality, many of whom are their competitors. While individual employers may well recognize the importance of skilled workers for their enterprises, they also know that if they incur the expenses for their training, their competitors can easily 'poach' their trained workers by offering them a higher wage, with their rivals' overall labor costs still remaining below their own. Since the rewards of his or her investment can so easily be 'socialized' whereas the costs remain his or her own, an employer in a competitive market will therefore be tempted not to train, or to train as little as possible, and buy in needed skills from the outside. As other employers are likely to perceive their situation in the same way, they will probably prefer not to train either. As a result, in the absence of regulation that suspends competition, there will tend to be an under-supply of skilled labor.

To increase their chances of internalizing the returns on their training investment, firms may choose to limit their training efforts to workplace-specific as opposed to general skills.[11] If what workers learn from their employer can be used only in their present place of work, 'poaching' becomes difficult, and the bargaining power of workers does not increase in proportion with their skills. Such concerns over the appropriation of skills may, however, easily become excessive and counterproductive. An employer who is anxious not to give away too many transferable skills, may fail to create enough overall skills. More specifically, as has been pointed out, where skills are to be used to increase product variety and process flexibility, it is precisely general and not specific skills that are needed. In such a situation, possessive individualism, as with other collective goods, is bound to result in shortage of supply.[12]

Diversified quality production seems to entail a dynamic of growing objective socialization of productive processes and assets (Adler, 1987) that is driven by the evolution of demand. This is why diversified quality production is facilitated by the joint, collective, obligated and regulated provision of vital, non-appropriable production inputs. Driven to the extreme, the argument, especially where it emphasizes the limits of private appropriation, resembles the dialectic of modes and forces of production that is at the core of Marx's theory of capitalist development. However, rather than buying into its far-reaching conclusions, the analysis of diversified quality production points to the competitive advantages of societies, regions or communities that have still at their disposal a residue of collective-communitarian institutions and values on which they can draw for the provision of collective production goods. It also does not in principle preclude the possibility of political institution-building replenishing the social dimension of capitalist production systems and thereby enabling them to reproduce themselves successfully on rising levels of objective socialization.

While grounded in and distilled from empirical research, the conceptualization of diversified quality production as an industrial order draws on a fundamental but often forgotten insight of social theory: that successful self-interested, utilitarian behavior requires cooperative relations, communitarian obligations and collective resources that individuals acting rationally on their own cannot normally generate, protect or restore even if they fully recognize their vital importance. This principle has for long been at the core of the sociological critique, both conservative and radical, of liberal laissez-faire capitalism, pointing out in varying ways that the capitalist freedom to pursue and appropriate private material gain depends on physical-environmental, social, moral or other foundations that cannot be privately owned, and that free markets and proprietorial hierarchies can therefore only consume but not reproduce. The analysis of the social conditions of advanced industrial production systems seems to confirm, in important respects, the continuing validity of core elements of the critique of liberalism.

Market and hierarchy failure in the formation and reproduction of an advanced structure of effective supply provide an example of the deficiency of a Spencerian social order based solely on contractual exchange between utility-maximizing individuals. The analysis forcefully underlines the productivity of a more-than-private, publicly and authoritatively enforced system of collective social rights and obligations – the economic uses, that is, of a society conceived and enforced as a reality sui generis beyond and above its individual members (Durkheim, 1964). An advanced industrial system with its potentials for synergetic growth, its needs for redundant capacities and its limits to individual appropriability, can fully unfold and efficiently allocate its productive forces only with the help of positive institutions that complement and control free markets and hierarchical property rights. Protecting, reviving or designing such institutions is an indispensable element of a supply-side strategy aimed at a qualitative restructuring of industrial economies.

Equity and Efficiency

The dependence of diversified quality production on an institutional exoskeleton constitutes an open door for political regulation and intervention. In this sense, politics forms an integral part of the rich social dimension of diversified quality production.[13] Unlike in a neo-classical production regime where the only constructive contribution of politics to performance lies in the de-politicization of the supply side through the establishment and protection of the zero-institutions of market and hierarchy, diversified quality production presupposes an affirmative polity in which major conditions of competitive performance are, and have to be, collectively created and maintained. It is for this reason that diversified quality production may offer an opportunity for a supply-oriented 'new deal' between efficiency and equity.

Equity can make an important contribution to each of the three requirements for effective diversified quality supply: congenial ecology, redundant capacity and collective production inputs. For all of them, political redistribution and egalitarian supplementation of initial factor endowments in favor of less well-equipped market participants may improve the performance even of those producers that were originally better endowed than their competitors.[14] For example, a more equal distribution of technological and design capabilities among firms than would emerge under a regime of competitive markets and unobstructed hierarchies increases the number of firms that may enter into joint ventures and strategic alliances with each other, and thereby extends each firm's range of strategic choices and alternatives. (This is the most compelling rationale for public or cooperative 'technology transfer' programs being financed by taxing already successful firms.) The result is a collectively enlarged repertory of individual responses to volatile markets for customized goods, and a greater likelihood that opportunities for profit and employment offered by the evolution of product markets can be fully exploited.

Similarly, redundant capacities are by definition factor endowments whose acquisition and deployment is not (yet) indicated by immediate market pressures. This, as we have seen, is why rational actors normally have insufficient incentive to invest in them. In the absence of conclusive market signals as to where redundant capacities are best developed, their generation and allocation might just as well be determined by political criteria of distributive justice. The reason why political pressures for equality may be a superior way of motivating redundant capacity building lies, of course, in the intrinsic difficulties of rationally calculating expected returns on long-term investment in 'fuzzy' capabilities, and the resulting inconclusiveness of 'economizing' as a principle of efficient allocation.[15] Similar problems also impede the production of collective factor inputs; here the contribution of politics to individual economic performance would appear to consist of either the authoritative provision of the required production factors, or of the creation of institutional settings that enable market-rational competitors to engage in cooperative non-zero-sum behavior. In both cases, the indivisibility and non-exclusivity of publicly provided factor inputs by definition entails an egalitarian redistribution effect. In addition, the furnishing of facilities to private gain-seekers by public authorities (of whatever kind) legitimates the latter charging a price for their services from the former through taxation. To the extent that public authorities are committed to equity as an objective in its own right, they may use the proceeds from the provision of collective factor inputs for further redistributive investment in an egalitarian organizational ecology or an evenly distributed pattern of redundant capacities.

It is important to emphasize that in the present context equity and redistribution refer not to entitlements for consumption, but to rights of access to and utilization of productive capacities. This is in line with, and follows from, the concern with the supply side of the economy and the productive contribution of its 'social dimension'. In standard economics, of course, redistribution occurs primarily on the demand side, with – mostly negative – repercussions for the efficient allocation of production factors, especially in the labor market. Since suboptimal factor allocation results in an overall loss of welfare, political redistribution is essentially seen as a mistake – a 'justice illusion' comparable to the 'money illusion' in collective wage bargaining – which in the long run hurts everybody, including those that it presumably is to benefit. Keynesian theory, again in line with orthodoxy, also viewed egalitarianism in terms of access to consumption, and as a consequence located it on the demand side. At the same time, it differed sharply from standard economics in that it assigned to the downward redistribution of incomes a productive function as a mechanism of increasing and stabilizing effective demand. In this sense, the Keynesian theory of full employment entailed the possibility of a combination of egalitarianism and productivism, which was why it was so universally embraced after the Second World War by trade unions and social-democratic parties (Przeworski and Wallerstein, 1982; Vidich, 1982). The left-Keynesian principle that 'wealth is like manure: it is useful only if it is spread around' provided reformist labor movements in Western democracies with an intellectual and strategic compass to avoid the deadly trap of the 'equity-efficiency-dilemma' posed by classical, 'bourgeois' economics: the claim, that is, that equity detracts from efficiency; that there can be only as much equity as does not seriously obstruct efficiency, or else everybody including the presumptive beneficiaries lose; and that the extent to which political redistribution undermines efficiency is determined by the response of the supply side, that is, by markets and managements.

Today, the new preeminence of structural and supply-side problems has reopened the question of the relationship between equity and efficiency in reformist politics. The principal reason for the present weakness of trade unions and labor parties in the mixed economies of the West may well be their failure to find an equivalent on the supply side for the Keynesian, demand-side-based reconciliation of equity and efficiency, or of egalitarianism and productivism – to establish, in other words, a similarly productive role for egalitarian redistribution in the creation of effective supply as was provided for in the Keynesian model of effective demand. The requirement for diversified quality production of a congenial ecology, redundant capacities and collective factor inputs, and the potential role of egalitarianism in their generation, may offer an opportunity for the Left to restore a productive function to redistributive politics and thereby re-capture for itself an independent role in the management of advanced industrial economies.

A proper understanding of the dynamics of diversified quality production could lead the way towards an alternative, non-classical supply-side response to the employment problem which would make productive use of institutional 'rigidities'. An egalitarian supply-side approach to full employment would aim at enabling marginal workers to earn the high wages prescribed for them by rigid institutions, by helping them increase their productivity. Rather than matching the distribution of incomes to existing productivity differentials, which would result in a high level of inequality, a non-classical strategy would undertake to match the level and distributional profile of productivity to a politically determined, socially acceptable pattern of income differentials, with marginal productivity being adjusted to rigid wages instead of wages being adjusted to given productivities.

Institutions as Constraints and Opportunities

To support a socially benevolent development of neo-industrial production, social and political institutions must simultaneously impose constraints on and provide opportunities for individual-rational actors. Constraints are necessary for the suspension of competition and the 'blocking of contracts' (Olson, 1983a), so as to protect profit-seeking individuals from the temptations of hyper-rationality and prevent them from seeking short-term, quick-fix solutions – which might lead to a Gresham's Law-type erosion of ecological conditions, redundant capacities and collective production inputs and generate a downward spiral of collective irrationality driven by individually rational choices. Constraints are also required to impose limits on the hierarchical exercise of property rights so as to force managements, in Karl Deutsch's (1963) famous formula, to substitute intelligence for power. Opportunities, in turn, have to be offered for firms and managements to be in fact able to adjust to diversified quality demand; they include, among other things, facilitating support for the creation of the three functional conditions of congenial ecology, redundant capacity and collective factor inputs. The difficulty is that the institutions that constitute an economy's social dimension must be so designed as to function as constraints and opportunities simultaneously; if they do just one and not the other, their capacity to drive diversified quality production is likely to be low.[16]

Institutionalized constraints and opportunities operate on a chain of interdependent micro-level decisions – on product ranges, production technology, work organization, skill formation, wages, and wage differentials – that link product markets to the social system of production. In the world of standard economics, product markets are seen as determining – that is, constituting overwhelming decisional rigidities for – the choice of product ranges. These, in turn, determine production technology, which then determines work organization, which determines skill requirements, from which, finally, flow wage levels and wage structures. The result is believed to be a production pattern that makes for an optimally efficient allocation of resources, provided that management – which is supposed to 'read' and follow product markets better than any other actor – is powerful enough to organize the decision sequence hierarchically from the product market 'down' to the labor market and the social structures underlying it.

Standard economics recognize that in the real world the decisional hierarchy that relates product markets to households as sellers of labor – the direction of the mutual conditioning of decisions – is contested in that 'lower' levels will always try to impose their own preferences on 'higher' levels, through institutional rigidities that interfere with the free play of markets and hierarchies. In empirical studies of industrial production patterns, observations of a reversal of decisional hierarchies are frequent, with existing product ranges conditioning market choice, a given technology determining a firm's product range, an established work organization affecting choice of technology, a present supply of skills shaping work organization, and rigid wages and wage structures affecting the skill supply. Such reverse conditioning is regarded in standard economics as a source of inefficiency – the more so the closer one gets to the social system end of the chain. The study of diversified quality production, by contrast, suggests that successful product diversification at a high quality level is not likely to come about if the decision sequence runs unidirectionally from product markets downward, without encountering on the way politically or culturally generated institutional rigidities, especially towards the social system end of the decision chain – like egalitarian wage settlements, employment protection rules, co-determination rights, standardized training profiles, mandatory job enrichment requirements, and technology agreements. Institutions like these may, if they function well, simultaneously force and facilitate fortuitious micro-economic choices of wages, skill patterns, work organization, technologies, product ranges and, especially, product markets that fit a given, or politically preferred, social system of production – rather than the latter having to be adjusted to the demands of presumably given markets and hierarchical decisions.

Not all institutional rigidities constraining markets and hierarchies are always and necessarily benevolent, and not all social systems of production can match the requirements of growing, turbulent and volatile markets for customized, non-price competitive goods. Not much is known on the generic properties of

institutions that prevent firms from following their natural inclina-
tions in times of economic stress – recovering profitability by cutting
prices to become more competitive; cutting wages to cut prices;
introducing labor-saving technology to cut employment; reorganiz-
ing work so as to cut the autonomy of skilled workers, as well as
their number; cutting training expenditures and procuring skills by
'poaching' from others through the external labor market; restoring
managerial prerogative to cut decision-time and make possible all
the other cuts – while at the same time enabling them to become
profitable diversified quality producers.[17] Of particular interest in
this respect is the contribution of trade unions, industrial relations
and collective bargaining. To the extent that it is necessary not just
to offer firms and managements opportunities but also to impose
constraints on them, some form of institutionalized conflict would
appear to be an indispensable condition of supply-side restructuring
towards advanced forms of demand. Understanding diversified
quality production thus requires analysis of the complex, 'dialectical' relationship between conflict and cooperation among organized
social classes in advanced political economies.

An example of how institutional constraints may create opportunities to move an economy into diversified quality production, and in
particular of the potential role in this of institutionalized social
conflict, is given by the German case. On the face of it, Germany
appears to be an advanced case of what used to be called 'Euro-
sclerosis'. Regulation of economic activities, by law and otherwise,
is dense, and 'deregulation', even after a decade of conservative
government, is not much of an issue compared to what it is in the
United States or Britain. Collective bargaining has remained centralized at the industrial level; the legal complexities of running
enterprises under co-determination continue to puzzle managers
and labor lawyers; involuntary dismissals of workers in large firms
are still very difficult by comparison with other countries; the
vocational training system with about 400 nationally standardized
occupational profiles, clearly a bureaucratic nightmare by liberal
standards, appears better established than ever; to enter a large
number of markets, small and medium-sized firms have to get a
license and join a quasi-public trade association with compulsory
membership, etc. But in spite of these and other institutional
'rigidities', Germany is one of the world's two or three most
successful economies.

The explanation appears to be that, whereas German institutional
rigidities have largely foreclosed adjustment to price-competitive
markets, they have at the same time and instead forced, induced
and enabled managements to embark on more demanding high

value-added, diversified quality production strategies (on the following see Streeck, 1987a). While making structural adjustment and the maintenance of competitiveness more difficult, German institutions have not made it impossible, and indeed they seem to have made more difficult adjustment strategies more possible. In particular, a range of egalitarian-distributive constraints seem to have operated as effective driving forces of a broad-based process of industrial upgrading. Among the most conspicuous examples of institutional rigidities in the German political economy that oblige economically rational firms and managements to contribute to collective goods needed for diversified quality production; prevent them from consuming such goods without replacement; and make them invest in a congenial organizational ecology, in redundant capacities, and in non-appropriable production inputs are the following.

(i) A system of 'rigid' wage determination, operated by strong and well-established trade unions and employers' associations, that keeps wages higher, and variation between wages, lower, than the labor market would determine. Unless employers are willing to move production elsewhere, this forces them to adapt their product range to non-price-competitive markets capable of sustaining a high wage level. A high and even wage level also makes employers more willing to invest in training and re-training as a way of matching workers' productivity to the externally fixed, high costs of labour. Moreover, as wage differentials are relatively small, employers have an incentive not to concentrate their training investment on just a few elite workers. In addition, fixed high and even wages make it attractive for employers to organize work in a 'non-Bravermanian' way, so that the labor extracted and performed justifies its high price.[18]

(ii) A policy of employment protection that compels employers to keep more employees on their payroll for a longer time than many might on their own be inclined to. Large German firms are subject to effective limitations on their ability to access the external labor market. High employment stability is imposed on firms through collective agreements, co-determination and legislation. To compensate for such external rigidities, firms have to increase their internal flexibility. By forcing firms to adjust through the internal labor market by redeployment, employment protection thus further encourages employer investment in training and retraining. Moreover, high employment security and the resulting identification of workers with the firm not only make for comparatively easy acceptance of technological change but also help create and support the cooperative attitudes among workers that are necessary for flexible organizational decentralization of competence and responsibility. By foreclosing ready access to the external labor market, institutional rigidities thus force as well as enable firms to invest in long-term human resource development, thereby making it easier for them to compete in non-price-competitive markets.

(iii) A set of binding rules that obliges employers to consult with their workforces and seek their consent above and beyond what many or most would on their own find expedient. Since German co-determination is enshrined in law, firms' 'consensus spending' is relatively fixed and securely protected from cost-cutting temptations. One effect seems to be confidence among workers and their representatives in the persistence of bilateralism regardless of whether employers find this to be in their immediate interest. Having an assured 'voice' in the management of the enterprise makes it possible for workforces to forgo short-term advantages for larger, longer-term benefits, without having to fear that they may not be around to collect those when they materialize. This, in turn, enables managements to invest more in longer-term projects. Co-determination thus insulates both management and labor from opportunistic pressures. It is made meaningful by, and in turn supports, long-term stable employment and internal labor markets, not least by providing for an equitable institutional mechanism to administer redeployment. Co-determination also seems to affect product and market choices in that firms, if they cannot avoid paying for consensus, are likely to find it expedient to shift towards quality-competitive production for which social consensus at the workplace constitutes an important asset instead of an unnecessary cost burden.

(iv) A training regime that is capable of obliging employers to train more workers and afford them broader skills than required by immediate product or labor market pressures. The result is an excess pool of 'flexible', polyvalent workers and skills that constitutes an important advantage in periods of fast technological change. A wide distribution of high and broad excess skills also underwrites high wages and strong employment protection, as well as a relatively even wage structure. The German training system with its nationally standardized and rigorously enforced curricula is governed in a 'corporatist' fashion, that is, by employers' associations and trade unions together under a state umbrella. Firms' training activities are closely supervised by quasi-public chambers with compulsory membership and far-reaching powers; in effect, these serve as conduits for pressures from the national level to increase and upgrade training activities. Training is also supported by co-determination drawing workplace trade unions into manpower management, with works councilors regarding it one of their main tasks to make firms train above and beyond short-term needs (to train, that is, as matter of 'social obligation'). Being forced to invest in expensive skills, firms find themselves further induced to move into non-price-competitive markets for high value-added products; use new technology in a way that makes the most of its potential for flexible retooling; adopt an organization of work that allows workers to use discretion; and comply with a regime of employment protection that also protects their human resource investment.

(v) A system of rules regarding the organization of work, created by trade union or government intervention and obliging employers to design jobs more broadly than many of them would feel necessary. Collective agreements, union-inspired government programs ('Humanization of Working Life') and co-determination in Germany have in a number of ways restricted managerial prerogatives in the design of jobs and the organization of the labor process. While the results are often less than satisfactory from the position of workers' representatives, together they amount to further pressure for 'de-Taylorization' of work through longer work cycles and job enrichment. Managements that have to live with unions pursuing higher 'quality of working life' as an independent objective may find themselves constrained to go for markets – of customized quality products – in which decentralized organizational competence is an asset. This holds in particular where workers have rights to co-determination and where therefore a stable working consensus with the workforce is a vital resource for management. Concessions on work organization are made easier by the fact that de-Taylorization not only facilitates flexible adjustment to changing technological and market conditions, but also enables employers actually to utilize the high and broad skills they are obliged to generate under the training system. In combination with high and even wages, high employment security, co-determination and training, the imposition on employers of non-Taylorist work rules thus impedes the use of new technology for 'rationalization' purposes and encourages a 'modernization' strategy of industrial adjustment that is highly conducive to diversified quality production.

German institutional constraints and opportunities seem to form an interactive pattern of mutual reinforcement and causation. On the basis of studies of industrial adjustment in the automobile industry in the 1970s and 1980s, it has been suggested that reference be made to this configuration as a 'virtuous circle of upmarket industrial restructuring' (Streeck, 1987a). While its dynamics and origins still await systematic exploration, two claims can plausibly be made: (1) that given the institutional constraints faced by German firms in their social system of production, managements, short of migrating to Southern Europe or the Pacific Basin, had not much of an alternative to seeking out non-price-competitive market segments; and (2) that given the available institutional opportunities, they may have been better able than their foreign competition to do so. Both observations together would explain why low volume/high-margin production has been found to be a characteristic not just of individual German firms but of entire industries or even the economy as a whole (Cox and Kriegbaum, 1980).

Germany, or any country for that matter, cannot possibly be a 'model' after which other political economies could be rebuilt or built. But this does not mean that there are no lessons in the German case that could fruitfully be applied, with different means adjusted to different circumstances. The need to drive managements to greater efforts beyond what they would do if guided by 'the' product market alone; the indispensability of social obligations complementing economic interests as guides of economic action; the synergetic contribution of generalization of advanced production patterns; and the central contribution of a particular kind of redistributive politics are examples of this. The question is not whether specific 'German' institutions are so specifically 'German' that they cannot therefore be transplanted to other 'cultures'. It is rather whether certain general principles that can be derived from the analysis of the institutional requirements of diversified quality production, and of the German 'virtuous circle' in particular, can be usefully applied to the design of a post-Keynesian institutional infrastructure on the supply side that can sustain socially benevolent industrial change.

Concluding Remarks

Further reflection on diversified quality production as an advanced production pattern would have to elaborate on subjects like the relative importance of culture and politics as sources of institutional differences between nations and regions, and the possibilities and limits of institutional design drawing on 'models' from other countries. Institutional analysis is, almost of necessity, comparative. Its practical application within a supply-oriented employment strategy therefore inevitably raises questions on the transportability of institutions and experiences from one 'cultural' context to another. The standard objection here is that what works in one 'culture' will not necessarily work in another, and that 'cultures' cannot be strategically changed. However, how difficult it is to determine whether institutions are culturally inert or politically malleable is illustrated by the example of the Japanese industrial relations system with its 'three sacred treasures', the enterprise union, life-time employment, and seniority pay. While some accounts empha-size the deep roots of this pattern in Japanese culture, for example, the structure of the family and the role of informal groups in Japanese society (Abegglen, 1958), others maintain that it has been deliberately designed and forcibly imposed upon workers by employers in the 1950s after the 'Red Purge' of the Japanese labor movement (Koshiro, 1979). Similarly, German co-determination has been described both as an innovative political construct and as an emanation of a presumed German 'culture' of consensus and incorporation.

Another of the many possible questions concerns the potential deficiencies and practical difficulties of an egalitarian supply-side industrial policy. For example, a clear disadvantage of an institu-tional design approach to supply-side economic policy, compared to neo-classical institutional minimalism, is that qualitative institu-tional intervention and innovation are simply much more difficult than deregulation. Moreover, an economic strategy of institutional design, or institutional gardening, needs time for experimentation, elimination of unanticipated side-effects, and maturation. Fast results cannot, but may have to be, promised. Given the short duration of political cycles, there should in fact be a strong temptation for policy-makers to have recourse to short-term solu-tions even if these, over time, erode crucial institutional conditions of long-term prosperity and stability.

In addition, a public policy that blocks contracts, apart from the risk of being held responsible for the less-than-full employment it tries to remedy, runs up against a voluntarist-libertarian mass consciousness, not least among the constituencies of left parties, for which the 'free choice' promised by neo-liberals has its strong attractions. Ideological resources to defend a non-liberal model of political economy are scarce at a time of proto-capitalist perestroika in the heartland of socialism. The idea of prosperity coming in joint supply, of collective investment taking precedence over private investment, of institutional regulation superseding individual liberty, and of opportunities being accompanied by constraints may sound too collectivistic for today's electorates – just as trying to protect collective investment from turning into collective consump-tion may be too productivistic to be acceptable.

It is also possible that a diversified quality supply-side strategy makes excessive and unrealistic demands on the homogeneity and sovereignty of socio-political systems. Blocking low-productivity and low-pay employment contracts may make sense only in a relatively homogeneous society without cultural divisions and mass immigration. Where cultural standards and expectations differ too much, preventing low-paying employment may result in societal dualism and a 'second economy' rather than equality. Moreover, if it is true, as Dore (1988) argues, that new technology gives greater weight to differences in natural ability as a basis for social stratification, the hope that marginal workers can be included into the core labor force through training and retraining may be in vain. Nor is it clear to what extent the generalization of diversified quality production as a production pattern requires a viable, that is, sovereign, national state – for redistribution between regional economies as well as to protect the social dimension of the supply side from erosion in and by border-crossing markets for capital, labor and final products. The completion of the European internal market in the coming years will offer an exciting opportunity to study these and other questions (see Chapter 7, this volume).

Notes

1 The chapter tries to avoid a long and very likely bottomless definitional exercise as to what is and is not an 'institution'. In a perfectly acceptable sense, a market is an institution no less than, say, a chamber of commerce, and a managerial chain of command is an institution in the same way as a trade union. For the purposes of this chapter, however, we find it convenient to distinguish between what we call 'neo-classical', 'minimal', 'zero' or 'economic' institutions on the one hand, and 'historical', 'political', 'cultural' or 'social' institutions on the other – sometimes, for simplification, reserving the concept of 'institution' exclusively for the latter. The generic difference between the two is that the first kind of institutions accommodate and facilitate rational-utilitarian voluntarism, whereas the second generate, impose and enforce social obligations that rational individuals would not voluntarily and contractually take upon themselves. In a strong Durkheimian sense, it is only institutions of the latter kind that make a society. Like Durkheim, we are in this chapter less interested in categoric distinctions than in the notion that the relative significance of the two kinds of institutions may vary between societies, with institutionally 'thinner' societies allowing a comparatively large space for free contract and individual choice in relatively unregulated markets and hierarchies, and institutionally 'thicker' societies subjecting the actions of rational individuals to a richer set of regulations and constraints.

2 In this respect the analysis of diversified quality production was informed by the study of industrial interest politics. Comparative research on the impact of trade unions and industrial relations on economic adjustment and competitive performance had revealed long and complex chains of causation and interdependence. Especially in a comparative perspective, the view that weak and accommodative trade unions, standing for the minimalist institutional environment demanded by neo-liberal and neo-classical prescriptions, are necessarily conducive to economic performance had been found to be simplistic and misleading (e.g., Cameron, 1984; Castles, 1987; Crouch, 1985; Hotz, 1982; Streeck, 1987a, Chapter 6, this volume).

While some economies seemed to thrive on institutional minimalism in general and the absence of organized industrial interests in particular, in others – and clearly not the least successful ones – strong and assertive trade unions performed a variety of, manifest and latent, positive functions. Indeed such functions were not limited to aggregate demand stabilization through 'aggressive' redistribution, 'rigid' wage fixing or 'cooperative' wage restraint in a Keynesian, demand-side-oriented sense. Among the most important discoveries in the neo-corporatist debate of the 1970s and 1980s, sometimes introduced under misleading labels like 'micro-corporatism' (Streeck, 1984b), was the supply-side dimension of neo-corporatist institutions: their actual and potential role in the formation and functioning of competitive production systems. Such insights helped prepare the ground for a re-orientation of the corporatist paradigm from the Keynesian concerns of the 1970s to the structural, 'qualitative' concerns of the 1980s.

3 In the work of Arndt Sorge in particular (see Sorge, 1985), the notion of different and alternative production patterns was derived from comparative studies of work organization and, later, responses to technical change. Sorge's work, often co-authored with Marc Maurice and Malcom Warner, undertook to link distinctive national patterns of work organization to different selections of product ranges and product markets, and to explain the resulting configurations with reference to different institutional endowments in the society at large. In this way, a society's specific 'culture', as crystallized in its institutional macro-structure, came to be conceived as a production factor in the widest sense, shaping both the process and the outcome of economic action. The objective was to account for the persistence of differences in work organization and technology use in the face of 'identical' technology, and in patterns of industrial output in spite of 'identical' market pressures, by explaining them as consequences of different institutional conditions generating alternative responses to similar technological and economic stimuli. As a consequence, the idea that there might have been something like a universal choice around the turn of the century between mass and craft production never appears in Sorge's work.

4 Or the 'industrial district' of Baden-Württemberg, the neo-regionalist description of which often somehow manages to overlook the dominant role played in it by a multi-national giant like Daimler Benz.

5 It is at this point that the present chapter's critique of rational choice as a sufficient basis for advanced industrial production patterns is particularly pertinent. The chapter's 'Durkheimian' concern with the regulatory, interventionist and non-voluntary elements of social institutions corresponds to a strong emphasis on prisoners'-dilemma-type coordination problems, and on the insufficiency and indeterminacy of rational individual calculations vis-a-vis complex, long-term decisions on the development of advanced productive capacities.

6 Which means that the concept, while not buying into all implications of 'flexible specialization', does cover and include the phenomena studied under this label. It therefore can fruitfully draw on the rich research tradition of the flexible specialization school.

7 In other words, diversified quality production requires a specific pattern of industrial organization; exhibits a particular investment function; and is characterized by a distinctive production function.

8 Indeed the analysis of the 'social dimension' of diversified quality production could entirely be phrased in terms of the preconditions of an advanced form of productive flexibility, in particular in terms of the difference between quantitative

(neo-classical) and qualitative flexibility, with the associated trade-off between different, corresponding forms of rigidity. More on this below, with reference to the constraints and opportunities for diversified quality production originating from the 'social system of production'.

9 If this was so, small firms would be much more important in the British and American than in the German and Japanese economy. The fact that in reality it is the other way around has to do with a number of status privileges for small and medium-sized firms in Japan and Germany that are hard to reconcile with the principles of free competition and unlimited market access. See Chapter 4 in this volume.

10 The strong claim of this chapter, and the theoretical core of its institutionalist argument, is that, to the extent that economic behavior is – or should better be – also social behavior, rational individual calculations of costs and benefits have inherent gaps that make them less than instructive and that need to be filled, for action to be possible at all, by socially institutionalized norms. While in certain relatively simple or historically established production patterns this fact may for practical purposes be negligible – which is why it is neglected in standard economics – it is observable, for example, in the persistent differences in structure and practice between presumably equally rational organizations embedded in different institutional contexts. It is also visible in the considerable 'space' economic exigencies regularly leave for cultural diffusion of organizational patterns and practices. Instrumental rationality, in other words, is not enough to 'close' organizational structures. This seems to hold in particular where 'the rational thing to do' would be the creation of an affluent supply of non-dedicated capacities and possibilities. While some organizations could be expected to understand the logic of redundant capacity-building on their own, many others may not and may require institutional pressures to behave in line with their rational interests. Moreover, since each organization's investment in a rich supply of redundant capacities is part of the other organizations' ecology of possibilities, the success of individual efforts at redundant capacity-building depends on effective institutions providing for equifinal behavior beyond the limits of individual rationality.

11 This distinction, of course, is at the heart of conventional 'human capital' theory.

12 This applies in particular in conditions when the kind of general skills that are needed cannot easily be generated outside the workplace in public schools (Streeck, 1989).

13 Strictly speaking, this is true only for 'modern' societies whose institutional substructure is not, or is no longer, traditionally given, and therefore needs to be reconstructed through collective action and organization. By and large, a case of a society whose 'thick' institutions are of a traditional kind is Japan. Sweden, by contrast, can be taken as an example of successful political reconstruction of social obligations in a modern society.

14 Productivist justifications of egalitarianism have a long history in European socialism, especially in Sweden. See Higgins (1985) on Ernst Wigforss.

15 Equity, in other words, performs a positive economic function insofar as it stands in the way of excessive rationalization of social and organizational structures. Diversified quality production, we have argued, requires that production systems be not fully rationalized, in the sense of completely dedicated to specific instrumental purposes. To be able to withstand and contain economic rationalization pressures, a society needs to institutionalize strong competing values that can successfully defy subsumption under the dictates of the 'economic principle'.

16 Institutions that are no more than constraints on firms, managements and workers will choke off economic growth and initiative; they are particularly likely to become strongholds of trade unions turned into rent-seeking 'distributional coalitions'. Institutions that merely offer opportunities will favor exploitation of the 'public' by the 'private' sector, for example by firms shopping around for subsidies.

17 The prime example of politically designed 'thick' institutions with negative – and, in fact, disastrous – economic consequences was, of course, 'really existing socialism' until 1989. For traditional societies, compare India to Japan.

18 Unlike Keynesianism, that is to say, the positive effect of high wages on diversified quality production takes place primarily through the supply side – where they operate as a 'productivity whip' and, to the extent that they are sufficiently rigid, as a barrier to low-wage adjustment strategies. To what extent diversified quality production also requires the contribution of a high and stable wage to effective demand is more difficult to determine, given that markets for diversified quality production are typically worldwide, and the overlap between producers and consumers is usually much smaller than in 'Fordist' mass production. In fact, large-scale adoption of diversified quality production in recent decades may well be interpreted, as it is in Piore and Sabel (1984), as a micro-level response to long-term declining institutional capacities – including those of trade unions – to make domestic demand stable and predictable. Product diversification and movement into quality markets are in this perspective insurance against permanently high local demand uncertainty and volatility – the assumption being that unsaturated demand for diversified quality production in non-local markets is, for whatever reason, large enough to be taken for granted. For a perceptive discussion of this topic that arrives at different conclusions, see Mahon (1987).

2

Revisiting Status and Contract: Pluralism, Corporatism and Flexibility*

On scarcely anything have the classics of modern sociology been so unanimous as in their criticism of the 'free labor contract'. The ironic formulation, reminiscent of Anatole France, that it 'is left to the "free" discretion of the parties [in the labor market] to accept the conditions imposed by those who are economically stronger by virtue of the legal guarantee of their property', comes not from Karl Marx but from Max Weber (1978: 731). The word 'free' appears in quotes because, according to Weber,

> the formal right of a worker to enter into any contract whatsoever with any employer whatsoever does not in practice represent for the employment seeker even the slightest freedom in the determination of his own conditions of work [. . .]. It rather means, at least primarily, that the more powerful party in the market, i.e., normally the employer, has the possibility to set the terms, to offer the job 'take it or leave it', and, given the normally more pressing economic need of the worker, to impose his terms on him. (1978: 729 f.)

Precisely the same idea can be found in Durkheim: 'If one class of society is obliged, in order to live, to take any price for its services, while another can abstain from such action thanks to resources at its disposal [. . .], the second has an unjust advantage over the first at law.' In the next sentence comes the famous verdict: 'In other words, there cannot be rich and poor at birth without there being unjust contracts' (1964: 383).

Arguments such as these are based on complex conceptual foundations. The market as an institution derives its legitimacy from its presumed ability to create a stable social order by balancing out the different interests of rationally acting individuals maximizing their own advantage. This requires, however, that the participants can enter into their relationships freely and shape them according to their discretion. The medium through which this takes place is the contract. But if the resources of the parties are distributed so asymmetrically that much more depends for one party than for the other upon the conclusion of a contract, then while contracts may still be concluded, they are contracts only in form; in reality they are commands. In particular, where 'market power' is as unequal as it is between owners of labor power and of capital, the market creates not order but conflict. In Durkheim's proto-functionalist ethical theory, 'injustice' is accordingly equated with social instability: it prevents the development of that 'organic solidarity' which alone can manage to hold a functionally differentiated society with an advanced division of labor together: 'The harmony of functions and, accordingly, of existence, is at stake. Just as ancient peoples needed, above all, a common faith to live by, so we need justice' (Durkheim, 1964: 388).

In Marx's analysis of the labor contract too we find the theme of the imbalance between the two sides of the market. But for Marx, what is important in the capitalist labor contract is not only that it is unequal, but also that it is indeterminate. The second point results from the central distinction between labor and labor power. It is not the former that is the commodity traded on the labor market, but the latter – which, incidentally, is why the market wage, which according to the theory of value on average corresponds to the expenditure necessary to reproduce the labor power, is in principle a 'just' wage. In the fully developed wage-labor system, labor contracts are concluded not about labor services stipulated in detail in advance (this distinguishes them from work contracts), but about the recognition of an institutionalized authority relationship, the employer's right to manage, in the framework of which the services expected in return for the wage can be, and are, continually redefined. The economic necessity and superiority of this arrangement results both from the high capital investment needed in the industrial mode of production, and from the fact that under modern conditions of economic action under uncertainty the precise nature of the activities required by the employer in the future cannot be known at the time of concluding the contract. At this point, the distinction between labor and labor power opens the door for a sociological theory of work organization, or indeed for an institutional theory of economics, and especially of contracts, like for example that of John R. Commons (1924). However, the Marxist tradition has mainly followed other lines that start from here, such as the theory of alienation and, as with Marx himself, the project of a political economy that seeks to deduce, from the development of the concept of surplus value as the difference between the value of labor and the value of labor power, the immanent contradictions and developmental trends of the capitalist social formation.

But of course the labor contract is only a special case of contract, and in fact the criticisms by early sociologists went quite generally against the market and contract model of society that had in the nineteenth century become the ideal of progress for the new class of the bourgeoisie on its way to social hegemony. Paradigmatic for the emerging new world view was the liberal optimism of Herbert Spencer, whose utilitarian-voluntarist theory of society (Spencer, 1961) represented an attempt to flesh out systematically Henry Sumner Maine's famous dictum that 'the movement of the progressive societies has hitherto been a movement from Status to Contract' (Maine, 1960: 100). For Maine, contract meant any voluntarily agreed relationship of rights and obligations between individuals with different resources and interests, each increasing their advantage by exchanging goods and services with the other. Status, by contrast, represented a complex of rights and duties imposed on individuals a priori as a consequence of their belonging to a particular social category – for Maine as a rule the family – independently of their own wills or actions. This distinction between the agreed and the preordained, the created and the grown, between consensual and obligatory order has, in manifold variations, remained fundamental for modern social theory until today. It can be found again for instance in Weber, who distinguished between rights that 'in a marketless community [rest] directly upon the prescriptive and prohibitory propositions of the law itself', and rights deriving from contractual 'legal transactions' (1978: 668). While Weber too locates the origin of status as a 'starting-point for [an individual's] further legally relevant activities' (1978: 669) in the family and the law of inheritance, his concept of status can be used more generally as it speaks of 'a special and intrinsic quality [that] is attributed to him by the law independently of his own acts of consociation' (1978: 669).

Those who doubted the possibility or indeed desirability of a social evolution towards a contractual society of Spencerian type could seek to show against Maine that even in early societies there had always been contracts – which seems to have been the main line of attack by anthropologists, as the specialists for 'premodern' cultures. However, much more promising strategically for an anti-liberal line of defense of either past or future 'community' against utilitarian market-plus-contract 'society' was the converse argument that status powerfully survives even and especially in modern society. Indeed, the concept of status in one form or another became the very watchword and *Leitbegriff* of sociology as it was forming as a discipline in defining itself more or less explicitly as the theory of the 'noncontractual conditions of contract' (Durkheim, 1964) and thereby from the outset turning polemically against the 'unconditional' contract theory of bourgeois economics. The attractiveness of the labor market specifically as a field for investigation in, and an object for illustration of, the persistence of status and the irredeemability of contract no doubt had to do with the possibility it offered for linking up with an existing general awareness of the 'social question'; ultimately, however, what was at stake was not industrial (contract) relations but modern society as a whole. Here three types of argumentation can be distinguished among the classics in which status is called upon as a counter-concept to contract (and these types were, as we shall see, to continue reappearing later, enriched by further permutations).

First, there is the demonstration of the survival in modern society of status orders antedating individual legal transactions which can make the conclusion of more than formally free contracts impossible: status prevents contract. As we have seen, this idea can be used for both a 'liberal' and a 'radical' critique of the power imbalance on the labor market; it was later taken up and popularized by the Webbs, Brentano and an innumerable multitude of subsequent authors. In this line of argument, status takes on a scalar dimension not inherent in it a priori or necessarily (Zelditch, 1968, 250); to the extent that it is seen as based on property rights, whose acquisition is in turn mediated or facilitated through family membership, it comes close to the concept of class. This connection has been made not only by Marx and Weber but also by Durkheim, who in his *Division of Labor* speaks of unjust status orders that can lead to 'class-wars' (1964: 374). As is well known, Durkheim deduces from this a radical postulate of equality, the social realization of which is for him the prerequisite for the functioning of freely agreed contractual relationships (1964: 374–88, passim).

Secondly, there is the demonstration that individual contracts may be the basis not only for specific and contractual, but also for unspecific and diffuse, rights and duties: contract establishes status. This was pointed to notably by Marx in his reconstruction of work organization on the basis of the labor contract, adding as we have seen an important facet to the asymmetry argument. For the fully developed wage-labor contract, as the basis of a hierarchical work organization, is an unequal contract insofar as it contractually specifies the rights of the worker and the obligations of the employer, while the rights of the employer and the obligations of the worker remain, and must remain, in principle 'open', that is, diffuse and status-like. In this way, contractually based organizational status reproduces the social class status that precedes it while at the same time, through its functioning as a 'relational contract' (MacNeil, 1974), translating it into legitimate rule. As will later be shown in our discussion of Fox (1974), this already highly complex configuration contains still other status components by which it is further socially stabilized.

Thirdly, there is the demonstration that contracts can emerge only against the background of a social structure of rights and duties that can be taken as given and that is not itself negotiable: status makes contract possible; contract presupposes status. 'For everything in the contract', thus Durkheim (1964: 211), 'is not contractual [. . .]. Wherever a contract exists, it is submitted to regulation which is the work of society and not that of individuals, and which becomes ever more voluminous and more complicated.' This is the core of the theory of the 'non-contractual terms of contract' – or, in other words, the normative, if one so wishes: 'constitutional', preconditions for rationally purposive instrumental action. These determine, for instance, who may, by virtue of a status as a subject of civil rights awarded by society and withdrawable by it, engage in contractual relationships at all. At the same time and additionally, a status-type determination of inalienable rights and duties of contractual parties ensures that the gaps in definition and risks in implementation that are unavoidable not only in labor contracts but in most other types of contract as well, do not render contractual exchanges impossible from the outset.[1] Where, in Oliver Williamson's terminology (1975: passim), the (transaction) costs of 'writing' a contract would be prohibitively high because of both the uncertainties lying in the matter itself and the 'bounded rationality' of the parties involved, uncertainty and mistrust can be decisively reduced by pre-contractual, but nevertheless and precisely because of that sanctionable, norms of, for example, 'good faith'. Where such status preconditions of contractual agreement have been eroded, the voluntarism of market and contract runs dry: instead of balancing of interests, there results a Hobbesian permanent conflict.

Status, we have asserted, is a key concept of sociological theory in its constitutive endeavor to incorporate the utilitarianism of the economic paradigm into a broader categorical frame of reference and thereby relativize it as a (highly) contingent special case of social action. However the concept may in each case be defined in detail – and T.H. Marshall has impressively described its degeneration in symbolic interactionism and social psychology (1964: 200ff.; see also Zelditch, 1968) – it cannot, at least in combination with its classical counterpart, the concept of contract, deny its kinship with that multiplicity of antinomies through which the 'sociological tradition' (Nisbet, 1967) has sought to understand the evolutionary, historical and functional bases of modern social orders: Tönnies' community and society (on Maine's influence on Tönnies, see Parsons, 1968: 687); Weber's *Wert-* and *Zweckrationalität* (whose relationship to Durkheim's analysis of contract has also been reconstructed by Parsons – 1968: 660); Redfield's 'Folk and Urban Society' (Redfield, 1955); Parsons's 'pattern variables' (Parsons 1951: 68–112); Blau's economic and social exchange (Blau, 1964), etc. The comparative advantage of status and contract as analytical categories possibly lies in the fact that they lead more closely and more concretely than others to both the institution of the market and, at the same time, the social embeddedness (Granovetter, 1985) of economic exchange relationships – which makes them seem particularly suitable for analyses of the empirical extreme case for a contract theory of social order, the labor market.

Fox: Unequal Contracts, Trust and the Status Obligation of Obedience

How was the system of trade in labor power as a commodity, mediated through the labor contract, so long able to survive the early diagnoses of its inherent instability? In his book *Beyond Contract: Work, Power and Trust Relations* (1974), Alan Fox, starting from a recapitulation of the sociological theoretical tradition of status and contract, tried to find elements in the historical development of the relationship between the two that might explain the robustness of the labor market as an institution. Fox's analysis represents a cross-fertilization of Marxian and Durkheimian lines of argumentation, linking up in the case of Marx particularly with his uncompleted theory of the relationship between labor contract and work organization, and of the foundation of organizational status on unequal contract. Contracts, according to Fox, following Durkheim, cannot beforehand include and specify all the modalities of their implementation; they therefore function only on a fund of extra-contractual 'goodwill' and diffuse mutual loyalty. This is particularly true of the labor contract and the entrepreneurial right of management, with the help of which the regulatory gaps of the former have to be closed. But wherever labor 'is seen as a commodity resource to be hired and discarded as required' (Fox, 1974: 88), the consensus between the contracting parties necessary for its utilization is exposed to constant erosion. The social locus of this erosion process is the organization of work. If the relationship between the owners of capital and the sellers of labor is so defined that the former must 'bend their efforts to maximize the return on the labor' of the latter (Fox, 1974: 88), then employers must use their contractually based right to manage to impose on their labor force highly structured and standardized role definitions, restricting their discretion and room for maneuver to the unavoidable minimum (Fox, 1974: 59, 96, passim) – an organizational principle which found its highest expression in the organizational technology associated with the name of Frederick Winslow Taylor (Fox, 1974: 191–5).

Now, to the extent that contractual trading in labor power entails a Taylorist work organization and a categorical status distinction between organization members with higher and lower freedom of decision, it gives rise to 'oppositional' forces (Blau, 1964), the effect of which inevitably tends to make the labor contract unusable as an instrument for the balancing of interests. For even a Taylorist organization of work requires an at least rudimentary readiness, even by the occupiers of extremely standardized positions, to identify with them and behave towards the organization as loyal members rather than mere external suppliers. Loyalty, however, can in the long run persist only if it is reciprocated (Fox, 1974: 102ff.). The problem of a work organization brought about through market-type trading in labor power lies in the fact that, while it requires the loyalty of its low-status members, it must, due to imperatives of economic efficiency, continually show them disloyalty by cutting off their freedom of discretion. The inherent dynamics of trust relationships, however, are such that any withdrawal of trust is seen as an expression of mistrust, which in turn leads to a defensive withdrawal of trust. A 'low trust spiral' is thus set in motion (Fox, 1974: 102ff., 145) which, beginning with the degradation of work at the bottom end of the hierarchy, brings about a decline in the workforce's identification with its work, which in turn leads to reactions by the management that amount to a further restriction of discretion. Other elements of the developing vicious circle are the typically ensuing attempts by the employees, as a counter-move to the ever stronger formal regulation of their own duties, to subject, through collective trade union action, managerial discretion to formal rules as well – so that we can observe a scissor movement between the steady increase in the amount of bureaucratic and formal regulations and a simultaneous shrinkage of the extra-contractual capital of trust which alone could make formal rules and contracts effective (Fox, 1974: 113, 125). The result is an 'overloading' of the contract, which leads – or at least should be expected to lead – to a progressive decline in the binding capacity of the formal rules, with a corresponding proliferation of conflicts and, simultaneously, growing rigidity of the regulatory system, giving rise to adjustment problems and losses of economic performance.

This brings us to Fox's real question: how can a system of contractual exchange that leads to such consequences have any permanence? Only as long, says Fox, as it has not yet been fully realized. The riddle of the labor contract and its tenacity so far is solved if one drops the assumption that the complete realization of a contractual order on the labor market has either already been achieved, or indeed is in the interest of the economically more powerful buyers of labor power. According to Fox, it is not only the imbalance of power in the labor market that made the labor contract from the outset more of an ideology than a reality. 'Application of the contract system to the employment relation, would have suggested implications alarming to property owners' (Fox, 1974: 183). Among these was the fact that 'contract theory included the notion of appeal by either party to some outside adjudicating body in the event of behavior claimed to be inconsistent with the contract' (Fox, 1974: 184). If this were taken seriously, then the continuous one-sided redefinition of the employee's duties of performance by the employer under the entrepreneurial right of management, which is essential to the utilization of labor as a commodity, would be made impossible by appeals to the voluntary agreement principle of contract, or at least made intolerably difficult in practice – as in fact happened in the 1970s in those British firms where shop stewards were able to impose the principle of 'mutuality', the renegotiation of pay and effort on even the slightest change in operations. Fox's underlying idea here is that there is a tension between the legal form of the contract and the principle of generalized authority, in that the essential voluntarism of a contractual order exposes any authority founded upon contract to the constant danger of a lapse back into barter-type, 'tit-for-tat' exchange.[2]

In fact, according to Fox, the contractual foundation of managerial authority was only the visible surface of a construction in which in reality, conversely, the regulatory gaps and legitimation deficits of the unequal labor contract had to be repaired by recourse to prior status orders – so that on the labor market it was not contract that founded status, but also, and primarily, status that founded contract. For illustration, Fox here refers to English common law which, while it had from the Middle Ages been structured in a comparatively individualistic and contractual way, had at the same time, and perhaps precisely because of that, for long underpinned the labor contract by applying the legal pattern of the traditional, diffuse status relationship between 'master and servant' to its interpretation – sometimes with the consequence of criminal penalties for breach of contract (Fox, 1974: 184–6). Traditional, feudal status law was construed in case law as an implicit element of the labor contract to fill its lacunae (Fox, 1974: 184) – 'status' in the sense of 'estate', with the buyer of labor power as 'Lord of the Manor' and not at all as occupant of a managerial function grounded in a (social) contract. Where in the course of time modernization brought about a contractualization of the employment relationship, this consisted primarily in a specification and 'voluntarization' of the diffuse obligations of the 'master' – not of the 'servant'. The result was 'a form of contract almost as far removed from the pure doctrinal form as the status relationship which had preceded it' (Fox, 1974: 184). To the extent that the status relationship between master and servant persisted between the lines of the written contract and was maintained either by legal coercion or through the internalization of paternalist ideologies by the sellers of labor power themselves, the realization of the labor contract remained incomplete, and it is only for that reason and to the extent that this is still the case that the labor contract, and with it the status order at the workplace that appears to be based on it, has been able to function until today.

Contract alone, Fox's considerations may be summarized, cannot organize work; the labor contract as an organizing contract must be underpinned by prior status. But by contrast with Durkheim, Fox allows the possibility that a status system suitable for legitimizing labor contracts need not, at least for a while, necessarily guarantee the 'equality of external conditions' that the author of the *Division of Labour* regarded as indispensable (Fox, 1974: 234). Instead, the legitimation of contracts that remain unequal can be brought about by construing into them premodern status definitions, the binding capacity of which can be guaranteed either culturally or by force – status definitions which, for both Durkheim and Fox, albeit in differing ways, are 'immoral'. At the same time, against Marx and his distinction between labor power and labor, Fox points to the residual necessity – remaining despite the de facto compulsion for sellers of labor to enter into a contract on the labor market – to equip the status-type, diffuse right of management, unlike the contractual, specifically stipulated price of the commodity of labor power, with cultural legitimations that go beyond the apparent voluntarism of the contract – legitimations which keep the obligations of the employees diffusely open while they relegate those of the employers largely to their own, interest-led discretion. The argument that the traditional cultural stock of modern societies has such legitimations to hand and that these may be much more tenacious than could be expected from a materialist position represents a sociological critique of the version of a theory of political economy that has become dominant after Marx.

There can, however, be no lasting reliance on the stabilizing effect of traditional status. Writing the master-and-servant relation into the 'free' labor contract has, if one follows Fox, bought the system of wage labor no more than a breathing space – corresponding to the time required by the spiral of low trust, being steadily wound further by the organization of work and the working of the labor contract, to demolish the traditions of obedience, acceptance of inequality and subordinate loyalty unreciprocated from above. This process of cultural modernization, in the course of which even the most loyal of servants realize that indeed, as Marx and Engels put it in the *Communist Manifesto*, the 'bourgeosie [. . .] has left no other nexus between man and man than naked self-interest, than callous "cash payment"' (Marx and Engels, 1964: 588) – this process ends in anomie (see Fox's interpretation, 1974: 370–5, of Titmuss's 1970 study *The Gift Relationship*). Maine's progress from traditional status to modern contract could proceed as long as, and only as long as, contract had not yet swallowed up its foundation in status, nor modernity its basis in tradition.[3] With the full realization of contractual society, contract finally loses its capacity to create order. Marx and Durkheim may have underestimated the resistance of traditions and the time needed to demolish them; but ultimately they were right all along.

Sociological theories, even those aimed at comprehensive generalization, cannot deny the historical circumstances of their emergence, and that is particularly true here. In 1974, when *Beyond Contract* appeared, the Heath government's attempt to reform the British system of industrial relations by legislation had just failed, after conflicts that at times resembled an industrial civil war (Streeck, 1978; Weekes et al., 1975). Instead of providing a framework for cooperation among employers and employees to increase the productivity and competitiveness of the British economy, the system of industrial institutions lay in ruins; the government that had been pushing the reform had collapsed over it; and the reform act, open contempt for which had done the legitimacy of the legal order harm that would take long to mend, was withdrawn by its successor. Fox had fought the Industrial Relations Act, mainly it seems because it was incompatible with the 'voluntarist' philosophy of the 'Oxford School' and its rejection of government regulation of industrial relations. At the same time, however, he was astute enough to recognize that both the Act and its failure were consequences of an advanced normative disintegration (see Fox, 1974: 288), and that this represented an insuperable obstacle even for those 'voluntary' reform programs in the conception of which he had once himself been involved. *Beyond Contract*, with its strengths and weaknesses, is a far-reaching justification of the author's break with the institutional reformism of the 'Oxford School'; at the same time, it is an expression of a turn, admittedly not with much hope, towards what the book calls the 'radical position' – a sociologically grounded Marxism (Fox, 1974: 248–96).[4]

At the end of his book Fox cites Durkheim, with the sentence, no doubt a critical paraphrase of Maine: 'The task of the most advanced societies is, then, a work of justice' (Durkheim, 1964: 387), and he closes by stating that, 'our definition of justice may not be his, but it is becoming increasingly harder not to agree with the feeling as such' (Fox, 1974: 369). The only way out of the advanced stage of social disintegration seemed to Fox to be a radical-egalitarian reform, not of the institutions of industrial relations, but of the class structure underlying them. Only that could end the 'galloping contagion of mistrust', the visible manifestation of which was 'galloping inflation' (Fox, 1974: 322). Today, at a time when despite a considerable increase in social inequality in Britain (O'Higgins, 1985) not only has inflation gone down but labor relations have become more peaceful than they have ever been since the mid-1960s, arguments of this nature appear antiquated.[5] But even if they were so in fact; and even if it were true that Fox's analysis is so marked by the peculiarities of British society that it can no longer recognize them as such, it would remain of interest if only because the failure of one of the furthest developed models of a sociological theory of crisis ought to be a source of productive disquiet for all those who, whether as 'conservatives', as 'radicals' or simply as sociologists, share and retain the model's conceptual foundations and traditions of thought.

Tannenbaum and Marshall: Reconstruction of Status through Collectivization of Contract

Another attempt to explain the resilience of the labor contract as the result of an underpinning by status can be found in a number of authors of the 1950s and 1960s who in part reach back to much earlier ideas, like those of the Webbs or Dicey. What they have in common is that, by contrast with Fox (1974: 246), they accept Maine's basic idea of a historical development 'from status to contract', but supplement it with the idea of an associated counter-movement 'from contract to status' in the course and with the help of which society is alleged to have contained and balanced the disintegrative effects of the contractual system (Friedman, 1972). Status here means, as before, a set of rights individuals possess as members of a social group independently of individual agreements, which they cannot negotiate away by contract; as well as a set of obligations from which those to whom they apply cannot be released by way of contractual agreement (Selznick, 1969). Unlike

Fox, however, the authors in this tradition are concerned, not with primary status orders historically preceding contract, but with secondary restrictions on private contractual freedom, created through rational law-making by which society, quite in Durkheim's sense, subjects the intercourse of private legal subjects to compensatory regulation that protects the weaker contractual partner. As examples from within civil law itself one might refer above all to the doctrine of 'good faith' (Teubner, 1980) or the idea of the 'immorality' of contracts. More specific regulations that restrict the negotiating freedom of particular categories of contractual partners in status-type fashion are legal minimum wages, obligations to contribute to social security, rent control, the legal regulation of general terms of contract, etc. (Marshall, 1964: 112f.).

As far as the labor market is concerned, the central mechanism for domesticating the contract through restoration of status is held to be the negotiation of collective agreements by trade unions. That status itself thereby becomes contractually created is only superficially a parallel with the foundation of managerial authority upon the labor contract as described, and ultimately found inadequate, by Fox. The decisive difference is the collective nature of the industrial agreement, which despite its private-law form makes it into an instrument of public law-making and thus into a special case of the general blurring of boundaries between private and public spheres – expressed among other things in the frequently observed interchangeability between law and collective agreement as instruments for regulating the individual labor contract in different countries and at different times.[6] The essential point about the collective labor contract is therefore not that it is a contract but that it sets bounds to the freedom of individual contracting and, as an 'inalienable' law, subjects the market-rational action of the parties on the labor market to binding regulation. As a consequence, according to Tannenbaum, 'the sum of the expanding rules adds up to a reduction of the area governed by contract, and an expansion of the area in which men's lives are ruled by status' (Tannenbaum, 1964: 145). Similar observations can be found in analyses of the development of labor-law theory (especially Selznick, 1969) where the change seems to have been particularly striking in Britain with its age-honored distinction between 'common law' and 'statute law' (for a summary see Deakin, 1985). A rough and ready formula for the modern trend 'from contract to status' was offered by the concept of 're-feudalization' – which is inevitably imprecise as it does not do justice to the high contingency of collectively bargained status rights – and in fact to an author like Frank Tannenbaum, the trade union movement appears as a 'counter-revolutionary' force

(1964: 3) within the liberal social order, simultaneously transforming and socially reintegrating it through the collective agreement towards the model of a *Ständestaat* (1964: 140ff.).

The concept of the embedding of the individual labor contract in a new status order through collective agreement has found its most advanced formulation in T.H. Marshall (1964). Marshall too joins Maine, whom he acknowledges to have expressed 'a profound truth' with his idea of an evolution from status to contract – a truth which, however, requires elaboration since, as Marshall argues, both status and contract are always present in all societies (Marshall, 1964: 87). This would have to be the case if only because contracts, even between unequals, presuppose an equal status right to conclude contracts and to demand their observance. Accordingly, at the beginning of the modern epoch, 'differential status, associated with class, function and family, was replaced by the single uniform status of citizenship, *which provided the foundation of equality on which the structure of inequality could be built*' (Marshall, 1964: 87, my emphasis). This newly institutionalized status of a citizen with contractual capacity was subsequently the starting point for the emergence of two further modern status orders that Marshall terms 'political' and 'social rights', which unlike general civil rights did come into conflict with the primary status structure of inequality (Marshall, 1964: 93). One aspect of this dynamic was the recognition of the right to collective bargaining as a consequence of the exercise of political rights by the labor movement. This development had a peculiar double face. On one side it meant 'that social progress was being sought by strengthening civil rights, not by creating social rights; through the use of contract in the open market, not through a minimum wage and social security' (Marshall, 1964: 93, my emphasis). At the same time, however, the new 'industrial' civil rights were exercised not individually but collectively, and were therefore 'not simply a natural extension of [existing] civil rights [but] represented the transfer of an important process from the political to the civil sphere' (Marshall, 1964: 94). To that extent, the development in the area of 'civil society' was precisely the converse of that in the political sphere, as it led from the representation of individuals to that of groups and not, as in parliamentarism, from the representation of groups to that of individuals. The trade union movement created 'a secondary system of industrial citizenship, parallel with and supplementary to the system of political citizenship' (Marshall, 1964: 94) – a formulation that was later reflected in Stein Rokkan's influential concept of a 'second tier of government'.

In Tannenbaum and Marshall, too, as in Fox, contract is legitimated by status; but the significance of status and its relationship to contract are of an entirely different nature. While Fox uses the concept of status as a key for a critical-analytical reconstruction of the premodern bases and preconditions for the modern institution of the free labor market, for Marshall and Tannenbaum status appears as the outcome of a creative, adaptive, integrative reaction of modern society to contradictions and conflicts of the modernization process. In both models, underpinning contract through status makes possible the spread of contract as a mode of transaction and the conversion of the indeterminate labor contract into a system of authority at the workplace. However, while for Fox (traditional) status has the function of keeping the rights of the employer and the obligations of the employee open, in Marshall's view both are circumscribed and delimited through the collectively bargained (political) status of industrial citizenship, while at the same time the dynamic law-making mechanism of the institutionalized bargaining system generates basically open and extensible legal entitlements of the sellers of labor power as members of an organized collectivity. To that extent, the institutions of industrial citizenship were to become a mechanism of social redistribution that functioned as an important vehicle of the secular trend to greater equality that Marshall, like Dicey and many others before him, had seen as the true content of modern democratic development.

In the upshot, at least in tendency, the significance of the individual labor contract itself changes. In the configuration described by Fox, as a consequence of the inequality of the contractual relationship and its cultural legitimation in the doctrine of 'master and servant', all that counted as obligations of the employer and rights of the worker was what was explicitly laid down in the contract, whereas to define the rights of the employer and the obligations of the worker the vertical status order was drawn upon. But with the collective contract this relationship is reversed in that now the definition of the worker's rights, and therefore of the employer's obligations, is turned over to a dynamic mechanism for producing political and social status, and thus kept open in the sense of a progressive elimination of social inequality, while the employer's rights and worker's obligations, that were formerly left open, become subject to specification in contracts. This, however, makes the question of reciprocity of contractual terms appear in a new light, and it is only logical for both Tannenbaum and Marshall – on the assumption of the historically successful exclusion, through the innovation of social civil rights, of the 'primary' status structure stressed by Fox – to locate the crisis potential of the new configuration in the absence of a collective 'responsibility' of unions that could be the basis for unspecific status obligations (Marshall, 1964: 112ff.; Tannenbaum, 1964: 160f.).[7]

Industrial Pluralism: the Institutionalization of Status through Institutional Differentiation

The main thrust of Fox's conversion was directed against 'pluralism'. That term has many meanings, in particular as it applies to collective labor relations. Indeed, even within the very special, and very British, variant of pluralism adopted by the 'Oxford School', there was, after Fox's defection from it, no longer even terminological agreement between Fox and his former associates (Clegg, 1975). At the same time, it is true that, for instance, Clegg on the one side and the American 'pluralist' school of industrial relations on the other (Dunlop, 1958; Kerr et al., 1960) had a number of important ideas in common, among them in particular that of the possibility of institutional pacification of the labor contract with and despite continued unequal distribution of ownership and management rights – and it was just this possibility that Fox had disputed, through recourse to Durkheim and reference to the constitutive 'injustice' of a class society.

For pluralist theory, too, equality of the parties to a contract is the precondition for contracts to claim legitimate validity. But in the fully developed pluralist paradigm, the social locus of equality is shifted from the level of the individual to that of the collectives negotiating with each other, or from the social structure to the 'rules of the game' of a specialized system of institutions, differentiated from its environment. Equality, necessary as ever, now appears as 'combat parity' of the parties to the collective agreement who in Dunlop's formulation 'jointly regulate' the labor market – where for Clegg equality is already realized once the outcome of a possible conflict seems uncertain (1975: 313). For both Clegg and the Americans, in this way the inequality of individual actors is compensated for by equal collective procedural status rights of the partners to the collective contract, which make it possible for trade unions to lay down status rights inalienable in the individual contract and thus as a result protect the labor contract against delegitimization.[8] The difference between the American and the British variant of pluralism seems to lie above all in the important role that Dunlop in particular assigns to the state – the role, that is, of so adjusting the bargaining power, or 'status' (Dunlop, 1958: 98), of the two sides that neither can force 'irresponsible' agreements on the other (Marshall, 1964: 115). The 'pluralism' of the 'Oxford School', by contrast, was always at the same time 'voluntarism', based on the unshakeable belief that it could or had to do without the status-defining and guaranteeing contribution of the state.

However that may be, the construction of an integrative status of industrial citizenship under pluralist premises calls in both cases for the differentiation of a system of institutions relatively autonomous from the social class structure. At this point Marshall's political theory of the formation of new secondary status orders – whether these undermine the 'structure of inequality' or not – converges with the functionalist tradition of a sociological theory of industrial relations, which found its clearest formulation, explicitly related to Talcott Parsons (1951), in John Dunlop's influential *Industrial Relations Systems* (1958). For Dunlop (1958: 5) the system of industrial relations is an 'analytical subsystem of an industrial society' in the same sense and 'on the same logical plane as the economic system'. While the latter is specialized in the adaptive allocation of scarce resources, the former serves for the production of a 'web of rules governing the work place and the work community' (Dunlop, 1958: 14). Systems of industrial relations consist of three categories of actors – managements of firms, workforces and governmental and private agencies specializing in the regulation of the work process (Dunlop, 1958: 7); and they interact with three environments: a technological, an economic and a political one. Although the environments of the system affect the results of (joint) regulation and are in turn affected by them, the system functions according to its own laws. This relative decoupling is necessary not only for the procedural rules that guarantee the 'pluralist', legitimation-creating autonomy of the institutional system vis-a-vis the primary status and class structure. Equally important is a high degree of indifference to the environment of the substantive rules generated in the system through which the freedom of the individual labor contract is restricted. This is because these can amount to status rights for the individual employee only to the extent that they are insensitive to temporal, sectoral and local fluctuations of labor and product markets. Examples of this are 'sticky' wages fixed by collective bargaining, with their 'insurance' properties; collectively agreed employment guarantees; 'job property rights'; rights to promotion in internal labor markets, etc. As long as these entitlements apply independently of economic fluctuations – as they must if they are to redeem the 'unequal' contract through status – the system of industrial relations produces 'rigidities' for the decisions of managements of firms and of national economic policy, to which these must adapt.

Among the preconditions and consequences of the pluralist de-economization of industrial relations through the demarcation of a partially autonomous domain of regulation was the formation of a clear boundary between the competencies of management (for 'economy and production', if one so will) and unions (for 'social policy and distribution'). In principle and ideologically, this boundary remained controversial, and had to do so because of the de facto interdependence of product and labor markets. That it has nevertheless, in the 'mature' model of 'industrial pluralism' (Kerr et al., 1960),[9] been on the whole tacitly accepted by both sides is an expression not least of the asymmetry of status rights and contractual obligations inherent in the model and discussed above in connection with Marshall. If workers' entitlements, as generated by union action, were to achieve status (*Besitzstand*) character, then the unions had to exclude, as much as possible, any but 'social' considerations – that is, above all 'economic' ones – from the subsystem's decision-making and regulatory criteria, and as it were expect management as a status obligation to ensure that workers' entitlements, created regardless of specific economic conditions, could be met through corresponding production results. Since acceptance of economic responsibility by the unions would have forced them to admit a higher degree of elasticity of the terms of the individual labor contract in response to market fluctuations, the formation of the subsystem implied recognition in principle of management's right to manage, not on the basis of consensus on common goals but, on the 'pluralist' pattern, through institutionalized mutual recognition of differing goals.

In return, employers under the 'pluralist' set-up reconciled themselves with a pervasive moral indifference by workforces to the firm's economic goals and a shift in their loyalties towards the union. This they could all the easier do where Taylorist work organization guaranteed them the in principle 'motivation-free' functioning of the productive apparatus – that is, above all among manual workers in contrast to white-collar workers. In this way, the decoupling of the subsystem of industrial relations from the firm extended into work motivation as well – which suited the strategic need for unions as negotiating agents to limit their members' contribution to production to the minimum formally specified in the labor contract (that is, without accepting any further, informal, moral and therefore potentially open-ended obligations). Moreover, it corresponded to unions' organizational interest in preventing as far as possible the integration of their members into the firm as a 'moral community'[10] – an interest from the viewpoint of which a 'paternalist' employer often seems more dangerous than one who is hostile to unions. Especially in the United States, but not only there, the result was more or less conscious union acceptance of

Taylorist work organization, and profound mistrust of management attempts – in the United States through such projects as 'Human Relations' in the 1930s and 1950s, or 'quality of working life' and 'worker involvement' in the 1970s and 1980s – to raise the identification of workers with their work and with the firm.

From Pluralism to Corporatism: the Institutional Arrest of the Spiral of Low Trust

Alan Fox, at least for a while, seemed not to have excluded the possibility of a political foundation for a 'just' status order through institutional differentiation on the pluralist-functionalist model (he sometimes used the status concept clearly in the sense of Marshall, Tannenbaum, Friedman or Selznick: 1971, 165; 1974, 265). In the end, however, he rejected the idea that the anomic decay of social relationships as a consequence of social inequality could be prevented by institutional measures. Unions and collective agreements were for Fox, entirely in the nominalist tradition of British social theory, not any different in principle from the individual contractual partners and the individual labor contract (so also Clegg, 1975); instead of aggregates that could be more than the sum of their parts, they appeared to Fox to be ultimately merely a new, advanced expression of the all-dominating, irreversible mistrust between the parties to the contract. They could therefore not do otherwise than drive the spiral of mistrust on further (Fox, 1974: 113, 125). Pluralist industrial relations arise for Fox as a substitute for the traditional status definition of master and servant, where this has lost ideological persuasiveness; but they are subject in principle to the same anomic disruption (Fox, 1974: 204–6). For management, collective agreements may represent something like a second-best solution; as the price for them, however, it has to accept a proliferation of formal norms at the end of which stands the contract in its purity, denuded of all cladding and therefore no longer manageable. As for the unions – and this view was shared by many at the time of the worldwide resurgence of trade-union militancy in the late 1960s, mainly forced by the rank and file upon a reluctant leadership (Crouch and Pizzorno, 1978) – any pluralistic cooperation with the other side would inevitably subject union leaders themselves to the all-pervading mistrust of their members. The institutional differentiation of an industrial citizenship status therefore fails, if for no other reason, because of the political impossibility for unions to act in a pluralist sense, that is, as though substantive inequality could be rendered obsolete by the formal equality of collective procedural rules (Fox, 1974: 264–70).

It is statements of this kind which, almost two decades after *Beyond Contract*, make Fox's theses look so out of date. That Fox's sociological crisis theory has failed seems all too obvious today when we have seen Margaret Thatcher become the longest-serving British Prime Minister this century and Tony Benn, the prophet of an egalitarian reconstruction of British society in the early 1970s, relegated to the political fringe. But hindsight reveals also the theoretical weaknesses of Fox's argument, foremost among them the absence of a comparative perspective already pointed to by Wood and Elliott (1977). This insularity Fox shares with the 'Oxford School' and the bulk of British industrial relations research and theory in the 1960s and 1970s – which were prevented by their concentration on the single, very special case of their own society from understanding the particularities of that society.

One example of the blindness of British industrial relations theory to the British *Sonderweg*, the normatively and emotionally heavily loaded principle of 'voluntarism', has already been mentioned. Closely connected with it was a widespread lack of understanding, shared by Fox, of those versions of the pluralist model of industrial relations in which the respective status collectives of workers and employers are organized not, as Marshall, Tannenbaum and Dunlop assume to be the rule (cf. also Kerr et al., 1960: 294), on the basis of occupations, enterprises or work groups in firms, but more or less comprehensively and unitarily as classes. Typical of this 'neo-corporatist' variant, or further development, of industrial status is a largely uniform definition of status rights and obligations, for 'employees' on the one hand and 'employers' on the other, that is based on an unambiguous assignment of each individual actor on the labor market to one of the two broad social aggregates.

Corporatism requires a system of 'monopolistic' (Schmitter, 1974) and 'comprehensive' (Olson, 1965) interest organization whose emergence presupposes the historical supersession of the fragmented 'craft unionism' of the nineteenth century by some form of 'political unionism' (Marks, 1989). In societies like the United States and Britain with a weak state and, because of open borders or imperial control of the world market, extensive opportunities for particularistic, market-type pursuit of interests, this could succeed only imperfectly. Moreover, corporatist forms of organization could normally not – because of the complexity and heterogeneity of the underlying interest structure – be sustained on a purely voluntary basis, that is, without external organizational assistance provided, as a rule, by the state. As a result this led in corporatist and neo-corporatist political systems to a manifold interpenetration of 'state' and 'civil society' which was more 'modern' than the British and Anglo-Saxon configuration in that it opened up a rich new repertoire of possibilities of control and stabilization. But this, of course, in no way changed the fact that from the perspective of British liberalism and the common law it remained difficult to perceive such arrangements as anything but premodern, undemocratic and, ironically, anti-union, and not to reject them from the outset as incompatible with the basic principles of both free enterprise and 'free collective bargaining'.

These considerations are relevant here because in the 1960s and 1970s the specifically neo-corporatist constellation of status and contract, though it too in principle leaves untouched the fundamental inequality between the classes, had proved much more resistant to Fox's spiral of low trust than the pluralist-voluntarist British system. Fox and the British school did not find this irritating, no doubt mainly because they, here entirely in the tradition of Maine, believed that the corporatist solution was in principle historically backward and that the countries concerned would sooner or later have to follow the British path of development.[11] Had they questioned these premises, they might have been struck by the fact that the relatively high stability of industrial relations in, say, West Germany or Sweden was based not on a premodern cultural acceptance of unequal primary status by unions or workers, but in large part on the realization of a comparatively high level of equality not only between the classes but also and especially – in the form of contracted status uniformity – within the two class aggregates interacting on the labor market. A comparison of the British system with systems of comprehensive corporatist organization, which largely exclude both competitive particularism on the union side (cf. the Swedish 'solidary wage policy') and the use of the labor market as a terrain of competition among firms, would have shown that a considerable part of the stability problems of pluralist-voluntarist industrial relations have nothing at all to do with vertical inequality between the classes, but result from horizontal inequality of privately contracted status and the 'sectional' militancy triggered off by it. Accordingly, it was not primarily the high salaries of managers that were, as Fox believed, responsible for industrial unrest in Britain, but rather the wage differences – by German or Swedish standards enormous and erratic – between regions, industries, firms, occupations and groups of workers. This view is supported if one looks again at the famous case of the failure of 'productivity bargaining' in the Fawley refinery, adduced by Fox as an example of the insuperability of the 'spiral of low trust' (1974: 129–30). In fact, Fox himself in a later book (1985) makes the marked particularism of the British trade union movement – rooted in the comparatively early spread of contractual forms of social intercourse in English society and history – responsible, as the major cause, for the growth of industrial anomie in the 1970s.

Like many other British authors, Alan Fox misunderstands corporatism primarily as a form of enterprise paternalism and patriotism.[12] This astonishing misperception seems ultimately to derive from a nominalist misunderstanding of the conditional character of the social context for the reality of the individual firm, the only reality recognized as such. The result is an incapacity to do justice to situations in which class cooperation at enterprise level comes about as a consequence of rational, interest-led action within an economic non-zero-sum game that is in turn made possible through class confrontation at the societal level and the organizational status achieved through it. Admittedly, the idea that the capitalist labor contract might be modified, and thereby legitimated, by membership status, however contradictory, for employees in their firm could not but seem strange in an environment in which industrial relations continued well into the 1960s to be conducted largely as rearguard actions over the institutional vestiges of the work contract and in which, therefore, the idea of the employee 'belonging' to the firm had to appear to both sides as incompatible with their contractual freedom – to one as 'socialism' and to the other as 'paternalism'. At any rate, against this background of experience it seems to have been hard to understand that societies in which the application of the labor contract and of management's right to manage had advanced faster than in Britain had for this very reason been able to respond by institutionalizing rights of industrial citizenship, through collective bargaining or by legislation, that not only guaranteed a high wage floor but also restricted firms' freedom of decision in hiring and firing and allowed workforces a right to participate in managing 'their' firm.

The significance of this relationship for the stability potential of corporate systems of industrial relations resulted from the fact that where workforces have status-like, assured rights of tenure and participation, assumption of 'responsibility' for the economic well-being of the firm need neither be directed against one's own rational interests nor necessarily lead to disappointment. The same is true, as Olson (1965, 1983b) was first to show, also at societal level for 'comprehensively' organized trade unions in relation to national economic policy. In both cases the institutionally produced and guaranteed status configuration allows the weaker party to the labor contract to act strategically in line with longer-term interests in economic performance and prosperity, such as prevail in particular in difficult economic situations and in non-extractive economies without politically privileged markets, that is, above all for working classes unable to draw imperial rents. The pursuit of such interests presupposes a lasting exchange, unspecific within limits and initially open in outcome, between management and workforce, that must be protected against being undermined by all sorts of impulsions to low trust. Under corporatist auspices, this takes place through institutionalized status definitions that prevent each side from yielding to opportunistic temptations and above all provide work-forces with the certainty that they will, if necessary, later be able to enforce their participation in the economic results of their coopera-tion. In such circumstances it may be seen as highly rational – and as anything but servile – for workforces not to act 'bloody-minded', and to refrain from exploiting every opportunity for short-term advantage. In principle, it even seems conceivable that the particu-larly marked societal differentiation of status in the corporatist model at least partly disposes of the need for motivational differen-tiation between work organization and worker loyalty typical of pluralism, thereby opening up for the firm, or for production, moral resources that pluralism had largely written off or else left to the trade union.

That Fox, at any rate, regarded class-collaborative trade unions as historically backward, and the resistance of corporatist systems to the spiral of low trust as no more than transitory emerges ultimately from his theory of work organization. Under 'normal' circum-stances, that is, where the working class has shaken off its feudal bond to its superiors at the workplace, for Fox the moral decay of the 'enterprise community' through erosion of trust is inevitable because of the economic compulsion to Taylorist fragmentation and degradation of work, 'codetermination' and societal corporatism or not. Just as for interest-conscious, that is, profit-conscious, employers there is no alternative to Taylorism for filling the gaps in the labor contract, so for a workforce aware of its interests and its human dignity, ultimately the only answer to Taylorism is refusal of cooperation.[13] The 'irresponsibility' of British unions might have been contributing to the ruin of the British economy; but for Fox it was incomparably more up to the demands of the time than the assumption of 'responsibility' in a context of 'codetermination' that was unable to alter the fundamental laws of capitalist exploitation.

Here again, at a point central for Fox's argument, the absence of any comparative perspective becomes painfully obvious. Nowhere did Fox spend a thought on the possibility that the organization of work, especially the degree of its Taylorization, might be modifiable through contingent cultural, economic or political factors[14] – like through suitable qualification structures or product ranges, or even the structure and conduct of unions themselves. Thus, indications are that sectionally organized, particularistic trade unions, by keeping the supply of skills scarce, defending jobs as 'territories' and insisting on strict contractual circumscription of work duties, promote Taylorism – whereas industrial trade unions like the Swedish and German ones can use their organizational status in the firms to secure not only higher wages but also less restrictive work conditions (thereby contributing to braking the spiral of low trust). Nor has Fox ever considered that in particular markets and under particular economic conditions the profitability of Taylorist organizational forms may decline, and decentralization and delegation of decisions may be more economic – an idea long in circulation before the contemporary debate on 'flexible specialization' (Piore and Sabel, 1984) and 'new production concepts' (Kern and Schumann, 1984). Instead, Fox keeps to a Taylorist convergence theory,[15] the determinism of which is expressed particularly crudely in those passages of *Beyond Contract* where first a connection is rightly established between the organic work organization and strong moral integration of Japanese firms, which is then, however, followed by the prediction that this configuration will sooner or later fall victim to 'Westernization', for reasons of economic necessity (1974: 131–5). The fact that today the pressure to adjust is going in precisely the opposite direction (Dore, 1987) need hardly be emphasized.

But have the pluralists, and among them above all the corporatists, therefore been correct against Fox's crisis theory? There can be no doubt that Fox keeps confusing the peculiarities of British society with general laws of Western capitalism[16] and that he grossly underestimates both the breadth of variation of industrial pluralism and the resilience especially of its corporatist version to anomic disruption. The question is, however, whether this is enough in itself to do away with Fox's central argument that a utilitarian social order founded on contractual exchange is not viable in the long term. There are indications that ironically Fox may today find himself confirmed precisely where in the early 1970s he was taken to task for a conservative concern with 'order for order's sake' and a 'unitary' view of the firm incompatible with his new radicalism (Wood and Elliott, 1977: 118): in his insistence, that is, that work and production cannot function without moral commitment and normative integration. It is here, and not in specific empirical problems of comparative industrial sociology, that the real point of dispute between Fox and the pluralists with their technocratic model of a motivationless social order lay – with Fox, as we have seen, being unable to recognize that the comparatively high stability of corporatist systems to a considerable extent derived from the fact that they at least gradually departed from the ideal pluralist model, in the direction of his own postulates.

Not only left radicalism, but also and especially the pluralist functionalism with which Western societies had sought in the 1950s and 1960s to order their production sphere, is today discredited. The new institutional crisis is manifested not in open conflicts and industrial ungovernability; to that extent it is not a continuation of 1968. Instead, it arises from specific economic performance deficits in competition with a capitalism of a new, Eastern type, the peculiarity of which lies precisely in the fact that it is founded much more than even the most corporatist Western systems on a status-type of order. Indeed, compared to the rising Asian societies, the differences among Western capitalisms, important as they may have been in the 1970s for explaining the failure of Fox's crisis theory, could in the long term pale into insignificance. The fact that Fox himself, as his discussion of the Japanese case shows, did not recognize this, is scarcely relevant here; what counts is that today in fact, as the 'sociological tradition' always suggested, the normative and moral emptiness of pluralist functionalism – the Taylorist differentiation of contract and obligation, organization and morality – has itself become pregnant with crisis.

Justice and Flexibility: the Neo-Liberal Depoliticization of Status and the Limits to Private Order

By the 1980s, the theme had become, not justice, but 'flexibility'. In changed economic, technical and political circumstances, the status-type standardization of the individual labor contract and its decoupling from the firm's economic performance through the differentiation of a specialized regulatory system have increasingly proved a barrier to adaptation and a threat to competitiveness. In the confrontation particularly with the comparative advantages of the Japanese production system, it became clear how much the pluralist answer to the social insufficiency of the unequal labor contract, even in its neo-corporatist variant, was dependent on the contingent conditions of the 'long boom': on stable and growing sellers' markets for industrial mass production; on a 'mature', largely standardized, uniform technology; and on a hegemonically ordered, liberal world economy that provided the conditions for national Keynesian economic policies. It was only under those circumstances, it emerges today, that the inertia of the Dunlop 'web of rules' was economically tolerable, and that the decision-making premises of managements and economic policy-makers could be robust enough to accept as an unquestioned datum any regulatory outcome generated in the industrial relations system under conditions of pluralist combat parity.

The new pressure for flexibility that marks the end of Fordist–Taylorist production methods and prosperity is driving a process of institutional de-differentiation and functional reintegration in the course of which the status-guaranteeing line of demarcation between the bipolarly organized subsystem of industrial relations and its (macro- and micro-) economic environment is steadily attenuated. Systems of economic action that in the absence of benevolent macro-regulation have to adapt fast to changing, unpredictable market conditions can no longer afford to leave labor relations, personnel planning, skills and work motivation to external agencies for central, standardized regulation. What in 'mature industrialism' (Kerr et al., 1960) used to be the domain of a specialized and semi-autonomous system of rule-making, is therefore increasingly today being pulled back into the area of general, integrated company strategies (Strauss, 1984). In the upshot, the pluralistic-corporatist configuration of status rights and contract obligations, described already by Marshall as rife with economic crisis and, because of its inherent 'rigidities', proving today to be a fetter on the competitive development of the productive forces, is broken up – with industrial relations tending to disappear as an autonomous area of action decoupled from the overall strategy of the firm.

The present institutional crisis, just like that of 1968, affects the various national capitalisms to different degrees. Instability and adjustment pressure seem, at least initially, to be greatest, and institutional change to proceed more discontinuously, where the pluralist regulation of the labor contract had failed to develop into its corporatist variant. Economies like Germany and Sweden seem to have reserves of flexibility that are all the greater the more their institutional system deviates from the pluralist ideal type. In this way, the same national peculiarities that in the 1960s and 1970s acted against the 'spiral of low trust' seem today to be providing countries with more corporatist labor relations with a relatively high level of economic competitiveness. Nevertheless, the corporatist variant of the generation of status through collective bargaining is not spared from instability either. By contrast with pluralist systems, however, in which a long-term 'de-unionization' might well be on the agenda (Visser, 1990), the stability problems peculiar to the neo-corporatist configuration lie primarily in a, perhaps irreversible, decline in the social cohesion of the two big political status aggregates organized along class lines. One of the reasons for this is that growing turbulence and increasing differentiation of product markets and increased intensity of competition have drastically reduced the resources that in the past were available for redistribution to create, if not 'justice' and solidarity *between* the classes, at least common definitions of interests and solidarity *within* them, particularly within the working class (Olson, 1986). As a consequence, the integrative and regulatory capacities of the class organizations serving as institutionalized bearers of status has been severely damaged.

The decomposition of the pluralist-corporatist regulation of industrial relations can be interpreted as a decay of the specific balance between status and contract that had underlain the Fordist–Keynesian mode of regulation. In a first approximation one might speak here of a polarization in two opposite directions: 'back' to an overwhelmingly contractual and 'forward' to a primarily status-determined order.[17] While in the first case the removal of the pluralist status-contract blockade is being sought in a reduction of status rights accompanied by an extension of contractual obligations, the second model aims at an extension of status obligations in exchange for the protection or new creation of status (-like) rights of workers. What is common to both solutions is that they try to restore flexibility through renewed linkage of workers to the economic fate of the firm. The better understood road towards this, the 'neo-liberal' one, consists in intensified recourse to short-term, (status-) 'free' labor contracts as a means towards the quantitative and qualitative adaptation of workforces. This is made possible by changes in the statutory or collectively negotiated status of workers, which are conceded to firms by cooperative governments or weakened trade unions. Status survives in this variant at most in its traditional form as a moral obligation of obedience, the importance of which for the stability of a neo-liberal contractual order is, however, probably slight compared to the compulsion of economic circumstances under high unemployment.

At the same time, however, likewise in the name of flexibility, there appear elsewhere, or for other groups of employees, internal labor markets with high security of employment, the adaptive capacity of which is guaranteed by increased internal flexibility despite low or even further reduced elasticity of employment. Internal flexibility plus external rigidity on the basis of status-like employment thus appears as a functional equivalent to external flexibility plus, unavoidably in this case, high internal rigidity (Marsden, 1981). For the maintenance of the boundary between the internal and external labor market – which as a mechanism of status definition takes the place of the old boundary between economics and industrial relations – requires a high degree of acceptance by workers of tendentially diffuse, that is, flexibly re-interpretable, status obligations, from the assumption of unspecified, generalized responsibility in a de-Taylorist work organization, up to identification with the goals of the firm. In the background here is indubitably the Japanese example of a highly motivated, socially integrated, 'intelligent' production organization in which the motivational boundary between 'industrial relations' and the firm disappears and in which, consequently, the union merges into management (Deutschmann, 1987).

It would seem, then, that one can speak of a polarization of status and contract in two respects. Firstly, there are indications that societies in which socio-economic relationships were always primarily contractually formed seek to dissolve the status-contract blockade preferably through a neo-liberal return to the market, whereas less 'modern' societies with relatively strong status traditions tend more to go for an expansion of internal labor markets. As a consequence, and in contrast with the explicit hopes for convergence in pluralist theory of the 1960s as well as the possibly implicit convergence expectations in the corporatist debate of the 1970s, the differences among Western societies should today be increasing again (Goldthorpe, 1984). Secondly, polarization processes can also be observed within national societies between industries, within industries between enterprises, and within enterprises between groups of employees, with the emergence of 'good', that is, status-secured, jobs coinciding with growing disparities with a secondary labor market for 'poor', marginal and uncertain employment relationships. Segmentation of this type seems to have increased in nearly all societies. The Japanese example in particular is often adduced as evidence for the claim that the status-type safeguarding of 'core workforces' not only does not rule out the marginalization of a fringe workforce kept disposable through short-term contracts, but indeed economically presupposes it.

The empirically more valid and at the same time systematically more interesting variant of the polarization theory would seem to be the latter. Even corporatist countries, with perhaps the sole exception of Sweden, are today affected by segmentation. At the same time, in societies that place their hopes for overcoming pluralist rigidities on market and contract, the neo-liberal turn has in no way removed all long-term exchange relationships on the labor market. Precisely in Britain, one can observe in sectors and firms under high competitive pressure developments towards 'lifelong employment' in the context of long-term personnel strategies of firms, which at first sight entirely follow the status model – with structures developing which Dore (1987, 1988) has characterized as institutional 'rigidities' that are both economically efficient and socially dualistic.[18] Indeed, even in Goldthorpe's much-quoted 1984 article, it is not the 'free labor market' of neo-liberalism that appears as the counter-pole to societal corporatism on the Swedish pattern, but a 'dualist' society whose highly heterogeneous order is characterized by growing disparities between primary and secondary, internal and external, central and marginal labor markets. If it were true that even corporatist societies are not immune to segmentation, then what is happening today may not after all be a polarization between national societies with different development trajectories, but on the contrary a process of convergence around a more or less marked type of 'dualism' which for all the remaining differences in degree would profoundly question any categorical distinctions of the kind used by Goldthorpe (1984).

Another question is, of course, whether such a development could still be adequately grasped with the concept of a dualist polarization of status and contract within one and the same society. In a dualist context, corporatist and pluralist status change in social significance so fundamentally that their identity and continuity, and with them the further usefulness of the status concept itself, become more than doubtful. Modern industrial status which is, so to speak, 'particularized' in a dualist environment loses its constitutive character of a right of citizenship, as well as its function as a mechanism of political redistribution, and turns into an individual right of private property. In such circumstances, an adequate explanation of the 'survival, if such it is, of status might require a change in the conceptual paradigm along with the change in the real context, so as to account for the persistence of status-like, that is, long-term, stable, 'trustful' labor relations in the face of deregulation of pluralist or corporatist institutions, as an event not against but within market and contract, that is, as an outcome of interest-led individual action and without recourse to either (re-) distributional politics or residues of feudal status. If this were correct, we would be back at our starting theme of the viability of a contractual-voluntary social order. How topical this has again become today can be seen from the widespread interest in contract theory, above all the 'new institutional economics', which is nothing other than a renewed attempt to base social order, in the tradition of Maine and Spencer, theoretically, practically and ideologically on market and contract.

For the 'new institutional economics', in particular Oliver Williamson's theory of transaction costs (1975, 1979, 1980; Williamson et al., 1975), one-off, non-relational contracts providing solely for one single, isolated act of exchange ('spot market contracts') are rare, exceptional and extreme cases. From this, in thorough conformity with the sociological tradition, the theory derives the necessity and economic significance of institutions. Since as a rule, and at any rate in most contracts for the sale and purchase of human labor, neither the content of a contract can be precisely specified before it starts to be implemented, nor its implementation be supervised in detail, both contractual parties require as a precondition for maximizing their utility through mutual exchange, a minimum of guaranteed confidence and control ('governance'). Additionally, the establishment of a contractual relationship causes 'transaction' costs – that is, costs of searching and of contract-writing – which are lower if the 'goodwill' of the contracting parties can be assumed so that it is not necessary to write every conceivable eventuality into the contract. Moreover, in the (more complicated) normal case of a developed economy, a number of resources are transaction-specific, that is, exchangeable only with particular contractual partners. Investments in the generation of such resources are therefore only made where there is both the prospect of long-term contractual links, and a degree of certainty that the other side will not use the limited mobility of transaction-specific resources for extortion. In other words, so the thesis runs, if the long-dominant image in economic theory of one-off contracts about homogeneous goods with transaction costs tending towards zero and full information for all participants is abandoned, then for rational actors interests in institutions to bring about trust and protect long-term investments in transaction-specific goods can be found that appear to be strong enough to support a lasting social order. In fact, according to Williamson, if only one looks at empirical contracts sufficiently closely, one can see that typically they not only govern the exchange of specific services but also, implicitly or explicitly, establish a relationship between the contracting parties as such. If in this way one looks at 'contracting in its entirety' – instead of confining oneself to the manifest content of contracts – then the contract even appears as a privileged instrument for the consensual production of an 'efficient' order in a complex society that holds together, not despite but because of the high differentiation and specialization of the goods and services supplied and demanded in it.

The idea of a multiplicity of social micro-orders brought about through private contracts in the broadest sense ('private ordering'), the formation of which flexibly follows the situational logic of the interests and of the resource base of the individuals involved in each case, seems remarkably close to the morphology of post-pluralist or post-corporatist flexibilized labor markets. Indeed the transaction cost analysis of the contract starts from just that growing multiplicity and heterogeneity of interests and resources as a fact that today less than ever can be neutralized, far less homogenized, by corporatist-pluralist institutions under efficiency and flexibilization pressures. This is where its strength lies, not least vis-a-vis the sociological tradition of status and contract which implicitly always treats labor as a homogeneous commodity, or at any rate assumes that the common status of wage worker at least in prospect outweighs the differences in the qualifications being offered.

Today the trends towards the dissolution of the unitary, politically generated status system are unmistakable. Looking back at the 1970s, the neo-corporatist institutionalization of status and contract can be seen as probably the last attempt at a comprehensive ordering of the labor market. In its place there develops, more quickly in pluralist societies than in corporatist ones, a multiplicity of the most diverse contractual forms and contents, with the transformation of individual firms into closed moral status communities – into Piore and Sabel's 'plant community of multi-skilled workers' (1984: 213) – going hand in hand with the disintegration of company hierarchies in favor of market- and contract-type supply relationships between autonomous 'profit centers' or even firms. Where, as in the markets for occupationally specialized or firm-specific skills, idiosyncratic properties of the work force are dominant, the labor contract seems to lose its special features and become increasingly subject to the same laws as any supply or service contract – into which it often turns also in form. This suggests that the relations between the parties on both sides of the market and the developing differences in position, interests and behavior of the sellers of labor power can be explained as the result of a search for more efficient arrangements of rights of ownership and utilization over heterogeneous, transaction-specific resources – namely the simultaneity of the debate on 'subcontracting' and on stock ownership of workers – with the suppliers of mass commodities on the 'spot (labor) market' becoming increasingly exposed to fluctuations in demand, while at the same time long-term contracts for the hire of specialized qualifications come to give rise to status-like linkages and relationships.

Yet however great the similarities may be, it is important not to lose sight of the difference between long-term contracts emerging from the market and politically generated status. Long-term agreements on the use of specialized resources under 'private governance' do not constitute a foundation for citizenship. They are not designed for generalization, but are sub-elements of a hetero-geneous order with high variability, the most important characteristic of which is its privateness. In this, long-term trading relationships differ categorically from Marshall's public status orders that are opposed to, and imposed on, the market. Because of the absence of any public quality in 'relational contracting', it seems inappropriate to use the term of (sectoral, enterprise or micro-) corporatism for internal labor markets that are embedded in a 'dualistic', market-determined order and have emerged from the laws that govern it. What looks here like status is based not on citizenship but on property rights, and is therefore not only not transferable and generalizable through collective action, but also unusable as a motor for redistribution and redistributive justice. On the contrary, the formation of lasting labor contract relationships, especially in the formerly pluralist countries, goes hand in hand with growing social inequality. Correspondingly, the new, status-like privileges of core workforces can mostly be secured without trade unions, and result in a residual form of industrial relations termed by Garbarino (1984) 'unionism without unions',[19] which reflects and reinforces the social-structural fragmentation of the interests of suppliers of labor power instead of overcoming it. The corporatist conversion of the labor contract into a social contract, on the pattern of Sweden or postwar Germany and Austria, is ruled out under such circumstances.

'Dualism', the decay of the political status systems set up in Western democracies in response to the unequal labor contract, is not the same as anomie, and in a complex, heterogeneous, rich society a liberal return to the 'free' labor contract does not lead to the collapse of civil order. To that extent, social history has refuted the classical critique of contractual trading in labor power. But the self-selected success criterion of the new liberalism and its most advanced expression, the economic theory of institutions, is not the absence of civil war, but 'efficiency' understood as a combination of balancing of interests and optimal resource allocation. If this claim is taken seriously, then questions arise that reach from the present debate well back into the center of the sociological tradition of status and contract. How 'efficient' is 'private ordering' without public intervention, and how efficient can it be? Is it conceivable that flexibility without justice – defined with Durkheim as socially produced and guaranteed 'equal' starting positions for the parting to voluntary contracts – might come up against limits? Is the economic performance of a society in fact better if exchange relationships are shaped individually from case to case, according to the free discretion of the contracting parties and the interests and resources involved in each case? Or can the standardization of contractual relations through politically generalized, transferable status have productive effects – say by compelling participants in the market to seek more ambitious solutions than would in the short term be needed? Are there institutional restrictions that are not merely constraints but also opportunities, the removal of which by deregulation would economically weaken a society?

There is much to suggest that the theoretical and political program of a privatized social and economic order will not be able to accomplish its goal, the revitalization of Western capitalism for competition with its new Eastern rivals. The pluralist solution to the problem of contract may have turned organized groups into mere distributional coalitions, favored irresponsibility and impeded productive adjustment. But this in no way alters the fact that internal labor markets developed as special cases within an – in principle – contractual system of wage labor are more precarious and therefore fulfill their specific functions in flexibilizing labor less well than internal labor markets in societies in which they constitute the institutionally guaranteed normal case (Dore, 1988). Nor does it alter the fact that the conscientious execution of open labor contracts is more likely where, as in Japan, differences among incomes are smaller (Dore, 1983, 1987); that unequal development, typical of non-regulated market economies, makes it harder for firms to have recourse, for the flexible solution of production problems, to strategic alliances with a rich range of competent suppliers and partner firms; and that, particularly in advanced societies, there is a need for collective, non-appropriable production factors which, without status-type regulation of rights and obligations of the individuals involved on the market, can be generated only with difficulty and inadequately (Streeck, 1989). The sociological debate on status and contract is alive today in the political debate on the productive contributions of politically redistributive, that is, status-generalizing, institutional rigidities and the influence of equality and industrial citizenship on economic performance; however much the terminologies may have changed, Durkheim's problem has not in the slightest become obsolete.

Notes

* This chapter was originally written in German. The English text is based on an excellent translation prepared by an anonymous translator at the European University Institute in Florence. Since the author revised this translation extensively, it is only he who can be blamed for any remaining flaws.

1 The 'openness' in principle of all contracts was, as is well known, stressed already by Durkheim (1964: 212ff.). More recently, above all Williamson (e.g. 1979) has pointed out that one-off 'sharp in, sharp out' contracts ('spot-market contracts') arise only in exceptional cases and that 'soft contracting' – the conclusion of repeated, incompletely described, imperfect contracts on the basis of a lasting (status) definition of relationships between the contracting parties ('relational contracting', following MacNeil, 1974) is the more frequent and the more important case. It is the indisputable merit of the new institutional economics to have once again pointed out the vital role of social institutions for the bringing about and implementation of 'soft', underdetermined contracts.

2 This idea is, rather surprisingly, not far from resolving the ambivalence of the contract as a means of liberation from feudal status and as an instrument of dominance of capital over labor, in the liberal direction. It further seems to point towards the utopia of a contract-based, voluntarist-individualist social order, although conditioned on the assumption of equal starting positions for all contracting parties. And, finally, it implies that a just, that is, 'really' liberal-voluntarist social order is inevitably bound up with whatever losses of efficiency may result from an absence of 'organization' – all very 'British' themes.

3 This topic is dealt with by Hirschman (1982).

4 The fact that Fox's argumentation so much reflects the spirit of a time of apparently unceasing social polarization need not necessarily mean that it is opportunistic – as Clegg implies by characterizing it as an attempt 'to grab the coat-tail of the "radical" shop steward' (1975: 315). More plausibly, the radicalization of Fox's position could be understood as a consequence of the interaction of certain conceptual limitations (*Denksperren*) of the 'Oxford School', among them for instance Kahn-Freund's rejection, directed against the continental tradition, of any statutory regulation of collective bargaining (see below), with the high political ambivalence of the sociological tradition. In fact Wood and Elliott showed in their reconstruction of Fox's turn that he largely remained faithful to central premises of the 'pluralist' school and that in particular he never abandoned their 'commitment to trust and order' (1977: 118). Wood and Elliott point out in particular that Fox's response to Durkheim's theory of anomie originally remained entirely within the framework of Oxford institutionalism and was confined to the call for institutional reforms as means towards the restoration of moral integration (Fox and Flanders, 1969/1975). The shift to the 'radical' position of *Beyond Contract* seems to have taken place above all under the influence of Goldthorpe's critique (1974a, 1974b) that Fox and Flanders had failed to see the connection in Durkheim between anomie and inequality. The fact that although Fox was not deaf to this criticism, he still could be reproached by Wood and Elliott (1977) for being at bottom (still) concerned with conservative themes like 'trust', 'cooperation' and 'order', shows his closeness to the 'sociological tradition' with its ambiguous political orientation. Apart from that, he must be credited for having written in a situation in which even such an unshakeable 'pluralist' as Clegg felt compelled to state that Western societies were affected by a 'disease' apparent in 'increasing failure of the pluralist stabilizing mechanisms to contain inflation, competitive greed and social disorder' (1975: 316).

5 The same is of course true of Goldthorpe's (1978) sociological explanation of the high inflation rates in Britain in the mid-1970s. In this connection the hostile dialogue, reported in the collective volume issued by Hirsch and Goldthorpe, between Goldthorpe and two economists, one of them Samuel Brittan, is of interest (Goldthorpe, 1978: 214–6):

BRITTAN: But it is a reasonable inference from your paper, isn't it, that, as a sociologist, you do not think anything can be done about inflation under the present system?

GOLDTHORPE: No – I don't discuss the matter of 'what can be done' at all. I object to this definition of the problem, as if it's a leak in my pipes – so summon up lots of institutional plumbers . . . [etc. etc.]

6 Since Weber, the concept of the 'status contract' has been available for this. Unlike a normal contract, a status contract is not concerned with the exchange of specific goods and services but with 'a change in what may be called the total legal situation (the universal position) and the social status of the persons involved' (Weber, 1978: 673). The original model for this is marriage, a 'contract' by which one of the partners, in becoming a member of another family, changes their social identity.

7 Otto Kahn-Freund has pointed out that Maine's concept of status differs from that of Dicey and other authors after him in that status obligations in Maine's sense are unavoidable for the individual who is subject to them, whereas legal restrictions on contractual freedom always leave open the possibility of not entering into a contract in the first place. To that extent, according to Kahn-Freund, however legally regulated an employment relationship may be, it remains a 'legal relation based on agreement' (1967: 640) that has nothing to do with status as in Maine. Kahn-Freund explains the, to him, wrong use of the concept of status in twentieth century Anglo-Saxon legal theory on the grounds that common law, by contrast with the Roman-law legal systems on the Continent, found the idea of a shaping of individual contracts through statutory *jus cogens* so alien that the legal regulation of contracts, when it did set in gradually and belatedly, was perceived as a fundamental change – 'hence the tendency to think of anything that is imperative or compulsory as imposed in the way status is imposed' (1967: 642). The details of this conceptual controversy need not be gone into here as long as we are concerned solely with the common ground, undisputed even by Kahn-Freund, between status in Maine and status in, say, Selznick – consisting in the fact that neither can be bargained away. Moreover, the legal-political thrust of Kahn-Freund's argument should not be overlooked: as a British labor lawyer, it had to be his concern to free substantive regulation of the content of labor contracts by statute from the odium of a lapse behind Maine's 'progressive society'. This explains the repeated assertion that even in the event of legal intervention in the free labor contract 'the worker's duty to work and the employer's duty to employ' still remain founded upon 'an act of their own volition and not [. . .] a *character indelibilis* imposed upon them by the law' (1967: 643).

8 With, for Marshall and others, formal equality of organized contracting parties drawing its meaning from the expectation that it would allow a stepwise expansion of substantive equality; so that the unequal labor contract was ultimately rendered effective, if not through actual elimination of 'unjust' status differences, then at least through its prospect.

9 For which there has increasingly emerged the idea of a 'subsystem' (Batstone et al., 1984) within the economic system, limited to regulating the personnel policy and work organization of firms, or to social and distributive policy at national level.

10 On the contribution of modern trade unions to the moral detachment of their members from 'older ethical motivations to work' in the name of a primarily redistributive demand as opposed to supply-side orientation, see the remarkable article by Vidich (1982: 767). Vidich makes a plausible connection between the

indifference of the moral orientation of (organized) workforces to production needs on the one hand and the Keynesian welfare state on the other, which 'represented the state administration of a new ethic wherein the ultimate productive aims of the older Puritan ethic could be achieved while detaching them from the moral and ethical strictures originally identified with work' (1982: 779).

11 That is, move 'from status to contract', and thereby to low trust and anomie.

12 Cf. Fox's later excursion (1977), without further consequences, into comparative industrial relations.

13 Where nothing of the sort occurred, as notably in the German case, the usual exogenous explanations, in particular the familiar national stereotypes, had to be called in. Among Fox's witnesses in this respect were Dahrendorf ('pervasive ideology of social harmony and national community') and Kendall (1975). Co-determination appears in this light as an element of a system imposed on the working class by management in the latter's interest, characterized by 'the protection–dependence equation; the insistence on obedience and collaborative working; the pay/off in the form of upper-class acceptance of responsibility for working-class welfare' (Fox, 1977: 29). The most important elements of co-determination are listed as: 'the way in which the power of the union as a collective body is virtually excluded from the workplace; [. . .] the "peace" and "company interest" obligations bearing upon the works council; and [. . .] the separation of "works community" issues from "managerial" issues, as embodied in the works council and supervisory board respectively' (Fox, 1977: 29).

14 Among many, see Tolliday and Zeitlin (1986), Sorge and Streeck (1988).

15 In part, this may reflect the fact that by the early 1970s most British firms were still fighting the battles of the 1920s and 1930s against traditional forms of factory organization – at a time when other societies, notably Japan and Germany, were getting ready to move beyond Taylorism. The slow progress of Taylorist 'rationalization' and 'modern' mass production in Britain can certainly in part be related to the politically privileged position of British firms in the world economy in the nineteenth and early twentieth century.

16 Or, put otherwise, that he saw the peculiarity of the British case in it being particularly close to the ideal type of a capitalist society – so that it could be treated as a general case.

17 Whereby ultimately it is a matter of taste whether one prefers, again following Maine, to regard the first variant as the 'progressive' and the second as the 'backward' one.

18 Note also the corresponding, highly selective tendencies towards 'life-time employment' in the United States (Gutchess, 1985).

19 Where trade unions involve themselves in the organization of particularized status, they lose not only their autonomy – since the new order could in principle also function without them – but also their political quality: a backsliding from 'political unionism' to the 'craft unionism' (or even 'yellow unionism') of the pre-pluralist phase. For an example, see the exclusive contracts of the British electricians' trade union with 'modernizing' firms.

3

Interest Heterogeneity and Organizing Capacity: Two Class Logics of Collective Action?

Among the problems that have from early on figured prominently in the 'corporatist debate' is the question of symmetry between capital and labor. In Gerhard Lehmbruch's work, this theme is addressed primarily with respect to the outcomes of political exchanges at the national level, in particular in the context of incomes policies. Others have looked at the organizing capacities of the two classes, in an attempt to determine whether there are differences in their ability to act as organized social categories: to formulate collective strategies, negotiate collective obligations and implement collective policies by preventing free riding of individual class members on the efforts and sacrifices of others in the pursuit of collective interests.

There always were suspicions that the two dimensions of symmetry, political and organizational, were in some way related, and that on both of them capitalists were better placed than their opponents. From early on, students of incomes policy have pointed to the fact that usually it was only one kind of income, wages, that became subject to regulation, and prices, profits and dividends remained free to rise either by design – where incomes policies were intended to reduce the real wage – or for lack of adequate enforcement machinery. Perhaps for this reason, incomes policies often included deals between trade unions and the state – for example on taxation or social policy – that were to compensate labor for wage restraint in the absence of price or profit restraint, or of binding commitments on employment and investment (Lehmbruch, 1979a, 1984). But doubts remained as to the equity of such exchanges. More recently, the very necessity of political rewards for trade union conformity with restrictive policies has been questioned, most forcefully by the theoretical and practical proponents of monetarism, but also, at least implicitly, in recent work by Fritz Scharpf (1987).

As indicated, economic asymmetry was thought by some to be related to the two classes' respective organizing capacities. Sometimes trade unions demanded that prices and profits, or employment and investment, were included on the agenda of national incomes policies and tripartite negotiations. But invariably they were told by their direct counterparts, the national peak associations of business, that these were not among the subjects on which business associations have a mandate from their members to negotiate. While firms were, more or less enthusiastically, willing to engage in collective regulation of the labor market, this in their view was and had to remain an exception, and under the rules of a market economy all other prices and incomes were to be determined by the individual decisions of competing firms judging independently their market environments.

This organizational delimitation of the scope and domain of incomes policies, modified only in exceptional cases like the Austrian *Paritätische Kommission*, always appeared as an important source of strength for capital and contributed to the impression of political and economic asymmetry. What was remarkable about it was that, in this case, political strength seemed to be associated with and protected by organizational weakness, as reflected in the strict limitation of the mandate under which business associations were permitted by their members to take part in tripartite negotiations. More precisely, the structural power of the capitalist class, expressed in its ability to pursue important objectives through individual action in the market, translated into political power through an absence of organizational power at the level of collective action. Being located in a privileged market position, capitalists could afford weak associations, and thereby they could escape the dialectical logic of interest intermediation that may turn against its original beneficiaries by subjecting them to negotiated discipline. Organizational weakness, in that it prevented a spill-over of collective-political intervention to subjects of 'managerial' or, for that matter, 'proprietorial privilege', thus served, paradoxically, as a source of strength.

If this was so, however, an intriguing question was bound to arise. If the equity problems of incomes policies – and generally of a negotiated trilateral management of democratic capitalism in the 1970s and 1980s – were related to limitations on the scope of corporatist political bargaining, and if such limitations derived at least in part from deficiencies of capitalist associations in intermediating the full range of interests of their members, should it not then in principle be possible to increase the symmetry, and thereby the legitimacy, and as a consequence the efficiency, of the 'bargained economy' by strengthening the organization of capitalists? Was it not then, to add to the paradoxes, in the interest of trade unions and social-democratic governments to increase the organizational power of business associations as a way of controlling the market power of the individual capitalist? To weaken – or discipline – capital by strengthening its associations?[1] The answer depended on how one resolved a theoretical problem located at that crucial intersection between class theory, organization theory and political science that had been notoriously neglected by the mainstreams of the various disciplines bordering on it: the problem of whether the organization of capitalists is just lagging behind the organization of workers for some reason of historical sequence or due to lack of attention paid to it by governments and states as principal agents of political-organizational design – or, alternatively, whether there is a specific class logic behind capitalists' organizational weakness that makes for categorical differences in organizational forms and dynamics between capital and labor. While in the first case the deficits of interest intermediation, incomes policy and, ultimately, neo-corporatism might be rectifiable, in the second the prospects of doing much about both the organizational asymmetry of capital and labor and the resulting lopsidedness of the political management of capitalist economies would appear extremely inauspicious.

Astonishingly enough, the question of a class logic of interest associability has received little explicit and systematic attention, probably because the subject is so very difficult. One important exception is the much-quoted essay of Claus Offe and Helmut Wiesenthal titled 'Two Logics of Collective Action: Theoretical Notes on Social Class and Organizational Form' (Offe and Wiesenthal, 1980) which comes down strongly in favor of inherent, class-specific differences in organizational capacity, precluding by implication an equitable corporatist management of advanced capitalism through tripartite bargaining. The present chapter will undertake to relate some of Offe and Wiesenthal's propositions to a body of empirical evidence. While it will arrive at conclusions quite different from the hypotheses put forward in the 1980 essay, this is not to detract from its importance or, indeed, its theoretical accomplishment. In fact, this chapter deliberately abstains from offering a final judgment on the project of a class theory of organizational form as such; if at all, it argues that the substantive propositions of such a theory will likely differ from those suggested by Offe and Wiesenthal, but, in the light of the pioneering status of their effort, this is far from surprising. (In any case, given the limited scope of the evidence available and the measurement difficulties involved, a claim to have empirically rejected a theory of this breadth and sophistication would be more than premature.)

Taking Offe and Wiesenthal (1980) as a point of departure, the present chapter will, however, try to throw some light on the problem that dominated so much of the political and social science debate in the 1970s: the possibility of symmetrical corporatist management. In a nutshell, it will argue that, at least under the historical circumstances of the 1980s and 1990s, there may well be a degree of convergence in organizational form between capital and labor, albeit not in the sense of a corporatist transformation of business associability but vice versa: with labor organizations undergoing transformation on the model of capitalist associations. While it is not at all clear what the possible implications of this may be for the distribution of political power, such a development would seem to reflect more general changes which are likely to preclude a resurgence of the kind of economic policy that was at the center of the 'corporatist debate' of the 1970s. As a consequence, the problem of symmetry in incomes policy in particular and in centrally bargained economies in general, rather than being resolved by organizational convergence, would fall by the wayside due to convergence occurring in an unexpected direction. While this would not necessarily eliminate corporatism as a form of interest organization and policy coordination, it certainly points to it assuming a more fragmented, decentralized and functionally specialized structure ('local', 'sectoral', or 'policy arena' corporatism).

A Class Theory of Organizational Form

The central message of Offe and Wiesenthal (1980) can be summarized as yet another paradox adding to that of organizational weakness and political strength: a supposed coincidence, in the case of business interests, of a lower need for with a greater ease of interest organization. For Offe and Wiesenthal's class theory of organizational form, the new paradox is what the old one was for the class theory of political exchange; in fact, both reflect the same underlying condition projected on different conceptual planes. Since capitalists can successfully pursue most of their interests individually through market relationships, they need collective action and organization only for a subset of their interests. In this sense, capitalist associations are organizationally weaker than trade unions. At the same time, the interests they have to represent are less complex and thus comparatively less demanding to treat inside collective organizations. Capitalist interest associations should therefore find it easier than trade unions to become strong organizations, as building and maintaining an organization of which little is expected is likely to be less difficult than building and maintaining an organization that has to perform important functions. As a consequence, capitalists – also because they have superior material resources – tend to be better organized than workers given the limited purposes their associations are to serve, and this holds regardless of the fact that they require collective interest representation much less urgently.

Why exactly is it that capitalists need interest associations less than do workers? Rooting their analysis firmly in the Marxist theory of the capitalist class structure,[2] Offe and Wiesenthal (1980) start from the fundamental condition of inequality underlying the formally equal contract of employment: the fact that the commodity traded in labor markets, labor power, is not detachable from its seller. Wage labor therefore inevitably gives rise to a relationship of social control and domination between a small number of owners of 'dead labor' who, in organizing the labor process, combine their physical capital with the 'living labor' of a large number of workers – whereby the latter, to become party to an 'equal' and 'voluntary' commercial exchange, have to accept a subordinate position in a relationship of authority. Small group size and control over the labor process, Offe and Wiesenthal argue, each give capitalists access to a specific 'form of collective action' that workers do not have at their disposal: 'informal cooperation' on the one hand, and 'the firm itself' on the other (1980: 75). For capitalists, interest associations are therefore just one of three alternative instruments 'to define and defend [their] interests' (1980: 75), and, compared to capitalists' everyday command over the organization of the enterprise, they are unlikely to be regarded by them as very important.

This is different for workers. Large group size, Offe and Wiesenthal imply, increases dependency upon formal arrangements for collective action. Moreover, as trade unions are organizations of those that have no power over the organization of work and the enterprise, they are the only organizational means available to their members to protect their interests – given that the labor 'market' and the 'free' employment contract are inevitably biased against the 'seller'. While business associations cover, process and pursue only a limited segment of the total interest range of their members, 'unions are confronted with the task of organizing the entire spectrum of needs that people have when they are employed as wage workers' (Offe and Wiesenthal, 1980: 75).

The narrow range of interests that need to be fed into and represented by capitalist associations provides, according to Offe and Wiesenthal, for a comparatively homogeneous organizational input that does not make difficult demands on the organizational process (see Figure 3.1). On the labor side, by comparison, organizational input is highly heterogeneous, and its processing requires more complex arrangements that are always at risk of

Capital	Labor
Class structural conditions	
Small group size	Large group size
More important alternative Modes of collective action: firm, collusion	No alternatives modes of collective action
Organizational input	
Narrow	Broad
Homogeneous	Heterogeneous
Specific	Diffuse
'Pure'	'Contaminated'
Organizational process ('logic')	
Simple	Complex
Bureaucratized	Political
Empirical	Discursive
'Monological'	'Dialogical'
Substantive interest definitions	
Given	Chosen
Negative	Positive
Quantitative	Qualitative
Additive	Non-additive
Individualistic	Collectivistic
Utilitarian	Normative

Figure 3.1 *The class theory of interest organizational form: an ideal typology of differences between capital and labor (abstracted from Offe and Wiensenthal, 1980)*

failing or breaking down. In particular, Offe and Wiesenthal suggest three mechanisms that reduce input heterogeneity for capital associations and increase it for trade unions:

1 the fact that 'the powerful are fewer in number' and are therefore 'less likely to be divided among themselves' (Offe and Wiesenthal, 1980: 78);

2 the 'multitude of needs of "living" labor' – the complexity of life interests as opposed to capital interests, and of a life-world entangled in a relationship of social control by the inseparability of labor as a commodity from the person of its seller – which, if only 'for quantitative reasons', is 'comparatively more difficult to organize' (Offe and Wiesenthal, 1980: 75);

3 the asymmetrical dependency of workers' interests on capitalists' interests – being just another expression of the basic asymmetry of a class society – which forces workers to consider

and take into account the interests of capitalists much more than capitalists in turn have to consider the interests of workers. This 'increases the lack of homogeneity of those interests that working class associations have to accommodate and the concomitant difficulties of the intra-organizational decision-making process' (Offe and Wiesenthal, 1980: 76)

Differently heterogeneous inputs, then, result in differently demanding organizational process requirements. The small group size of the capitalist class entails low transaction costs and less divergent interests needing internal reconciliation; high functional specificity of interest associations and the absence of contamination by the opponent's interests further relieve the internal process. It is here that Offe and Wiesenthal ground their idea of two different class logics of collective action. To the extent that interests become the subject of organized representation, those in a dominant structural position are argued to have far simpler interests that can be handled in what Offe and Wiesenthal call a 'monological' mode of interest politics. Domination generally implies 'a clearer view of what [one wants] to defend' (Offe and Wiesenthal, 1980: 78) as interests can be largely negatively defined in terms of a preservation of the status quo. A dominant capitalist class, in particular, has an especially simple and easy-to-apply criterion by which to define its interests since 'all the relevant questions can therefore be reduced to the unequivocal standards of expected costs and returns, i.e. to the measuring rod of money' (Offe and Wiesenthal, 1980: 75). Capitalist interest politics, strictly speaking, can be conducted without a preceding or accompanying political discourse. In the limiting case, determining and aggregating the interests of capitalists can be delegated to a staff of experts, and indeed according to Offe and Wiesenthal, capitalist collective interests, narrow as they are, lend themselves particularly well to 'rational' and 'efficient' processing inside highly bureaucratized associations that are, and can be:

> confined to the function of aggregating and specifying [. . .] interests of members which, from the point of view of the organization, have to be defined as given and fixed, the formation of which lies beyond the legitimate range of functions of the organization. (Offe and Wiesenthal, 1980: 79)

Offe and Wiesenthal admit that the capitalist class, 'under the competitive pressure that its individual members put upon each other, has to seek constantly to find the *means*, or the most rational purposive behavior, by which its interest is to be met' However:

> the interest itself (the *end*) can safely remain remote from any conscious

reflection or effort to learn on the part of class members [since] in order for his interest to be his 'true' interest, the individual capitalist does not have to consult with other capitalists in order to reach a common understanding and agreement with them as to what their interests are. In this sense, the interest is 'monological'. (Offe and Wiesenthal, 1980: 91)

Non-political, bureaucratic, 'individualistic and purely instrumental', or 'utilitarian' associability (Offe and Wiesenthal, 1980: 78) is not a liability for capital but its natural and optimal form of collective action. Labor, on the other hand, is described as depending on a 'dialogical' mode of interest politics as the only way of dealing to its political advantage with the wide and heterogeneous range of 'life interests' arising from workers' disadvantaged position in the labor market and the class structure. Labor, therefore, is the really political class in that the 'real' interests of workers cannot be determined empirically but, unlike those of capital, *can only be met to the extent they are partly redefined* in a political discourse (Offe and Wiesenthal, 1980: 79; authors' italics). Not only do trade unions face a much greater heterogeneity of interest 'inputs' than do business associations; what is more, since the interests of workers are functionally diffuse and need to be positively clarified in terms of some normatively acceptable alternative to the status quo, there is no simple 'common denominator to which all these heterogeneous and often conflicting needs can be reduced' (Offe and Wiesenthal, 1980: 75). Moreover, because of their structural position of dependency workers are much more likely to perceive their interests in a 'distorted' way, and unless such distortions are 'rationalized' in a political dialogue, collective action through trade unions is more likely to prolong than to overcome labor's disadvantaged position in the class structure.

Interest heterogeneity, then, makes 'the problem of creating and maintaining unity among members and of mobilizing members' resources [. . .] considerably more serious' for labor than for capital associations (Offe and Wiesenthal, 1980: 83). In addition, the substantive content of working class interests and its normative contestability require a dialogical internal process which, especially if the number of participants is large, is intrinsically more difficult to operate and more likely to fail. Associative action of labor is thus handicapped not just by higher underlying interest heterogeneity but also and at the same time by lower organizing capacity. This interpretation is confirmed by Offe and Wiesenthal's use of the concept of 'opportunism' (1980, 103ff.). Trade unions, the authors observe, tend to fall victim to a temptation to adopt the same 'monological' and 'bureaucratic' organizational process that serves capitalist interests so well, in an attempt to avoid the effort required by, and the crises inherent in, the dialogical mode, and thereby to expand their organizing capacity in relation to their heterogeneous interest base. But this, Offe and Wiesenthal argue, comes at a high political price. While an 'opportunistic' shift to a monological process may indeed enable labor to overcome some of its comparative organizational disadvantages, it inevitably eliminates the categoric difference between capital and labor interests, reducing the political quality of the latter to that of the former. The result is a formal-organizational, that is, superficial, symmetry between capital and labor which places the latter at a political disadvantage, thereby reproducing the underlying structural asymmetry. This is why 'opportunistic' trade unionism is bound to be unstable: it is subject to cyclical crises and transformations as suppressed needs for normative interest definition revolt against the monological suspension of politics in a more than technocratic sense (Offe and Wiesenthal, 1980: 103ff.).

Implications for Encompassing Organization: Mobilizing Empirical Evidence

There are a number of ways in which one could discuss a theory as wide-ranging and ambitious as that of the 'two logics of collective action'. One possible, and quite plausible, approach would be to scrutinize Offe and Wiesenthal's various assertions on the structure and internal life of trade unions. This is not what the present chapter will do.[3] Having reconstructed in some detail the Offe and Wiesenthal theory, the argument will instead focus on one specific implication of that theory that appears to be empirically testable. This relates to differences in the capacities of capital and labor to set up what in Mancur Olson's widely used terminology (1982) are called 'encompassing organizations' – organizations which both include a large proportion, and ideally all members, of their social category *and* are capable of developing and implementing a centrally determined, common policy for their entire constituency.

While Offe and Wiesenthal (1980) do not explicitly address the subject of encompassing organization, it should be clear from our account that on their premises, the capitalist class is likely to find it much easier than the working class to build and maintain encompassing organizations. This follows directly from the theory's two main propositions: the lower interest heterogeneity among capitalists – at least insofar as interests enter the arena of collective action – and their higher organizing capacity, as expressed in the greater ease and confidence with which capital can allegedly make use of the 'monological' social technology of functionally specific, bureau-

cratic organization. Centrifugal tendencies that give rise to pluralistic organizational fragmentation and internal decentralization
should therefore be weaker among capitalists than among workers;
internal conflict and dissent resulting in secession and separate
organization should occur comparatively rarely; there should in any
population of capitalist interest organizations be fewer lines of inter-
organizational differentiation reflecting structural interest cleavages; and thus the number of capitalist associations in any given
'interest space' should be clearly lower than the number of trade
unions.

Extracting empirically testable propositions from a complex
theory is always hazardous. However, in the present case it is the
authors themselves who, if only by implication, offer strong confirmation. This is where they attribute, by logical deduction rather
than on empirical evidence, a different 'optimal size' to trade unions
and business associations. The latter, Offe and Wiesenthal argue,
can grow almost indefinitely since, due to the high simplicity and
commensurability of capitalist interests, increasing size does not add
much to their internal heterogeneity. (Put in a more technical
language, business associations have more favorable economies of
scale than have trade unions.) Another reason why business
associations can grow without limits is that they do not depend on
their members' marginal propensity to act – as opposed to pay – to
mobilize sanctioning power against their opponents. 'What there is
in terms of sanctioning potential of the [business] organization',
Offe and Wiesenthal (1980: 80) maintain, 'can be put into effect by
the *leadership* of the organization alone.' By contrast, the sanctioning potential of trade unions 'becomes effective only through the
organized members and their explicitly coordinated action' (that is,
the strike). From this results a curvilinear relationship between
organizational size and organizational effectiveness:

> As union size increases, heterogeneity of members' positions, occupa-
> tions, and immediate interests tends to increase, too, which makes it
> more difficult to formulate generally agreed upon demands and to
> mobilize a common willingness to act that flows from a notion of shared,
> collective identities and mutual obligations of solidarity. (Offe and
> Wiesenthal, 1980: 81)

The maximum size of a trade union is therefore not its optimal
size. Limits exist for the growth of union organizations that do not
exist for business associations. There is, according to Offe and
Wiesenthal (1980: 81), an 'optimum size beyond which union power
decreases', and there is a dilemma 'between size and collective
identity' (1980: 82) that is quite unknown to business.[4] From this it
follows, as Offe and Wiesenthal themselves indicate (1980: 111),

that membership density should generally be lower for trade unions than for business associations, as organization size can come much closer to group size among capitalists than among workers. But given the significant economies of scale that exist for bureaucratic formal organizations, the optimal size argument also implies that, everything else being equal, the higher aggregate organizational density among capitalists is likely to be achieved by a smaller number of more encompassing organizations. A trade union, by comparison, can achieve, and in fact afford, high density only if it defines its organizational domain narrowly and specifically, thereby excluding from it potentially large segments of the working class which then can, and have to, be organized by other, competing unions. For the working class as a whole, this means that it can reach a high level of aggregate density – which will likely still always be lower than aggregate density among capitalists – only if it organizes itself in a large number of small organizations rather than, like capital, in a small number of large organizations. It also implies that however labor may at some point escape from its position of structural disadvantage, it will not be able to do so through the use of encompassing organization. It is at this point that Offe and Wiesenthal's theory deviates most strongly from the mainstream of the neo-corporatist debate.

How can one mobilize empirical evidence, keeping 'everything else equal', on the relative degree of organizational inclusiveness of social groups as different as capital and labor? For example, it seems self-evident that capitalists are always 'fewer' in number than workers, so even if their 'logic of collective action' or the political quality of their interests were not different from labor, they should have both 'fewer' interest organizations and, due to lower trans-action costs, 'higher' organizational density. (This point is, in fact, made by Offe and Wiesenthal themselves although group size, as we have seen, is not their most important explanatory variable.) But to make sense for empirical analysis, comparative terms like 'fewer' or 'higher' must refer to some common universe. Which collectivity of capitalists is to be compared to which collectivity of workers? If the comparison is to be valid, the respective populations of capitalists and workers must be so defined that they in some way correspond to each other. For one thing, this raises the question of what a capitalist is – rather a tricky one indeed. Secondly, it requires identification of social spaces – defined as sets of economic processes and political activities – in which coterminous sets of capital and worker interests can be assumed to emerge that can meaningfully be compared in terms of their scope, complexity, heterogeneity, etc.; these will in the following be referred to as interest spaces. And, thirdly, to count the number of interest associations on either side of the class divide, a common criterion is needed as to what an association is and, in particular, where it ends: at which point, in other words, a set of interrelated organizational units begins to constitute one encompassing organization rather than a system of several, independent organizations.

The empirical evidence introduced in this chapter is based on the following operational decisions (Schmitter and Streeck, 1981).

First, 'capitalists' are ideal-typically not individuals but firms, and the chapter will be looking exclusively at such capitalist associations under whose rules members are defined as, or stand for, independent production units competing in markets for goods and services. While this, as any, decision may appear debatable, it is clearly in line with Offe and Wiesenthal's description of capitalist interests as functionally specific, impersonal and dissociated from the life-world of individuals. In any case, defining capitalists in this way places, as it should, the theory being tested at an advantage since it eliminates from the universe of capitalist associations those based on the *Weltanschauung*, religious beliefs, gender, leisure activities, etc. of individual members of the capitalist class – inclusion of which would increase the observed degree of organizational fragmentation.

Secondly, a possible 'interest space' for comparing organizational patterns of capital and labor could be a country as demarcated by the boundaries of a nation-state. However, given Offe and Wiesenthal's close recourse to Marxist class theory, even more appropriate appear to be economic sectors, defined as any population of firms producing a similar range of products for the same product market using similar inputs of raw materials, technology and labor. Assuming, as class theory undoubtedly does, that actors' positions in the division of labor and the system of economic exchange significantly affect their interests, the set of capitalist interests originating in a given sector can plausibly be regarded as 'corresponding' to the set of workers' interests originating in the same sector.

Finally, in distinguishing between the borderline cases of a specialized associational subunit on the one hand, and an independent association affiliated to an association of associations (or 'higher order' association) on the other, the criterion will be the presence or absence of a, statutory or customary right of the lower-level unit to secede from the higher-level unit. A highly decentralized interest organization whose subunits do not have a right to secede is thereby counted as a unitary, and potentially encompassing, organization. A highly centralized 'association of associations', on the other hand, whose affiliates can however decide to disaffiliate, is treated as a set of different, autonomous organizations. The assumption is that the reservation by organized subgroups of a right to secede is a meaningful tool to protect their interest-political autonomy, and that it therefore is likely to reflect a higher degree of interest heterogeneity than even the most advanced decentralization inside a unitary organization.

To test one aspect of the Offe and Wiesenthal theory, then, this chapter will compare the number of trade unions and business associations representing the interests of capitalists and workers located and producing in identical economic sectors. To control for the impact of special market conditions and technologies, the chapter will look at seven different sectors: chemicals, pharmaceuticals, construction, dairy, meat processing, fruit and vegetable packing, and machine tools. To control further for the influence of national specificities and peculiarities, the chapter will use evidence from sectoral associational systems of nine countries: Austria, Canada, Italy, West Germany, the Netherlands, Spain, Sweden, Switzerland and the United Kingdom.[5] Class theory of organizational form predicts that sectoral interest spaces will be populated by clearly more trade unions than business associations, with business associations being more encompassing with respect to their sectoral interest base than are trade unions. It also predicts that the capitalist class will achieve a higher organizational density ratio. Since this prediction is derived from a general theory of the class structure under capitalism, by and large the same results should be expected in all countries and sectors.

Size, Fragmentation and Density: the Role of Domain Choice

At first glance at least, it is hard to see how empirical data could more forcefully contradict a theory than in the present case. In the 56 sectors on which data are available, there are on average no fewer than 16.4 business associations to 1 trade union. Even if the two extreme cases are deleted – two West German sectors with a high number of local artisanal associations – the relationship reduces only to 8.1 to 1. More unions than business associations can be found only in three cases: the machine tools industries of Austria, Canada and Switzerland. These, however, are clearly exceptional in that they are extremely small and narrowly defined subsectors of the metal-working industry.[6] The basic numerical relationship between business associations and trade unions remains unchanged even if 'associations of associations' – or 'higher-order associations' – are excluded. In this case, the ratio of business associations over trade unions declines to 6.7 to 1.[7]

Assuming that sectoral interest spaces for business and labor are comparable, the observation that on the labor side a given interest space is populated by far fewer associations than on the business side would seem to justify the conclusion that trade unions are more, rather than less, encompassing than business associations. Taking into account that the number of firms in a given sector is always much smaller than the corresponding number of workers, it appears that either the range of interests represented by business associations is much more heterogeneous in spite of it being associated with a smaller number of individuals – so that a capitalist association that was of the same size as a trade union would incorporate much greater interest variety – or the organizing capacity of business associations is much lower than that of trade unions, resulting in disproportionately greater aversion to hetero- geneity, or both. This follows if one assumes, as Offe and Wiesen- thal do, that organizational boundaries are determined by limits to the internal heterogeneity that an organization can process. Put otherwise, the addition of one more member to a capitalist associa- tion seems to increase its internal heterogeneity to a much greater extent than the addition of one more member to a trade union. In fact, since there are many more business associations than trade unions for fewer capitalists than workers, the extent to which one marginal member of a business association detracts from its internal cohesion exceeds, going by our empirical data, by a factor of at least 7 the centripetal effect in a trade union caused by a group of marginal members equal in size to the average number of workers per firm.

There are no good data available on the comparative organiza- tional density of capitalists and workers by sector. However, assuming for the sake of argument that Offe and Wiesenthal are right and that capitalists are universally more densely organized than workers, the strongly different patterns of organization that we have found suggest quite a different explanation from the one offered by class theory. If capitalists do achieve higher density, this seems to be because their interest organizations are much more fragmented than trade unions, enabling them to make dispro- portionate use of their general advantage of small numbers. Rather than being due to 'the dual advantage of greater commensurability and calculability of what the "right" demands and tactics are, and [of] a comparatively smaller probability of internal conflict' (Offe and Wiesenthal, 1980: 84f.), high organizational density among capitalists appears to be explained by small numbers generally, plus a class-specific response to interest heterogeneity through high organizational specialization and fragmentation. Thus, it is precisely not some 'advantage of greater commensurability and calculability' (Offe and Wiesenthal, 1980: 83) that makes for high organizational density among capitalists, but rather a pattern of organization that decomposes the sectoral class interest into a number of less than encompassing, separate subinterests – the very pattern that Offe and Wiesenthal would have expected for trade unions. And neither is it 'a comparatively smaller probability of internal conflict' (Offe and Wiesenthal, 1980: 84) but the elimination of conflicts through organizational fragmentation from the domain of any one association that seems to account for a larger proportion of capitalists than workers joining interest associations.[8] Far from being 'easy to organize', capitalists seem to be willing to join associations only if these are narrow enough to cater to their immediate special interests, and if they are small enough to make for low transaction costs and a strong incentive against free-riding.

These conclusions still hold up if one takes into account that membership in the various business associations representing sectoral capitalist interests is not necessarily mutually exclusive, and that capitalist firms are often members in more than one association. While the majority of business associations specialize by product at the subsectoral level, some of them, and sometimes in addition, specialize by function, for example as employers', trade or technical associations. Multiple membership of firms is common in the latter case but also occurs in product-differentiated associations, for firms that operate in more than one product market. The difference to trade unions is that union members have to subscribe to a collective action, or interest, 'package' which they cannot easily modify, whereas the high organizational differentiation of capitalist associations gives individual firms the choice to select and create their own custom-made combinations of memberships and – specific – collective involvements. The result is a highly varied and idiosyncratic pattern of associational activity, quite unlike what one would expect if capitalist interests were indeed as narrow, homogeneous, commensurable and easy to determine as Offe and Wiesenthal claim. Actually, judging from observed patterns of associability, capitalist interests rather appear so broad, heterogeneous and complex that, to become narrow, homogeneous and simple enough for organization, they must be subdivided in a large number of specialized (sub-) domains. This need not mean that the interests contained in these domains are necessarily in conflict or incompatible with each other although they very well may be; what seems clear, however, is that they are not as easy to trade off and aggregate as Offe and Wiesenthal suggest and as, in contradiction of their theory, seems to be the case for labor.[9]

Looking at the process of organizing as distinguished from the pattern of organization, the empirical data suggest that business associations tend to 'find' a larger number of heterogeneous categories of potential members in any specific interest space than do trade unions. This is reflected in the fact that organizational and interest-political leaders in the capitalist class tend to cut the domains of their organizations more narrowly than their counterparts among labor. Domain decisions, however, precede optimal size decisions, and the way Offe and Wiesenthal's optimal size problem poses itself to an established interest association depends crucially on how it has originally demarcated its domain. The reason, that is, why business associations do not appear to have an optimal size problem, and why they can appear to be straightforward size maximizers, is that they have in the first place defined their domains so narrowly that even complete organization of their (comparatively very small) potential membership would not overburden their internal process with excessive heterogeneity. In reality, business associations have 'optimized' long before they have begun to 'maximize': namely at the point when they decided to limit their organizing activities to a narrowly defined subcategory of interests. Trade unions, on the other hand, in defining their domains more encompassingly, indicate a comparatively high degree of confidence that they will be able to internalize whatever interest diversity may exist in their respective constituency. (Not to mention the fact that trade unions refusing to organize workers within their domain, so as to not exceed their 'optimal size', are extremely rarely observed these days – to put it mildly.) Seen this way, and considering domain choice as well as actual organizing behavior, business associations, in contradiction of the class theory of associability, appear to be facing a much stronger dilemma 'between size and collective density' (Offe and Wiesenthal, 1980: 82) than trade unions.

Groups organized in a fragmented pattern of associability frequently, although by no means always, rely on institutionalized inter-organizational links as an alternative way of coordinating encompassing collective action. Particularly important in this respect are higher-order associations – especially sectoral or national peak associations – which may strengthen inter-organizational relations by adding a hierarchical dimension to them. In some countries and sectors, a typical difference between capital and labor is that while trade unions are by and large organized in a unitary, encompassing way, on the business side one finds a multitude of small, regional or product-specific associations which, while independent and autonomous, are joined together in often complex pyramids of higher-order associations.[10] Although inter-organizational coordination through this kind of mechanism can be quite effective, it appears reasonable to regard a 'federative' pattern of collective action and organization as less encompassing and more fragmented than one based on unitary organization. A group that, rather than coordinating its activities by internalizing their external effects in a unitary organization, relies for this purpose on inter-organizational diplomacy – breaking up, as it were, a potentially encompassing organization into a set of smaller, more homogeneous subunits that may or may not cooperate with each other – thereby documents the existence of tensions between subinterests that are too strong for an encompassing organization to manage internally. Unless one assumes that the social 'meaning' of the distinction between internal and external ways of coordinating collective action differs for capital and labor, it seems legitimate, and indeed compelling, to read the apparent preference of the capitalist class for external coordination as an indication of higher interest heterogeneity or, correspondingly, lower organizing capacity.

Organizational Form and Substantive Interests: Unity by Opportunism?

Trade unions, class theory has been shown to imply, should be organizationally more fragmented than business associations because of a coincidence of greater heterogeneity of underlying interests with lower organizing capacity. Empirically, however, trade unions turned out to be much less fragmented than their capitalist counterparts – raising the double question of where the theory may have gone so wrong and, more importantly, how the observed organizational pattern can be accounted for. Two possibilities appear particularly interesting.

First, that trade unions are more encompassing not because their interests are less heterogeneous but because their organizational process is superior in managing internal diversity. If this was so, Offe and Wiesenthal could still be right with respect to class differences in organizational input, and their mistake would have been to underestimate the integrative capacity of the 'dialogical mode'.

Secondly, that trade unions are more encompassing because their interest base is simpler than that of business associations. Even if there were differences in organizational processes between classes, and even if the 'dialogical' mode was less conducive to encompassing organization than the monological one – as the authors clearly believe – this would be overridden by the greater simplicity of labor's organizational input. Offe and Wiesenthal would be right on the organizational process; where they would have erred would be in their assessment of the impact of class position on interest variety.

Could it be that the greater inclusiveness of trade union organization is due to a superior organizing capacity associated with the 'dialogical mode'? While this might 'rescue' the theory's assumptions on the differential heterogeneity of class interests, it is clearly not what class theorists should believe to be possible. And indeed Offe and Wiesenthal are far from being idealistic here. As their optimal size hypothesis makes clear, for them dialogue presupposes that the range of admissible arguments and interest perceptions has been narrowed beforehand through collective identity-formation and organizational boundary maintenance. Unity, for Offe and Wiesenthal, is built on elimination. This is confirmed by a quite remarkable passage on the means by which liberal democracies allegedly try to keep trade unions from arriving at unified and undistorted conceptions of their members' interests – namely by forcibly increasing unions' internal organizational diversity through:

> the imposition of regulations that make it more difficult for unions to deny access and/or to expel dissident members and thus to narrow the spectrum of positions within the membership. Such regulations, commonly advocated in the name of 'intra-organizational democracy' or 'pluralism', appear, *in the light of the argument we have developed about class-specific distortions of interest perception*, as measures to paralyze *those associational practices which could help to overcome interest distortions or 'fetishism'*. (Offe and Wiesenthal, 1980: 103; italics added)

Placing legal restrictions on the expulsion of members with deviating interest perceptions, the authors continue in a remarkably euphemistic conceptualization of Leninist organizational *realpolitik*, is a technique of trade union enemies designed to make it:

> more difficult for unions to partially suspend the individualistic orientations of members *in a dialogical process of collective interest articulation*. (Offe and Wiesenthal, 1980: 103; italics added)

There are also empirical indications that, quite in line with Offe and Wiesenthal's skepticism on the unifying power of dialogue inside encompassing organizations, the second explanation for the mismatch between theory and reality is more appropriate, and that lower interest heterogeneity accounts for a much larger proportion of the greater organizational encompassingness of trade unions than does higher organizing capacity. This conclusion emerges if the business associations that are included in the comparison are limited to those which, either solely or in addition to other activities, act as direct counterparts of trade unions in industrial relations (the so-called 'employers' associations'). Of the 55 sectors on which we have data, 23 have more employers' associations than trade unions; in 6 sectors the numbers are equal; and in 26, trade unions outnumber employers' associations. Differences in national industrial relations systems play an important part and have to be taken into account. For example, in 6 of the 26 sectors where trade unions prevail numerically (all of them in Canada), there are no employers' associations at all as collective bargaining takes place solely at the enterprise level; here, business associability is not more encompassing than trade union organization but is non-existent. Of the remaining 20 sectors with fewer employers' associations than trade unions – those sectors, that is, which exhibit a pattern relatively close to that predicted by class theory – 3 are in Austria with its uniquely compact system of compulsory business associability monopolized by the *Bundeskammer der gewerblichen Wirtschaft*; 5 each are in the United Kingdom, the Netherlands and Switzerland with their fragmented trade union structures; and 2 are in Sweden. In the 23 sectors where, in contradiction of class theory, employers' associations prevail numerically over trade unions, on average there are about two employers' associations to one trade union, which is still low compared to the overall ratio of business associations over trade unions.

In other words, while the evidence on employers' associations by no means conforms with the Offe and Wiesenthal theory, it is considerably more favorable to it. Where the substantive concern of business interest associability is limited to the interaction with organized labor in the labor market and in industrial relations, the degree of organizational fragmentation varies much less between the two classes, and the organizing capacity of capital – the ability to make firms join comparatively encompassing organizations – is not necessarily much weaker than that of labor. One may note in passing that Offe and Wiesenthal in their paper frequently leave the impression that they treat all business associations as though they were employers' associations – which may be understandable coming from a class theory of associability, although it can, as we have seen, lead to serious misperceptions.[11]

What does the relative degree of symmetry between employers' associations and trade unions, compared to the asymmetry between all business associations and trade unions, imply for the problem of heterogeneity versus capacity? Employers' associations are business associations that interact with one out of several 'task environments' facing capitalist firms and the capitalist class. Either exclusively or together with other functions, employers' associations represent business interests vis-a-vis the labor market and the industrial relations system regulating it, including those national institutions of economic and social policy-making that affect the content of employment contracts. Important as the labor market may be for capitalist firms, however, capitalists also have interests relating to product markets and their regulation through, for example, tariffs, taxes, standards, etc. Although some business associations represent their members both as employers and producers, or traders, a frequent pattern is for producer interests to be represented by separate, specialized 'trade associations'. A sectoral or national system of employers' associations, being no more than a subset of a typically much larger sectoral or national system of business associations, thus covers only a subset of the full range of organized interests of capitalist firms. By definition, a subset is less internally heterogeneous than the universe, and therefore it is easier to organize comprehensively with a given organizing capacity. The evidence thus suggests that the comparatively low overall capacity of business to organize comprehensively is a function of comparatively high interest heterogeneity, indicated by the fact that if such heterogeneity is reduced, business associations do seem to have roughly the same capacity as labor to make their members form encompassing organizations.

If the high overall fragmentation of business associability is to be accounted for by comparatively high interest heterogeneity, then the similarity in the level of inclusiveness of employers' associations and trade unions would indicate a similar degree of interest heterogeneity for these two categories of associations. From this it should follow that the universe of interests that business associations have to cover in any given sector is broader and more complex than the respective interest range on the labor side. Capitalist associations, in other words, would represent not only different but, above all, more interests than associations of workers, and, going by the differences and similarities in organizational fragmentation, such interests as they do represent in addition are those represented by trade associations. (In fact, these interests are being organized and represented even in sectors where there is no need at all to confront trade unions above the individual firm level.)[12] Trade unions, on the other hand, would appear to have an interest base that is simpler and narrower than that of capital, and this would account for their higher inclusiveness. As Offe and Wiesenthal have predicted, low-interest heterogeneity results in encompassing organization; but, contrary to their theory, interest heterogeneity turns out to be lower, and organizational unity therefore higher, among labor than among capital.

Pursuing further the distinction between trade associations and employers' associations, the problem for business associability which prevents it from taking advantage of encompassing organization – and which Offe and Wiesenthal's class theory seems to have overlooked – appears to be that the members and clients of business associations are not just buyers of labor but also sellers of products, and that they have collective interests not just in relation to their workers but also to their customers – and, one might add, their suppliers of raw materials, finance and other production inputs. These additional interests, as reflected in their pattern of organization, are more specific, diverse and divisive than labor-market interests. And indeed, there are clearly fewer categories of labor than there are products, and in any given (local) labor market firms producing different products compete for the same category of workers (or at least for workers whose wages are highly interdependent). It is true that different conditions in product markets may reflect also on the interests that firms have in industrial relations. Where employers' associations are still more fragmented than trade unions, this could probably often be accounted for by the fact that many business associations are simultaneously trade and employers' associations, with the more centrifugal product-related interests tearing apart organizations that could be more comprehensive if they were organized only around labor-market interests.

The distinction between employers' and trade associations invokes an important generic difference between two kinds of collective interests of business: class interests and producer interests. Both originate in markets. But whereas the axis of interest differentiation in competitive product markets divides sellers from sellers, labor markets give rise to a categoric cleavage between two groups of actors: capitalists and workers. Employers in labor markets, just as workers, face a 'common enemy' whose interests differ so much from theirs that they find it comparatively easy to develop a common identity and policy. Usually, the categoric difference between the two groups is strong enough to supersede internal diversity by (sub-) sector or product on the capital side and by skill or occupation on the labor side. As a consequence, class interests are typically easier to aggregate than product or occupational interests. Where trade unions have relatively simple organizational structures, this would be explained by their being essentially organized around class interests whereas business associations have in addition to incorporate the more heterogeneous 'producer' interests that originate in product markets. Trade union organization can be more compact because the ('class') interests it exclusively incorporates are less diverse and, consequently, the obstacles

	Capital	Labor
Class interests *Labor market*	Employers' associations	Unions
Producer interests *Product market*	Trade associations	?

Figure 3.2   *Organizational types by interests and classes*

to collective interest formation lower. Nothing quite so compact and simple seems to suffice for capitalists.

Why, then, should it suffice for trade unions? Is it, in other words, really the case that workers' interests relate exclusively to class and not to production issues (Figure 3.2)? Without going into too much detail, it would appear that labor has not always been without organizational equivalents to trade associations – and in fact there still exist a variety of organizations that, in one way or other, could be seen as such: professional associations, like those of technicians or accountants; some craft unions; firm-specific staff associations; 'yellow' or 'house unions'; works councils; enterprise unions. What they have in common is that they do not primarily define the interests of their constituents as labor-market-based class interests but rather in terms of their members' specific contribution to successful production and its match with specific product markets. The reason why especially 'industrial' or 'general' trade unions view such organizations with such suspicion and hostility is that they represent a range of interests which modern unions, striving to organize workers exclusively on the basis of their status as sellers of labor and regardless of their occupation, skill or place of employment, had to submerge or suppress in their long struggle for organizational unity[13] – that is, against a pattern of organization and organizational fragmentation similar to that which Figure 3.2 shows for capital.

The purge of labor's organized interests of production-related concerns is a fairly recent phenomenon which involves the historical defeat not just of 'craft' and 'yellow' unionism but also of guild-socialist and radical socialist traditions ('workers' control'). In the course of accepting the rules of the game of 'mature', 'pluralist' industrial relations systems under a Taylorist work organization and a Keynesian economic policy regime, modern trade unions have focused their interest definitions, ideologies and activities on distribution as distinguished from production matters; they have found it more comfortable politically and organizationally to deal with the demand side rather than the supply side of the economy; and their primary policy orientation has turned towards the macro- as opposed to the micro-level of the economy. One expression is the de facto recognition by most trade unions of managerial prerogative on production issues, especially product strategy, which lies behind the refusal of trade unions in many countries to become involved in managerial matters through 'co-determination'. Where unions, especially large and encompassing ones, cannot avoid being drawn into production politics, for example in industrial policy, they usually perform poorly, not the least reason being that they find it difficult to deal with the internal divisions of interest among their members that immediately emerge on such occasions.

Distribution, of course, is not independent from production; demand and supply are interrelated; and macro-policies are conditional upon micro-level performance. However, trade unions have more often than not been careful not to recognize such interrelations in their ideology. They have preferred to influence production, supply, and the micro-level, if at all, through distribution, demand and macro-policies – even though knowing that such instruments were far from ideal for the purpose. In fact, there can be no doubt that trade unions and workers – as indicated by the resilience of certain non-class organizations of workers, as well as by the constant vigilance of industrial unions against 'plant egoism' or 'craft syndicalism' – do have quite significant product- and production-related interests. In many cases, however, these are similar to the respective business interests in the same firm or sector, whereas they differ from the interests of workers employed in other firms or sectors, or from the interests, of workers as consumers or citizens. Examples of this are industrial subsidies, problems of legal regulation of economic activities, taxation, foreign trade protection or regional development policies. Trade unions find such issues difficult to take up since they would likely undermine the 'class unity' of their members as sellers of labor power. They therefore tend to leave their representation to business, both in relation to the state and to other producer groups. Seen from this perspective, trade associations function, in important areas of their activities, as though they were vertical associations organizing both labor and capital. Since the diversity of production-related interests is largely absorbed within their (fragmented) organizational structures, their presence relieves unions of the problem of having to formulate and act on such interests. This, in turn, enables them to confine themselves to class interests and, thereby, to build up more encompassing and comprehensive organizational systems.[14]

It is at this point that we may briefly return to Offe and Wiesenthal's concept of 'opportunism'. For class theory, opportunism involves implicit acceptance of structural subordination through elimination, for organizational convenience, of a range of 'systemically unsafe' interests from collective action. The present analysis has shown that something like that may indeed exist. But the differences are crucial. While Offe and Wiesenthal believe that trade unions reduce their range of organized interests in order to become *like* business associations, in fact it appears that opportunistic trade unionism eliminates interests to become organizationally *different* from, especially *more encompassing* than, business associations. Opportunism, in other words, appears as an attempt precisely *not* to assume the organizational properties of business associability. And while Offe and Wiesenthal believe that opportunism reinforces dependency and subordination by leaving a range of (anti-capitalist) interests unrepresented, it seems that in reality dependency and subordination are cemented by leaving specific (production-related and therefore more heterogeneous) interests to capitalists to represent on their terms.

Rising Interest Complexity and the Prospects of Class Organization of Workers

If it is true that the comparative organizational unity of modern trade unionism is made possible by tacit delegation of production-related interests to the 'trade' interest politics of employers, one might feel tempted to speculate whether this is likely to remain viable in the future. This will not be so if the concentration of labor organizations on class interests is premised on contingent historical circumstances that will, or are about to, change. For example, the greater simplicity and comprehensiveness of trade unions might reflect an experience or belief that structural economic change either can be satisfactorily handled through redistributive class politics in a growing economy, or can be prevented by collective worker action without loss of wages and employment. Elimination of production interests from trade union organizational domains also seems to assume that there is no need for union intervention in the qualitative direction of economic change since this is predetermined by market and technological forces.

Today it appears that assumptions of this kind are becoming unrealistic (Sorge and Streeck, 1988; Streeck, 1987b). The center of gravity in political economy is shifting from distribution to production, from demand to supply management, and from the macro- to the micro-level. Structural adjustment of firms, industries and economies has taken precedence over the control of inflation or the creation of domestic demand. The high pliability of the new technology has opened new options for structural change, making space for alternative concepts of productivity and economic revitalization that are subject to strategic choice and may be affected by collective-political action. Moreover, unions in many countries today are faced with new, more divergent, more specialized and more 'qualitative' demands by their members and clients. This is reflected in growing pressures to participate in production- and supply-related policy areas which are difficult to conceive in terms of traditional, labor-market- and distribution-centered trade union ideology.

This development can also be described in more abstract terms. Modern trade unionism is premised on the existence of a separate, semi-autonomous socio-economic subsystem of industrial relations that generates rules and entitlements relatively independent from product markets, entrepreneurial production strategies and technology (Dunlop, 1958). The pluralist-functionalist 'system of industrial relations', established and 'matured' in the era of mass production and steady growth, implied an institutional boundary between worker interests to be regulated through industrial relations, and production interests that were the domain of management and trade associations. 'Modern' industrial relations thus entailed a recognition not only of a right to collective bargaining but also of managerial prerogative. This 'historical compromise' has today become unstable, as a result not of labor radicalism but of management demands and production needs for 'flexibility'. In pursuit of the latter, labor relations are being (re-) integrated into comprehensive production strategies at the company level, pulling more closely together previously separate functions such as marketing, research and development, engineering, work organization and manpower management (Strauss, 1984). The consequence is progressive 'dematurity' of industrial relations – to apply a concept introduced to describe changes in industrial organization towards higher innovativeness and flexibility (Abernathy, 1978) – characterized by declining differentiation and increasing integration and interdependence between remuneration, working conditions, work motivation and worker attitudes on the one hand, and the operation and performance of the economic and production system on the other.

A case could be made that in today's economy and polity the

traditional indifference of trade unions to production issues has ceased to be functional for an adequate representation of the interests of workers. If this were so, trade unions would have to learn to involve themselves more directly and intentionally than in the past in production politics. In the course of this they would become immersed in, and infested with, problems and cleavages among their constituents far more diverse and divisive than unions' traditional themes of class and distribution.

As the axis of industrial relations shifts from class to production interests, trade unions may have to become more similar organizationally to business associations. As the interests with which they are confronted by their members and clients change to become more diverse – so as to resemble the heterogeneous interest-political 'raw material' that business associations have long been used to – unions might have to adjust their structures. One possibility would be to rely more than in the past on *inter-* instead of *intra*-organizational mechanisms and arrangements of managing interest diversity, with encompassing 'industrial' unions turning de facto, and later perhaps even de jure, into loose federations of workplace and enterprise organizational units. In any case, there may be developing in the future something like a convergence between business associations and trade unions, with the latter learning from their opponents how a high level of collective action can be achieved in spite of a highly diverse interest structure and highly instrumental, functionally specific, non-ideological and idiosyncratic attachments of members to their organizations.

Conclusions

'Labor and capital', according to Offe and Wiesenthal, 'show substantial differences with respect to the functioning and performance of their associations. These differences [. . .] are consequences and manifestations of antagonistic class relations' (1980: 72). But the effects of different location in the class structure on organizational form differ greatly from, and in fact are the reverse of, what class theory expects. Being a privileged social class is not concomitant with easy formation of consensus *on* common interests or with lower interest *in* common interests. To the contrary, the evidence suggests that a dominant structural position entails the dubious privilege to make decisions that are difficult to make and therefore may be divisive. A subordinate position, by comparison, may under favorable conditions permit its occupants to concentrate their collective action on a selected range of simple, easily identified objectives and leave aside more complex interests that would divide them. In fact, they may be able to delegate the representation of such interests to the dominant class and thus achieve greater organizational unity at its expense.[15]

An important part of the argument revolves around the concept of opportunism. While for Offe and Wiesenthal this denotes a change in the organizational process of trade unions that makes them similar to business associations, this chapter suggests that opportunism should be conceived as elimination of production-related interests from trade unions' interest base, in order to make unions organizationally different from, and in particular more encompassing than, business associations. There is agreement that opportunism entails a limitation of collective action to interests compatible with 'the system'; but whereas for Offe and Wiesenthal this system is capitalism, the evidence suggests that it is, more precisely, the established industrial relations system of democratic capitalism. There is also agreement that opportunism may be a source of institutional instability; but, unlike Offe and Wiesenthal, this chapter maintains that such instability is likely to be initiated not by militant trade union members but by management punctuating, under changed economic conditions, the institutional fence around 'industrial relations' and thereby forcing opportunistic unions to choose between two opposite alternatives: being relegated to insignificance under management-controlled 'flexibility', or preparing themselves organizationally to invade the domain of managerial prerogative in a market economy.

As opportunities for opportunism recede, workers and their associations will find it increasingly hard to resist entanglement in supply-side interests. The consequences of this for organizational patterns and the distribution of power are far from clear. While in some cases assumption of responsibility by trade unions for production matters may entail just another version of political subordination to capitalist interests, in others labor may become the driving and guiding force of strategic economic adjustment. But regardless of whether management takes over labor or labor takes over management, functional interpenetration of interest representation and economic decision-making is likely to be accompanied by disintegration of monolithic class structures of collective action. With class organization weakening or withering away and other, more complex lines of interest differentiation taking precedence, the important contribution of class politics to social order and social integration may with hindsight be generally recognized, and new, functionally equivalent solutions to the problem of governability are likely to be urgently required.

Notes

1 'Perverse' projects of this kind came to be far more than just speculation. Well in advance of the 1987 general election in Britain, a group of economists and social scientists close to the leadership of the Labour Party were working on an economic policy for the first year after a potential Labour victory. Central to their considerations was a return to the Keynesian full employment commitment of the time before the Conservative government – which if successful would certainly have curtailed the power of employers in the labor market. To prevent expansionary policy measures from resulting in another outburst of inflation, an incomes policy was seen as indispensable. Aware of the limited capacity of trade union leaders to keep their members from settling old bills with their employers to make up for their income losses since 1979, the group discussed methods of improving the organizational strength of the CBI, the British peak association of business, and in particular its control over the wage-setting behavior of the 100 or 200 largest British firms, as a way of precluding these from making concessions to their workforces that would have preempted an increase in employment.

2 In fact, as will become apparent, in a rather more orthodox version thereof than is normally invoked at least in Offe's writings.

3 Nor will it deal with the question of whether economic 'profit' objectives are in fact as clear cut and easy to define, at both the individual firm and the collective class level, as Offe and Wiesenthal believe – which would be another promising line of attack.

4 And that, as we have seen, can at most be temporarily removed by 'opportunistically' suspending the dialogical organizational process, at the price of assimilating the political quality of worker interests to that of capitalist interests, thereby eliminating the very specificity of the interests of a subordinate as opposed to a dominant class, with the result of submission to capitalist hegemony.

5 Due to missing values, the number of cases available is not 9 x 7 = 63, but only 56. The data were collected in the course of the 'Organization of Business Interests' research project directed by Philippe Schmitter and the present author (Schmitter and Streeck, 1981).

6 In fact, the machine tools sector as defined for the purposes of data collection comprises only two types of machine: metal- and wood-working machinery (Schmitter and Streeck, 1981).

7 Since associations of associations are more likely to exist where there are many independent associations, their inclusion increases the difference between large and small sectoral associational systems.

8 It is, by the way, precisely the fragmented pattern of capitalist interest organization that makes it so difficult to determine aggregate density ratios for capitalists. Nevertheless, in countries like Britain where there is – unlike in Germany, to which Offe and Wiesenthal refer as their only example – no compulsory organization of small (artisanal) firms, one may have doubts as to whether aggregate density among capitalists is indeed (much) higher than among workers. To the extent that the two density ratios differ less than in West Germany – which they should in many countries – the comparatively fragmented pattern of capitalist organization becomes difficult to account for as an organizational technique to raise density. Instead, fragmentation would even more clearly be recognizable as a reflection of high interest heterogeneity, clearly in contradiction to a principal assumption of Offe and Wiesenthal's class theory of organizational form.

9 This applies already at the level of the individual firm. Anecdotal evidence on

the internal politics especially of multi-product firms suggests that individual capitalists have a much harder time developing a consistent and comprehensive image of their interests than do workers, largely because they have to make more, and more uncertain, strategic choices. This uncertainty may be reflected in conflicting or at least inconsistent commitments in the different product-specific business associations to which such a firm is likely to belong.

10 From which they reserve a formal right to secede (cf. our operational definition of organizational independence, above).

11 On the other hand, precisely because they are so preoccupied with employers' associations, it is remarkable that Offe and Wiesenthal should have overlooked the fact that there are business associations, in some countries at least, which do greatly depend on their members' 'willingness to act' – namely, when they impose a lock-out. A successful lock-out presupposes as much internal cohesion in an employers' association as does a successful strike in a trade union.

12 While 6 of the 56 sectors studied have no employers' associations, there is no single sector without a trade association.

13 A unity which, by the way, is based on extremely simple decision rules which, in their simplicity, remind one strongly of the image that Offe and Wiesenthal have of the internal process of – in their expectation, encompassing – capitalist associations. For example, industrial unions tend to secure their internal cohesion by freezing existing wage structures, thereby avoiding the divisive 'moral' problem of a 'just' reward for work and skill. Or they settle on a policy of incremental wage equalization through identical or degressive wage increases for higher and lower paid members – although this already, if applied over more than a very short term, normally overtaxes their political cohesion.

14 The pattern of organization in Figure 3.2 can thus be recognized as the macro-level equivalent of the acceptance of managerial prerogative at the micro-level. Just as rejection of responsibility for a firm's competitive performance turns management de facto into the fiduciary of a fundamental interest of the workforce, the absence of labor organization in the lower right cell of the figure implies tacit agreement with the organizations in the lower left cell covering labor's collective production interests. While trade union indifference to production issues can at the ideological level be presented as an expression of radical rejection of capitalism, it is easy to see that in reality it involves acceptance of subordination since it leaves the responsibility for the productive preconditions of labor's redistributive successes to its opponent.

15 This is what one could call the white man's burden theory of interest representation. One could also see it as an organizational reflection of subordination under a hegemonic social interest.

4

The Logics of Associative Action and the Territorial Organization of Interests: the Case of German *Handwerk**

Associations mediate between two principal 'task environments' (Thompson, 1967): their members on the one hand and their collective interlocutors – state agencies and organizations of contending social interests – on the other. Elsewhere (Schmitter and Streeck, 1981) we have suggested that interaction with each of the two environments is determined by a particular 'logic', which we have referred to as the 'Logic of Membership' and the 'Logic of Influence', respectively. Briefly, the 'Logic of Membership' is governed by the values and interest perceptions of the groups and individuals that an association undertakes to represent, and in particular by both the sense of collective identity and the 'rationality traps' that emerge in collectivities of a given size, spatial distribution, internal composition, resource base and 'primary', informal social structure. The 'Logic of Influence', on the other hand, consists of the constraints and opportunities offered to associations by their institutional environment, and it is experienced by associations as a set of strategic imperatives, rules of political prudence and norms of reciprocal political exchange that collective actors in a given institutional context have to obey, and to internalize in their structural make-up, in order to be successful.

To acquire sufficient 'relative autonomy' for effective intermediation, interest associations have to build internal structures that respond to both logics equally and simultaneously. An association dominated by the 'Logic of Membership' resembles a social movement in that it is likely to be organizationally unstable and incapable of formulating and pursuing long-term political strategies. Similarly, an association ruled by the 'Logic of Influence' is likely to become so closely coopted into the state apparatus, and so strongly identified with its characteristic means of control, that it will appear to its constituents like a state agency; as a result, its capacity to mobilize active support from them will decline. The problem is, however, that striking a balance between the two logics is not easy as these may not always be compatible, and in some cases may even contradict each other. This possibility has been systematically underestimated in the 'pluralist' tradition of interest group theory which has viewed interest associations as the exclusive, 'democratic' creation of their members. But given the status of the results of collective action as 'public goods', stable organizational exchange with the membership depends not only on the authentic expression and successful pursuit of member interests but also on the ability of the association to punish free-ridership and to apply authority to extract a continuous and reliable flow of resources. Similarly, successful political exchange with interlocutors requires an ability not just to mobilize but also to compromise – that is, to moderate the demands of the membership and to ensure that they abide by negotiated agreements. Organizational structures, however, that are capable of enforcing policy, bringing about moderation and applying sanctions are not likely to be equally well-suited to expressing interest perceptions authentically and to mobilizing internal consensus and support. While institutional interlocutors are frequently willing to 'lend' associations sanctioning power and grant them monopoly status in exchange for 'delivering' their members; and while members are willing to offer support in exchange for authentic representation, associations are likely to find it difficult to produce their two tradable commodities, compliance and representation, at the same time and through the same structural arrangements.

To add to the complications, interest associations are formal organizations, and as such they are subject to yet another, specific set of forces. Drawing on Child et al. (1973), we have suggested (Schmitter and Streeck, 1981) that organization, just as intermediation, involves two potentially contradictory logics: a 'Logic of Goal Formation' (which Child et al., 1973, call 'representative rationality') and a 'Logic of Efficient Implementation' (referred to by Child et al. as 'administrative rationality'). The two 'organizational' logics operate independently from, and can in fact be seen as running orthogonal to, the logics of intermediation. The 'Logic of Goal Formation' informs the process by which, both through member participation and through consultation with, or imposition by, external interlocutors, an intermediary organization selects its manifest and latent objectives. The 'Logic of Efficient Implementation', on the other hand, relates to the way 'that specified tasks or outcomes', vis-a-vis both institutional targets and the membership, 'are attained with certainty and economy'; it involves such parameters as 'routinization of operation, specialization of functions, directness of communication and speed in decision-making' (Child et al., 1973). The tensions between goal formation and efficient implementation have often been analyzed, for example in Weber's famous antinomy of substantive and formal rationality, and there is no need to introduce them further here. In addition, there are also inherent tensions in each of the two organizational logics, in goal formation between the needs for comprehensive representation and for avoidance of decisional overload, and in implementation between pressures for rationalization and the 'sunk costs' of existing organizational arrangements.

Organizational structuring of interest intermediation proceeds along several dimensions, one of which is by territory. Differentiation of organized interests by subnational territories is an almost omnipresent phenomenon. Nevertheless, it has remained understudied, due probably to the traditional preoccupation of interest group research with the national (and, incidentally, the intersectoral) level. Just as any other organizational dimension in the formation of collective interests, territorial differentiation is subject to the contending demands of the four 'logics' that have been identified above.

Firstly, under the 'Logic of Membership' the pattern of territorial differentiation in organized interests is shaped by different territorial identities and identifications of subgroups of members, as well as by the degree of their local concentration and dispersion and by the constraints of spatial distance on their face-to-face interaction. It is also affected by the need for organized collective actors to be physically close to their membership base, both for delivery of services and for gauging members' perceptions of their interests and of the policy of their association.

Secondly, under the 'Logic of Influence' territorial subdivisions are required for, and have to be capable of, representing the membership in relation to subnational governments and regional authorities, as well as territorial subunits of other collective interlocutors. Moreover, territorial differentiation may also be imposed on organized interests by regional authorities trying to create for themselves coextensive systems of functional representation that they can turn into auxiliary bodies of the subnational state.

Thirdly, under the 'Logic of Goal Formation' intermediary organizations may use territorial differentiation as one way of managing the heterogeneity of their members' interests. Interest associations are faced with the perennial difficulty of having both to accommodate political diversity and to generate and protect organizational unity. Legitimate goal formation under the condition of diversity requires structured opportunities for a variety of potential organizational goals to be put forward by the members, and for relevant demands of the institutional environment on the organization's goals to be perceived and properly processed. Differentiation into territorial subunits is one possible way of generating and absorbing such 'requisite variety'. At the same time, the organizational subunits that take part in the process of goal formation must be so structured and institutionalized so that variety does not stand in the way of unity, and that organizational goals can be found that are legitimate as well as manageable under both the 'Logic of Membership' and the 'Logic of Influence'.

Finally, under the 'Logic of Efficient Implementation' the structure of territorial subunits has to satisfy organizational needs for an efficient use of scarce resources. This requires that territorial units are sufficiently large and functionally specialized to permit the realization of organizational economies of scale, both in the provision of services to members and in their interaction with collective interlocutors. It also requires an (inter- or intra-) organizational hierarchy that optimally balances the needs for manageable spans of organizational control on the one hand and short lines of communication and command on the other, so that territorial subunits can be efficiently integrated into the encompassing organizational structure and activity.

The present chapter utilizes the model of the four contending logics of interest organization in an attempt to offer an improved understanding of a specific, in many ways extraordinary, set of intermediary associations, and especially of its territorial structure. The associations that will be discussed comprise the universe of organizations that represent the business interests of artisanal firms in the Federal Republic of Germany. These organizations are so densely linked and so interdependent with each other that they can be properly analyzed only in their inter-organizational context. In this respect, the chapter offers support for a strategy of inquiry which, rather than looking at individual interest associations in isolation, conceives of them as of elements of associational systems through which the interests of categories of socio-economic actors are articulated (Schmitter and Streeck, 1981: 125).

Handwerk as an Institution

Most of what is called 'small business' in other countries falls in Germany within the legal category of *Handwerk*. The least awkward equivalent of *Handwerker* in English is probably artisan; a close competitor might be independent craftsman.[1] Difficulties of translation may point to differences not just in perception but in reality, and indeed a case could be made that *Handwerk* is so peculiarly German that the concept is simply not translatable.[2]

National idiosyncrasies are often explained by 'history' and 'tradition'. In fact, the present German *Handwerk* system has more or less continuously evolved since the late nineteenth century, during a period which was otherwise characterized by traumatic historical discontinuities (Chesi, 1968; for an excellent discussion of the peculiar social history of small firms in Germany, see Doran, 1984). Today, its cornerstone is a comprehensive piece of legislation, called *Gesetz zur Ordnung des Handwerks* or, in short, *Handwerksordnung* (HwO – Statute of Artisans) that was passed in 1953. This section of the chapter will present a brief description of *Handwerk* as a legal institution, as established by the 1953 legislation.

It may be useful to mention at the outset that German artisans are by no means an economically marginal group. In 1983, the artisanal sector in West Germany, as defined by the HwO and as represented by *Handwerk* associations, comprised 496,100 firms with 3.9 million gainfully employed (including owners and active family members). Together, these firms accounted for a turnover of DM 381,000 million – which was larger by far than any single 'big' industry like, for example, chemicals (153,899 million) or automobiles (156,569 million). On average, each *Handwerk* firm employed almost 8 people, and as many as 26 percent of those employed in the *Handwerk* sector[3] worked in firms with more than 50 employees (1.7 percent of all *Handwerk* firms). If Germany is widely considered a country in which large-scale industries coexist with a healthy and competitive sector of small and medium-sized firms, this is primarily due to the presence and performance of its artisanal economy (Doran, 1984).

As has been indicated, *Handwerk* in Germany is above all a legal concept. German law defines *Handwerk* as a particular mode of production in which only specifically licensed establishments or self-employed individuals are permitted to engage. The two elements of the definition correspond to two different bodies of law. First, the HwO and a number of court rulings have laid down criteria that distinguish *Handwerk* from other forms of economic activity, in particular what is called *Industrie*. Secondly, the HwO has specified the conditions under which an establishment is entitled to be licensed to engage in artisanal activities.

At first glance the matter looks fairly straightforward. The HwO, in its 'Appendix A', lists 125 trades in which artisanal production may occur (*handwerksfähige Gewerbe*). Outside these trades there can by definition be no *Handwerk*, whatever other legal criteria an activity or an establishment may meet. The 125 trades – the list may be amended by ministerial decree – cover a wide range of economic activities. The law groups them in seven categories: building trades; metal-working trades; wood-working trades; clothing, textile and leather trades; food processing trades; health care, cosmetics, chemical and cleaning trades; glass, ceramics and other trades. In addition, there is an 'Appendix B' which specifies 40 'minor trades' (*handwerksähnliche Gewerbe*) that are regarded as 'similar' to artisanal trades but do not enjoy the full legal privileges of artisans. One example in this category is scaffolding. In the following, we will for reasons of simplicity focus mainly on the 125 trades listed in Appendix A.

Not all activities in the 125 trades are necessarily artisanal, and here is where the conceptual and legal complications begin (Britze, 1964; Wernet, 1965). An establishment that operates in one of the Appendix A trades is an artisanal establishment only if it is '*handwerksmäßig betrieben*', that is, if it is operated 'in an artisanal fashion' (Section 1, 2, HwO). The HwO abstains, however, from giving any further details as to what this means, which in effect delegates the subject to the courts. This solution is widely applauded both by legal scholars and by artisanal interests since it permits the continuous adjustment of the *Handwerk* concept to changing economic conditions and to the specificities of individual cases. In legal and political jargon, this highly flexible arrangement is referred to as the 'dynamic concept of *Handwerk*' ('*dynamischer Handwerksbegriff*').

German courts have a long tradition of jurisdiction on what does and does not constitute an artisanal mode of production (on the following, see Fröhler, 1965). Going back to the Prussian Administrative Court in 1904, they have consistently refused to interpret the concept of *Handwerk* restrictively. The prevailing opinion at the turn of the century was that *Handwerk*, as distinct from the emerging modern, large-scale *Industrie*, was characterized by small size of establishments, active participation of the owner in the process of production, exclusive employment of skilled labor, an absence of both a formal division of labor and machines, customized production for local markets, no formal book-keeping and no specialized administrative staff (Fröhler, 1965: 6f.). Each of these criteria was later eroded or abandoned by successive court rulings. The typical question that was put before the courts was whether a particular establishment that had moved away from one or more of the original *Handwerk* characteristics and developed in the direction of *Industrie* was still to be considered *Handwerk*. This the courts have tended, wherever possible, to answer in the affirmative, arguing that *Handwerk* as a social category must not be excluded from economic and technical progress. It was this evolving legal doctrine that helped prevent the disappearance of *Handwerk* as a socio-economic category in the course of industrialization.

Today, due to the particular development of the law, it is much easier to say what does not exclude an establishment from *Handwerk*, than what includes it in it (Fröhler, 1965: 28f.). For example, in Germany, unlike in France, small size is no longer seen as a necessary characteristic of an artisanal establishment, and in fact there are artisanal firms in the construction industry with a workforce of 500 and more. Nor does an establishment necessarily become *Industrie* if its owner no longer personally takes part in production; if it employs unskilled in addition to skilled labor; if it uses modern machinery; or if it produces standardized products in large numbers for non-local or even international markets. Whether or not an establishment operates 'in an artisanal fashion' cannot under present legal doctrine be determined by any single criterion. Recent court decisions have emphasized the internal organization of establishments and the role of skilled labor in it. While the use of machinery is not necessarily indicative of *Industrie*, in the artisanal mode of production there must remain an important 'manual core' (Fröhler, 1965: 28). Also, while employment of unskilled labor does not mean that an establishment is no longer an artisanal one, *Handwerk* is seen as characterized by an organization of work that requires a sizeable and dominant presence of skilled workers. And finally, where work is so subdivided that each worker performs only repetitive and recurrent tasks, an establishment is likely to be regarded as non-artisanal (so the Federal Administrative Court in 1961; adapted from Fröhler, 1965: 31ff.).

For an individual firm, whether or not it is legally classified as artisanal in character may be a matter of life and death. As has been said, establishments that operate 'in an artisanal fashion' can participate in one of the 125 trades only if they are licensed. A firm that is not licensed but, in the opinion of a court, is '*handwerksmäßig betrieben*' commits the statutory offense of 'illegal engagement in an artisanal trade' ('*unerlaubte Handwerksausübung*') and can be prosecuted. To avoid this, such a firm has to show to the court that it is organized in a non-artisanal way, in other words, that it is *Industrie*. This, given the openness of the legal definition, may not be easy. A firm without a license that wants to compete with *Handwerk* firms in Appendix A trades has to invent a way of production that is clearly and demonstrably non-artisanal; if it cannot do so, it has to get a license or otherwise becomes subject to legal prosecution.

The second set of legal rules on which *Handwerk* as an institution is based regulates the licensing of individuals and establishments to work, 'in an artisanal fashion', in one of the 125 trades. In principle, a *Handwerk* license is identical to a Master certificate and can thus be held only by individuals. To become a Master artisan one has first to serve a three-year apprenticeship after which one has to pass an examination. Following this, one normally works for several years as a journeyman. Thirdly, one attends a two-year *Meister* course at a special school after which one, again, has to pass an examination. The period of training varies somewhat between trades, and sometimes it is not necessary to absolve the *Meister* curriculum in one piece. Nevertheless, the curriculum is exactly as demanding, long-drawn and difficult as it looks from this brief description.

Individuals who have passed the *Meister* examination have the right to become active in their trades as self-employed workers. They can also set up firms which then receive a license on account of their *Meister* certificate. While this is the simplest case, there are a number of exceptions and qualifications, some of which again serve to facilitate the adjustment of artisanal establishments to economic, technical and organizational change (Fröhler, 1971). For example, the (prestigious) university degree of *Diplom-Ingenieur* (graduated engineer) now carries the same entitlement to run an artisanal business as the *Meister* certificate. More traditionally, there always was the provision that if a certified artisan died, the family was entitled to carry on the business for a limited time (during which the heir was expected to complete the *Meister* training). But firms can also be licensed if their owner has never had and never will have a license – which makes it easier for the artisanal economy to attract investment capital. In such a case, a firm becomes eligible to practice an artisanal trade if it employs a certified artisan as production manager (*Betriebsleiter*). If the firm is a company, the license is awarded if one of the partners is a certified artisan and if he is in charge of technical operations (Section 7, HwO).

To foreign observers, all this is likely to look like one giant conspiracy in restraint of trade, and indeed in a sense it is. Historically, the development that culminated in the HwO started as a backlash against free trade (*Gewerbefreiheit*) after its introduction in the middle of the nineteenth century. Especially in the 1870s and 1890s, when modern industry increasingly entered the traditional markets of the small artisans, free trade began to be perceived by these as a threat to their independence and as a first step towards their being absorbed by the new, large-scale factories. Fortunately from their perspective, their growing concerns were shared by the Bismarck government, for which the possible 'proletarianization' of a group which was one of its staunchest allies presented a formidable political threat. Offering the independent artisans legal and economic support was seen by Bismarck as an ideal opportunity to cultivate a *Mittelstand* constituency that would for a long time be immune to the lures of Social Democracy and provide a stable base of support for conservative governments. It was this specific political exchange which started the legal institutionalization of *Handwerk*. While regimes changed frequently in the twentieth century, none of them could or would afford seriously to antagonize the *Mittelstand*, and this made it possible for the artisanal lobby to win and consolidate step by step its two central institutional privileges – the *Handwerksprivileg* and, fully formalized for the first time in 1935 (Chesi, 1968), the *Meisterprivileg*.

But this, in spite of its intuitive Machiavellian appeal, is not the whole story. German *Handwerk* legislation undoubtedly limits market entry and creates (group) monopolies, and in this respect it is indeed likely to result in welfare losses for the economy and the society as a whole (Olson, 1982). On the other hand, the benefits for a society of a healthy sector of small and medium-sized firms may not be limited to the political contribution of the *Mittelstand* to 'social stability' in the conservative sense. While it is difficult to assess the costs and benefits of *Handwerk* as an institution quantitatively, it would be premature to dismiss the arguments of its advocates as entirely ideological. In one way or other, these arguments all revolve around the notion that there continues to exist in modern economies a significant market for customized quality goods and services that can only be served by small firms with highly qualified labor and management. Firms and individuals, however, will invest in the generation of such qualifications only if they are protected both from 'free-riding' competition in the labor market and from low quality-low price competition in the product market. The main defense for the institutional privileges of artisanal firms is that they offer exactly this kind of protection. Indeed, at the core of both the ideology and the organization of *Handwerk* in Germany is training, and cultural sociologists would probably characterize the German *Handwerk* system as an institutional representation of the (Lutheran) idea of *Beruf* (vocation), defined as a set of acquired skills around which a person's individual and social identity is organized.[4]

The economic importance of vocational training in the artisanal sector is commonly emphasized under two aspects. Small firms seem to be more likely to survive in competition with large industry if their products and services are of high quality and if their owners and managers not only know their trade but also command sound managerial skills. The long training that Master artisans have to undergo in Germany, and in particular the curricula at the *Meisters-chulen*, ensure that there is an ample supply of people who meet these preconditions.[5] Between 1970 and 1983, a total of 399,000 young artisans – an average 28,000 per year – passed their *Meister* examinations, adding to the pool of individuals both licensed and trained to set up or manage artisanal firms. While it is difficult to prove that the success of small firms in the West German economy is in part accounted for by the presence of this large reservoir of technical and managerial skills, recent efforts in Germany to promote small business as a potentially important source of employment are certainly not constrained by a shortage of qualified potential entrepreneurs. Indeed, employment in the artisanal economy was higher in 1980 than in 1970, and its decline by 200,000 to its 1983 level is almost exclusively attributable to the severe structural crisis of the construction industry, to which about one tenth of artisanal firms belong. To the extent that the ability of owners and operators to discover market niches, use advanced technology, ensure high product quality and manage an enterprise efficiently has contributed to the sector's employment performance, the latter is at least in part explained by the *Handwerk* training system.

The second contribution of artisanal vocational training to the performance of the German economy relates to its central role in the training of skilled workers. In 1983, the 492,100 *Handwerk* firms accounted for 676,078 apprentices, which represented an increase by 85 percent over 1970. In the same year, 202,799 artisanal apprentices passed their journeyman examination and entered the labor force at a high level of qualification. Since many of the *Handwerk* apprentices later go to work in large industrial firms, the training efforts of the artisanal sector benefit not only the *Handwerk* itself but also the economy at large. As a matter of fact, the training system in the 'modern' sector of the German economy was deliberately modeled, in the 1920s, on the artisanal system, with apprenticeships of three years and the opportunity for skilled workers to advance to the level of *Industriemeister* (Stütz, 1969). High qualification of the workforce is a vital resource for a country like Germany which is short of raw materials and which needs superior products for export in highly competitive world markets. The role of *Handwerk* in generating this resource is one of the main reasons why this peculiar institution continues to be so firmly established and why it is unlikely to lose its political or cultural legitimacy in the foreseeable future.

Another reason for the persistence of the artisanal economy in Germany is that on the whole it has relied surprisingly little on its legal privileges to shield itself from pressures for modernization.

Today more than ever, *Handwerk* associations discourage the use of the HwO as a weapon against technologically and organizationally superior *Industrie* competitors. Underlying this is the conviction that legal protection cannot in the long run keep non-competitive firms in the market, and that trying to use it for this purpose would only erode its public and political support. Instead, *Handwerk* firms and their associations have successfully made aggressive use of the fact that there is no legal limit to the growth of artisanal establishments and that in practice technical and organizational modernization is unlikely to lead to a loss of *Handwerk* status. Legal privileges which on paper may look like protection from competition have in the process turned into instruments of support in competition. One indicator of the modernization that has taken place in the *Handwerk* sector is the continuous decline in the number of firms from 734,600 in 1960 to 492,100 in 1983, which coincided with almost steady employment (4.072 million in 1963 compared to 3.906 million in 1983).

In modernizing their operations, *Handwerk* firms are strongly and effectively supported by their associations which continuously upgrade training methods and curricula, offer assistance in collective marketing and cooperative research, help with the introduction of electronic data processing – often on a cooperative basis – provide credit facilities, run government support programs, etc., in addition to their classical tasks of administering examinations, keeping the register of licensed artisans and protecting the *Handwerksprivileg* by prosecuting the illicit performance of artisanal *Berufe*. These associations are far from peripheral to the *Handwerk* system – which is why the HwO devotes detailed attention not just to the legal status of artisanal firms but also to the structure of their representative organizations. In fact, it is arguable that without its interest organizations the artisanal economy would not have survived in its present strength, legal privileges or not. It is instructive in this context that Doran, in proposing measures to improve the situation of small firms in the United Kingdom, above all advocates the introduction of a German-style chamber system with compulsory membership (1984: 201ff.)

The Organization of Artisanal Interests in Germany

Artisanal firms in Germany are represented by one of the most complex, most comprehensive and most densely legally regulated systems of interest organizations anywhere in the Western world. Among its many unique features is the way in which the system combines elements of private and public law, of voluntary and compulsory organization, of social autonomy and state regulation. Private-law organizations with voluntary membership coexist with statutory associations of which each artisanal firm has to be a member, and at strategic points in their multi-layered structure private and public organizations of *Handwerk* are so closely intertwined that they become in practice indistinguishable. The organizational system also includes a sophisticated mix of trade-specific organizations – some of which function as employers' associations – and those that represent the entire category of *Handwerk*. Moreover, artisanal interest associations in Germany have managed, in important respects, to remain 'vertical corporations' in the sense that they do not represent just employers but also workers – much to the dismay of trade unions. As we shall see, this is related to the crucial role of *Handwerk* organizations in the artisanal training and examination system.

At the center of the organization of artisans in Germany are the regional chambers of artisans (*Handwerkskammern*, HWK) of which there were 42 before reunification, together covering the entire territory of the Federal Republic. Chambers are public-law institutions with compulsory membership. One of their main tasks is to keep a register of the licensed artisans in their territory. Registered Master artisans are by law members of the chamber and both obliged to pay dues and entitled to vote and serve on chamber committees. Firms that are owned by a registered artisan are exempted from the general legal obligation for business enterprises – and in fact are no longer qualified – to join the local chamber of commerce and industry. As chambers organize all 125 artisanal trades, they represent and incorporate the identity of *Handwerk* as a social and economic category distinct from *Industrie*.

Chambers of artisans differ considerably by size. In 1983, the smallest chamber was Coburg in Bavaria with 1,460 firms, while the largest, Munich, represented 37,754 firms. Due to their public law status, the internal structure and many of the activities of chambers of artisans are narrowly circumscribed by the law, in particular by the *Handwerksordnung* (Sections 90–116). There is also a wide range of activities that are optional and over which the governing bodies of the chambers have discretion. In this sense, chambers of artisans are a mixture between a para-state agency and a voluntary interest association. For example, chambers – that is, their representative assemblies – make their own budgets and statutes and set their dues, but their decisions require the approval of the respective *Land* ministry for economic affairs. Similarly, while their leading professional staff have the status of (senior) civil servants, they are appointed by the president and the governing body of the chamber who are elected representatives of the membership.

Just as the compulsory column of *Handwerksorganisation* is based on the chambers, the bottom layer of its voluntary column consists of local guilds (*Innungen*). The territorial domain of guilds and the artisanal trades they comprise are, to a certain extent, left to their members to decide. While the HwO stipulates that, as a rule, different trades should be organized in different guilds and the territory covered by a guild should be coterminous with a city or county (Section 52, 3), exceptions are possible. In no case, however, can there be two guilds for the same trade in the same place. Decisions by guilds on their territorial and trade domain require the approval of the chamber of artisans. While guild membership is not compulsory, guilds are public-law institutions and as such subject to legal control by the chambers – in the same way as these are under the supervision of the respective ministry of economic affairs.

All in all, there were 6,202 *Handwerk* guilds in West Germany in 1983. Although guild membership is voluntary, an estimated 85 to 90 percent of eligible firms are organized in guilds. One reason for this extraordinarily high density ratio is certainly the strong social cohesion of the artisanal community that is rooted in the long period of training and socialization. Also important seems to be informal organizational assistance by the chambers of artisans which, for example, often urge their members to join the guild representing their trade. In addition, there are two other factors that are interesting enough to be specifically mentioned.

First, under German legislation employers have to provide for comprehensive health insurance for their workforce. Insurance premiums are based on wages, with the employer and the worker each paying one half of the rate. Within limits, employers and workers can choose between a variety of insurance funds. *Handwerk* guilds traditionally operate special insurance funds for their members and their workers. Since absenteeism is lower in artisanal firms than in large industrial enterprises, the percentage of the wage that is charged by the guild insurance funds is also lower. However, membership in these funds is open only to employers that belong to the respective guild.

Secondly, again unlike the chambers of artisans, guilds are not only trade associations but also employers' associations that have the right to engage in collective bargaining with trade unions. One of the reasons why compulsory guild membership – which had been introduced in 1934 – was abolished after the war is that under the German constitution collective bargaining can be engaged in only by voluntary associations. Apart from their role in the negotiation of collective agreements, German employers' associations advise their members on matters of labor law and represent them in labor court cases. Since litigation is an everyday event in an industrial relations system as thoroughly regulated by law as the German one, expert legal advice and representation is essential for employers, and in fact they constitute one of the most attractive resources employers' associations have to offer to potential members (Streeck and Rampelt, 1982).

Chambers of artisans may cover large regions, and the number of firms that they serve may be very large. Guilds, on the other hand, are small; in 1983, there were no more than about 80 firms to each guild. As an intermediary between chambers and guilds, the HwO provides for a third institution, the so-called *Kreishandwerkerschaften* (KHS). In principle, county artisan bureaus – which seems to be the most appropriate translation – cover the territory of either a county or a city (that is, a local community large enough not to be included in a county). County bureaus are associations of associations in that all guilds based in their area of jurisdiction are, by statute, affiliated to them. There were 272 such organizations in 1983, an average of 6.5 per chamber, each serving, again on average, 2,143 firms. County bureaus are supervised by the chamber, which also pays their expenses. Although they have their own elected bodies, for all practical purposes they function as 'field offices' of the chamber. Their importance for the system of artisanal organizations derives from the fact that guilds are entitled to have their current business administered by the county bureaus. Guilds also have the option of employing their own full-time staff to run their affairs themselves, and this was chosen by 1,143 of the 6,220 guilds in 1983. For the rest, however, the county bureaus were the only source of administrative support and professional manpower, with each bureau serving on average 28.7 guilds.

The county artisan bureaus perform crucial functions within and for the system of artisanal organizations. Above all, the joint administration of the affairs of affiliated guilds generates considerable organizational economies of scale without which smaller guilds could not afford a separate existence. Just how important the county bureaus are for the artisanal community is reflected in the fact that they are often referred to as 'the artisan's city hall'. In addition, the tight financial and administrative control of the chambers over the county bureaus reinforces the former's central position in the system. County bureaus also constitute a strategic link between the statutory and the voluntary element of *Handwerk* organization. Moreover, since their staff are not specialized by trade but conduct the business of – potentially – all guilds in their area, bureaus contribute strongly to preserving the identity of *Handwerk* and help prevent its fragmentation by different trades.

County artisan bureaus are something between an administrative convenience of the chamber of artisans and a higher-level association of local guilds. Purer forms of associations of associations exist above the county level, and indeed the inter-organizational hierarchy of the *Handwerk* system is at least as impressive as its organizational structure at the base. Under the HwO (Section 79), guilds of the same trade or of related trades may form regional guild associations (*Landesinnungsverbände*, LIV), normally at the *Land* level – for example, a Bavarian Association of Butcher Guilds. Guild associations are private-law organizations whose statutes do, however, require the approval of the appropriate *Land* authorities. The law precludes the existence of competing guild associations for the same trade and territory (Section 79, 2). In 1983, the 6,220 guilds were organized in 288 *Länder* guild associations, with an average membership per guild association of about 22 guilds.

Membership in guild associations is voluntary. However, as has been indicated, dissenting guilds are not permitted to set up their own association, and this may explain why the number of guilds that are unorganized at any given time is very small. Guilds that join a regional guild association normally have to sign over to it their right to collective bargaining, and indeed one of the most important functions of guild associations is to represent their members – and the firms represented by these – vis-a-vis trade unions. (In many artisanal trades, collective bargaining is still further centralized and negotiations are conducted at the national level by federal associations of regional guild associations – see below.) Again, the fact that membership in guild associations is voluntary corresponds to their role as employers' associations. One of the least known political accomplishments of artisanal interest organizations in Germany is that they have managed, in spite of a strong system of industrial unionism, to preserve their separate industrial agreements. Although artisanal employers' associations negotiate with the same trade unions as their counterparts outside the artisanal sector, their collective agreements differ from those in the economy at large in that they take into account the specific needs and conditions of artisanal firms. For example, since the metal-working artisans are not covered by the industrial agreement for the *Metallindustrie*, they were not affected by the (1984) strike for the 35-hour week. On the other hand, wage differentials between *Handwerk* and *Industrie* are not dramatic in Germany, and they certainly are much smaller than between large and small firms in the United Kingdom (Doran, 1984).

As the reader should by now expect, the chambers of artisans, just as the local guilds, also form associations at the *Land* level, the so-called *Landeshandwerkskammertage* (LHKT) – at least in the seven *Länder* with more than one chamber. Interestingly, although the chambers are undoubtedly the most 'public' institutions of all artisanal organizations, their associations are pure private-law organizations that are not even mentioned by the HwO – which gives them considerable flexibility in conducting their affairs. In particular, they are not subject to any form of state supervision. Although chambers can at any time withdraw from their associations, this seems never to have happened.

The dualism between the two pillars of artisanal organization, voluntary guilds and compulsory chambers, exists also at the federal level. All 42 chambers of artisans are organized in a federal peak association, the *Deutscher Handwerkskammertag* (DHKT, German Association of Chambers of Artisans). Again, just as its counterparts at the *Länder* level, the DHKT is not an institution of the HwO. But no individual chamber has ever seceded, and for all practical purposes the DHKT operates like a public-law National Chamber of Artisans.

The guild system organizes in two ways at the federal level. First, there are 65 trade-specific national guild associations (*Bundesinnungsverbände*, BIV) whose members are, in the normal case, the respective *Länder* guild associations. This organizational form is provided for under the HwO (Section 85), and guild associations at the national level are subject to essentially the same legal constraints and controls as their constituent regional associations. Secondly, there is a National Federation of National Guild Associations (*Bundesvereinigung der Fachverbände des Deutschen Handwerks*, BFH) which, among other things, coordinates collective bargaining between the relevant federal and regional guild associations as well as with the Federal Association of German Employers' Associations (BDA) of which the BFH is a member. The BFH is a voluntary association not envisaged by the HwO, and in 1983 51 of the 65 national guild associations were affiliated to it.[6]

As if all this was not yet astonishing enough, there is still a higher level of organization at which the voluntary and the compulsory branches of *Handwerksorganisation* meet and converge. This part of the organization of artisans is exclusively based on private law, and it has been politically controversial, especially with the trade unions, since its inception in 1966 (John, 1979; Perner, 1983). The Federal Association of Chambers of Artisans (DHKT) and the Federal Association of National Guild Associations (BFH) together form a third organization, the Central Association of German

Artisans (*Zentralverband des Deutschen Handwerks*, ZDH). DHKT, ZDH and BFH operate a joint office in Bonn with a full-time staff of about 100. The three organizations are so densely intertwined that in practice they function as if they were one, with the General Secretaries of DHKT and BFH serving at the same time as Deputy General Secretaries of the ZDH. The fact that ZDH, DHKT and BFH still have separate legal identities is important only insofar as it is convenient to have different letter-heads for activities of different legal status. For example, the BFH is in practice little more than the industrial relations department of the ZDH, but since chambers are not supposed to become even indirectly involved in collective bargaining or otherwise operate as employers' associations, the ZDH wears its BFH hat when representing employer interests. Similarly, the DHKT functions as a ZDH department specializing in subjects like vocational training that are legally under the jurisdiction of the chambers. Hardly surprising, the same construction is replicated, at least formally, in each *Land*, with a regional peak association of guild associations (*Landesvereinigung der Fachverbände des Handwerks*, LFH) and the respective association of chambers of artisans – or the chamber if there is only one – joining together to set up a *Landeshandwerks-vertretung* (LHV) on the model of the ZDH.

It has already been mentioned that some of the artisanal organizations in Germany are still 'vertical corporations' that organize both employers and employees. At the same time, there are also artisanal associations that are regular employers' associations negotiating collective industrial agreements with trade unions – which is possibly the most important change in the system to take place after 1945 (Chesi, 1968). In fact, much of the complexity of the organizational structure of *Handwerk* can be explained as resulting from an attempt to combine traditional elements of 'vertical', or sectoral, organization with modern elements of 'liberal', or class, organization where different class interests are expressed by separate, independent and potentially opposing interest associations.

The location, the structure and the functional jurisdiction of vertical representation within the artisanal associational system are prescribed in detail by the HwO (Sections 68–72, 98–9, 108). Organizations that are required to provide for internal participation of employees are the chambers of artisans and the local guilds. Representation of workers in chambers and guilds is limited to journeymen; apprentices and unskilled workers are excluded. Participation rights extend primarily to matters related to vocational training. Although they are not completely limited to this, the vertical element of the artisanal associational system represents essentially the common sectoral interest in maintaining a high standard of training.

As already indicated, most of the activities of both chambers and guilds, and certainly some of the more important ones, revolve around the regulation and administration of the vocational training and examination system. For example, local chambers keep a register of all apprentices in their domain. They can determine that a firm is not suited to train apprentices, and they can – and sometimes do – withdraw a firm's training license if legal rules are violated or if training is insufficient. In individual cases, chambers may shorten or prolong the required training period. Chambers also liaise with the public vocational schools that apprentices have to attend in addition to their training at the workplace. Furthermore, chambers regulate the examinations for journeymen and *Meister*; among other things, they appoint examination boards and administer their current business. They also organize courses for retraining and further training, and most of them run their own training centers. In all these matters, chambers cooperate closely with the guilds in their domain, making use of their specialized expertise and of their closer contact to individual artisans or firms. Guilds are charged by the HwO with basically the same or similar functions in the area of training as chambers (cf. Sections 54 and 91). This overlap, together with their clearly established legal primacy, permits chambers to delegate important tasks in the supervision of training to the guilds. The result is a highly flexible division of labor between the two organizations which permits for different arrangements between chambers and guilds by individual trades, depending on how well a guild is organized and how well it performs its functions.

That journeymen are represented in the chambers of artisans gives them a certain, however limited, degree of influence over the governance of the training system. The HwO stipulates that one third of the members of the assembly, the executive board and the committees of a chamber must be elected delegates of journeymen (Sections 93, 1; 108, 1; 110). The particularly important vocational training committee has to include an equal number of representatives of employers and journeymen plus the same number of vocational school teachers, the latter being appointed by the government (Section 43). Guilds, on the other hand, have to have a special journeymen committee whose members are entitled to vote in the guild assembly and to participate in deliberations of the executive board on subjects related to training (Section 68, 2). Decisions of the executive board on such subjects require the approval of the journeymen committee. If such approval is withheld, the matter is decided by the chamber of artisans (Section 68, 4). To keep vertical and horizontal mechanisms of interest accommodation between workers and employers apart, the law precludes participation of journeymen at the guild level on matters that are the subject of a collective agreement with trade unions (Section 68, 5).

The basic structure of German *Handwerksorganisation* is summarized in Figure 4.1. No two-dimensional schematic representation can, however, do justice to the full complexity of the system. Six main axes of differentiation have to be distinguished.

First, public- versus private-law organizations. Guilds, county bureaus and chambers are based in public law, as indicated in Figure 4.1. Regional guild associations and their national federations are private-law organizations whose statutes do, however, require the approval of the respective government ministry. The remaining organizations are founded in private law and are not subject to state supervision, although their constituent units may be public-law bodies.

Secondly, organizations with compulsory and with voluntary membership. This distinction is not identical with that between public- and private-law bodies due to the peculiar construction of the guilds as public-law organizations with voluntary membership. However, since they can draw on both highly developed informal 'community' bonds and strong selective incentives – some of which are 'borrowed' from organizations in the system with compulsory membership – their membership density is almost as high as if membership was compulsory.

Thirdly, organizations with and without 'vertical' representation. As we have seen, vertical representation exists in two of the three kinds of public-law bodies (chambers and guilds) and is closely associated with these bodies' functions in the governance of vocational training. It does not however extend to their private law federations.

Fourth, organizations that perform the functions of employers' associations and those that do not. Guilds, although they are public-law bodies, represent their members, among other things, as employers, and to this extent they are not vertically integrated. Regional guild associations and their national federations also act as employers' associations, under delegated powers from their constituent guilds. The same applies to the peak associations of regional and national guild associations (the BFH and its counterparts at the *Land* level).

Fifth, organizations that represent (one or more) individual trades, and organizations that represent *Handwerk* as a whole. This

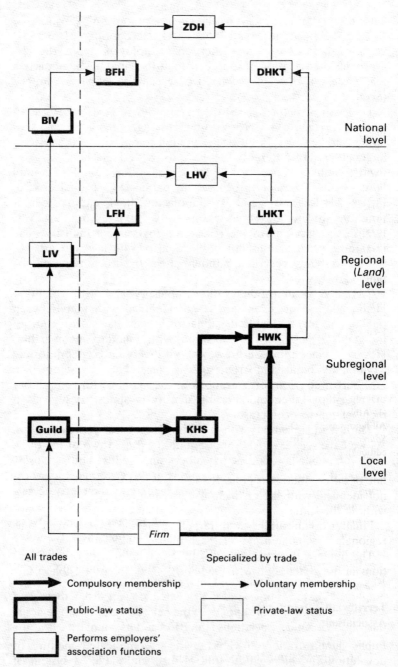

Figure 4.1 *The structure of the artisanal organizational system*

Table 4.1   *The structure of* Handwerk *organization, 1963–1983*

	National[a] federations	Regional federations	Guilds All	Guilds (1)	Guilds (2)	County bureaus	Chambers
1963	?	?	9,508	7,214	2,294	431	45
1964	63	387	9,449	7,383	2,066	430	45
1965	63	404	9,354	7,658	1,696	431	45
1966	63	402	9,240	7,561	1,679	430	45
1967	64	393	9,165	7,522	1,643	429	45
1968	64	389	9,044	7,414	1,630	427	45
1969	?	?	8,777	7,227	1,550	422	45
1970	?	?	8,492	6,985	1,507	413	45
1971	65	348	8,275	6,785	1,490	409	45
1972	65	333	7,884	6,502	1,382	386	45
1973	66	329	7,490	6,200	1,290	335	45
1974	65	310	7,080	5,799	1,281	320	43
1975	64	303	6,908	5,660	1,248	296	43
1976	63	311	6,695	5,512	1,183	288	43
1977	63	303	6,569	5,409	1,160	284	43
1978	63	312	6,453	5,292	1,161	277	43
1979	65	312	6,407	5,259	1,148	275	42
1980	65	302	6,358	5,219	1,139	274	42
1981	65	294	6,299	5,144	1,155	273	42
1982	65	295	6,243	5,097	1,146	273	42
1983	65	288	6,220	5,077	1,143	272	42

[a] Of regional guild associations or local guilds.
(1) Affiliated to County Bureaus. (2) With own office.
All figures as of 31 December.
Sources: Zentralverband des Deutschen Handwerks, *Handwerk* (successive editions); 1963–1965: Deutscher Handwerkskammertag, *Jahresbericht*.

line of differentiation is indicated in Figure 4.1; as can be seen, it is not identical with the distinction between organizations with and without the status of employers' associations.

Finally, organizations at different territorial levels (local, sub-regional, regional and national; see Figure 4.1).

The numerical development of the main categories of organizations in the system between 1963 and 1983 is given in Table 4.1.

Territorial Differentiation in Artisanal Interest Associations

Public administration in Germany is a complicated mixture of devolution and hierarchical control in a multi-layered system of subnational territorial jurisdictions. Before unification the Federal

Republic consisted of 11 *Länder*. Three of these, Hamburg, Bremen and Berlin, were actually large cities, and one of the others, the Saarland, had a smaller population than both Hamburg and Berlin. There is also a long tradition of self-government by local communities of which there were no fewer than 8,505 in 1983. All but 91 of these were included in one of 237 counties which functioned as a second tier of local government. The 91 cities that did not belong to a county – a category that includes the three 'city states' – had the same legal status as a county; we will in the following refer to the two categories together as 'localities'. Finally, six *Länder* – all the larger ones except one – operated an intermediate level of administration, the administrative district (*Regierungsbezirk*), which was used by the *Land* government to exercise its legal and administrative control over the localities. In 1983, there were 26 such districts. Unlike communities, localities and *Länder*, administrative districts do not have elected officials or assemblies. Where the system is fully developed, there are thus no less than five levels of government from the small local community to the national state.

The rich territorial differentiation of the artisanal system of interest associations clearly resembles the territorial structure of the German state. This correspondence is, not surprisingly, enshrined in law. Section 52, 2 of the HwO stipulates that the area covered by a guild 'shall as a rule be coterminous with a county or city' (locality). Of the county bureaus, Section 86 states that they are to be formed 'by the guilds based in a given county or city'. The territorial jurisdiction of a chamber of artisans is, under Section 90, 3, 'as a rule identical with an administrative district'. And regional guild associations are to be formed 'in the area of a *Land*' (Section 79, 1).

Legal intervention in the organizational design of intermediary associations is an element of what we have called the 'Logic of Influence'. This logic operates in two ways. Organized interests may themselves be interested in coterminacy with the subnational state to be able to lobby it more effectively. To establish themselves as institutionalized lobbies, they may go as far as to extract from the state a legal obligation for them to be present at the various levels of government. This appears particularly suitable for a social category such as *Handwerk* whose very definition and identity is based in, if not created by, the law. Governments, on the other hand, may want organized interests to be structured symmetrically to the structure of the state, to make them easier to govern and usable as paragovernmental institutions. Interest groups may have to accept such intervention in their organizational autonomy in exchange for legal recognition and state-guaranteed organizational security.

However, the reciprocal interest in effective subnational lobbying on the one hand and in functional control and devolution on the other can, even in extreme cases such as the one under discussion, not be expected to be the only factor shaping the territorial structure of associational systems. This is recognized by the HwO, which provides for exceptions from the rule and for other criteria of organizational design than that of jurisdictional symmetry. The territory of a chamber is defined by the *Land* government which may allow it to cross the boundaries of administrative districts (Section 90, 3). The territorial domain of the county bureaus is determined by the chambers, which 'may permit a different demarcation' from that of the localities (Section 86). Guilds, in addition to being required, 'as a rule', to be coterminous with a locality, have to be so organized 'that the number of members is sufficient for the guild to be capable of performing its tasks, and that the members can participate in the life of the guild and can have access to its facilities' (Section 52, 2). While the first additional criterion introduces considerations of organizational efficiency ('Logic of Efficient Implementation'), the second emphasizes the need for closeness to the members ('Logic of Membership'). Furthermore, Section 52, 1 demands that guilds organize members 'from the same trade or from such trades that are professionally [*fachlich*] or economically closely related'. This can be interpreted as a reference to the 'Logic of Goal Formation' in that it recognizes that there are limits to the heterogeneity of interests that can be successfully incorporated in the deliberations of a political organization.

The additional criteria of organizational demarcation point to interesting trade-offs in the design of interest associations in general and artisanal guilds in particular. A guild whose territory is coterminous with a large county may not be close enough to its members for them to participate. A guild that satisfies the latter criterion, coterminous with a locality or not, may not have a large enough membership base to be organizationally efficient. To increase its size, it may have to incorporate 'related trades' – with the result that it becomes too heterogeneous. This it may be able to avoid only if its territory is extended beyond one locality or even beyond the domain of a chamber. While the HwO stipulates that the territory of a guild 'shall not exceed that of a chamber', it provides for the possibility of guilds organizing beyond chamber boundaries, with the permission of the *Land* government (Section 52, 3). It even offers the choice, undoubtedly for the sake of internal homogeneity and organizational efficiency but at the expense of member closeness, for guilds organizing in more than one *Land*, with permission from all *Land* authorities affected.

The following discussion will explore in some more detail, drawing on the organizational unit of the guild as an example, how the pressures for coterminacy and symmetry between the state and intermediary organizations are modified by pressures emerging from Logics other than that of Influence. There is no direct information on the number of guilds whose territorial domain is coterminous with that of a locality. However, some conclusions can be drawn from the development of the number of guilds over time, in comparison with simultaneous changes in the structure of local government. The 1970s saw a dramatic reduction in the number of local communities, cities and counties due to a national drive to rationalize the administrative machinery. Between 1968, the last year before the reform, and 1978, the year when it was completed, the number of local communities declined by about two thirds, from 24,357 to 8,518. Most of this decline took place in the four years after 1971 when the number of communities was halved. The number of cities declined by one-third, essentially between 1972 and 1975, and the number of counties was reduced by 43 percent between 1970 and 1977.

The number of guilds also fell in the two decades between 1963 and 1983, although at a somewhat lower rate than that of localities, the corresponding unit of local government (35 as compared to 42 percent). Not all of this decline, however, paralleled the reform of local government. Between 1963 and 1969 when the number of localities was constant 731 guilds disappeared, and another 349 disappeared after 1977 when the changes in local government had been completed. The most rapid change in the number of localities occurred from 1972 to 1977 when it fell from 528 to 327, that is, by 38 percent; in the same period, the number of guilds fell by only 20 percent.

Some of the changes in the guild system that happened before 1970 may have been in anticipation of local government reform, and part of the changes after 1977 may have been delayed responses to it. But other factors which had nothing to do with the structure of local government contributed also to the decline in the number of guilds. Between 1963 and 1983, the number of artisanal firms dropped by 28 percent, from 686,440 to 492,100. Assuming, as does the HwO, that guilds need a minimum size to be organizationally viable ('Logic of Efficient Implementation'), one would expect this to have generated pressures for mergers, both in the territorial dimension and between guilds of 'related trades'. But one would also expect such pressures to have met with local resistance, and this is reflected in the fact that while the number of guilds did decline together with the number of firms, initially this decline proceeded

Table 4.2 *The structure of* Handwerk *organizations: selected parameters, 1963–1983*

	Firms/ guilds	Guilds/ localities[1]	Guilds[2]/ bureaus	Guilds/ regional federations
1963	72.2	16.8	16.7	?
1964	70.9	16.7	17.2	24.4
1965	70.1	16.5	17.8	23.2
1966	69.5	16.4	17.6	23.0
1967	68.6	16.3	17.5	23.2
1968	68.0	16.0	17.4	23.2
1969	68.4	15.6	17.1	?
1970	68.9	14.4	16.9	?
1971	68.9	15.3	16.6	23.8
1972	70.5	14.7	16.8	23.7
1973	72.3	19.1	18.5	22.8
1974	74.6	18.3	18.7	22.8
1975	75.1	20.1	19.1	22.8
1976	75.8	19.5	19.1	21.5
1977	76.4	20.1	19.0	21.7
1978	77.3	19.7	19.1	20.7
1979	77.5	19.6	19.1	20.5
1980	78.0	19.4	19.9	21.1
1981	78.6	19.3	18.8	21.5
1982	78.8	19.1	18.7	21.2
1983	79.1	19.0	18.7	21.6

[1] Cities (*Kreisfreie Städte*) and counties.
[2] Excluding guilds with own office.

more slowly. As a result, the average number of firms per guild fell steadily until 1971 (Table 4.2).

The principal proponents of rationalization of the guild system in the 1960s were the regional guild associations and, in particular, the chambers. Efforts by higher organizational levels to reduce the number of hierarchically inferior units are not unique to the system of artisanal interest associations or, for that matter, to the state; in fact, similar processes took place at about the same time in German trade unions (Streeck, 1981a). Organizational reforms of this kind tend to be resented by members defending established local identities ('Logic of Membership') and the interest-political homogeneity of their organizational units ('Logic of Goal Formation'). This is why the rationalization of German artisanal associations in the 1960s progressed more slowly than the decline of their potential membership. Its main achievement before 1970 remained the reduction in the number of guilds that conducted their business themselves, and the corresponding increase in the number of guilds serviced by county bureaus (Table 4.1, in particular 1963 to 1965). In the 1970s, however, the reform of local government offered chambers a legitimate opportunity to bring legal pressure to bear on the guilds to redraw their boundaries. That this was successful is shown by the fact that, beginning in 1972, the average number of firms per guild increased by 12 percent, to 79.1 in 1983, although the absolute number of firms continued to decline (Table 4.2).

The forces in favor of organizational rationalization were assisted not only by the reform of local government but also by social-structural changes. The possible territorial domain of the base units of interest associations or associational systems is limited by the spatial mobility of the membership. The same general increase in mobility that permitted the introduction of larger units of local government – and larger local units of trade unions – made it possible to extend the territorial domains of artisanal guilds and thereby to ensure an efficient minimum number of members. Here, three of the 'Logics' of intermediary organization coincided: those of Influence, of Membership and of Efficient Implementation. We do not know directly whether this development was accompanied by increased or reduced internal heterogeneity of guilds in terms of artisanal trades. However, the increase in the average number of guilds per locality from 14.4 in 1970 to 19.0 in 1983 (Table 4.2) suggests that rationalization did not occur at the expense of the 'Logic of Goal Formation' as the increased territorial domain of guilds seems to have permitted on average higher specialization by trade without a decline in average size or a loss of economies of scale.

The Public Organization of Private Interests and the Four Logics of Intermediary Organization

The remarkable stability of the basic parameters of inter-organizational structure (Table 4.2), in the face of rapid environmental change, sheds new light on the dynamics of territorial differentiation in the associational system under study. Pressures for equilibrium in inter-organizational, and in particular hierarchical, relations seem to affect the demarcation of territorial domains as much as the structure of subnational governments or changes in the member population. Territorial differentiation thus needs to be explained not just in terms of the adjustment of individual units to their political and institutional environment but also in terms of their 'fit' into the encompassing inter-organizational system.

The system of artisanal associations in Germany corresponds closely to Schmitter's (1974: 93) seminal definition of the structure of corporatist interest representation: its 'constituent units', the firms, 'are organized into a limited number of singular, compulsory [or de facto compulsory], noncompetitive, hierarchically ordered and functionally differentiated categories, recognized or licensed (if not created) by the state and granted a deliberate representational monopoly within their respective categories'. The state figures prominently in this definition, and indeed it would be difficult to find a system of interest associations in a liberal democracy where the traces of state intervention are as omnipresent as in the associations of the German artisanal sector. To be sure, the HwO has been asked for by the organized artisans themselves, and to this extent it is the outcome of effective lobbying and pressure politics. However, under the 'Logic of Influence' that governs the exchange between private organized interests and the state, once public status has been achieved the rules of the game change. For interest organizations as firmly established in the public realm as German *Handwerk* associations, the principal modus operandi can no longer be to lobby the government from the outside but to use to the advantage of their members and clients that part of public authority that they have brought into their possession. At this stage, the extortion of favorable decisions from state agencies as a mode of interest politics is succeeded by devolved self-government in the realm of public policy.

The organizational structure of artisanal interests in Germany is far too complex to be accounted for solely in terms of a lobbying instrument. While it does respond, through a bewildering number and variety of organizational units at the base level, to the special sectional interests that dominate the 'Logic of Membership', it has at the same time developed a hierarchical capacity to transform these into aggregate, categoric interests, thereby making it possible for the sector as a whole to engage in long-term political exchanges with the state. Undoubtedly, these exchanges are a way, and a successful one, of promoting sectoral interests. But the (state-sponsored) organizational mechanisms of authority and control through which such interests are determined turn their pursuit into a process of collective sector self-governance, involving among other things the passing down of detailed regulations on a wide range of matters from the national level to the individual firm. In this respect, the system is a perfect example of what we have elsewhere called a 'private interest government' (Streeck and Schmitter, 1985). In a mature corporatist arrangement and under a fully developed 'Logic of Influence', private governance is the most advanced form of what Schmitter refers to as the observance by organized interests, in exchange for representational monopoly, of 'certain controls on their selection of leaders and articulation of demands and supports' (1974: 94).

The hierarchical component of inter-organizational relations is essential for the integration and the governing capacity of corporatist associational systems. In the case under study, the institutionalized hierarchical links between the different types and levels of artisanal organization serve to connect a large, heterogeneous collectivity of small firms into the national polity – making it possible for the collectivity as a whole to defend its long-term economic and political interests by accepting responsibility for the implementation of negotiated public policies vis-a-vis its membership. Examples are the role of artisanal associations in promoting, under government-sponsored programs, the technical and economic modernization of the sector and in increasing the quantity and quality of vocational training (Hilbert et al., 1986; Streeck, 1983). In particular, the various campaigns of the ZDH and its constituent organizations in the 1970s and 1980s to raise the number of apprenticeships responded to both political concern over youth unemployment and the common interest of artisanal firms in a large supply of skilled workers. While it is true that an important motive on the part of artisanal associations was to defuse political pressure on the existing 'dual system' of vocational training, sector-wide concertation of this intensity and effectiveness would have been difficult to achieve for a state agency. Private interest government, while undoubtedly motivated by particularistic, 'special' interests, thus helped solve, or at least alleviate, a public policy problem which might otherwise have been intractable.

Long-term political exchanges with the state under corporatist arrangements require that associational systems develop 'top-down' inter-organizational control structures that satisfy the 'Logic of Efficient Implementation'. It is this requirement which lies behind the *Eigendynamik* of vertical inter-organizational relations and their capacity to affect the demarcation of system subunits. Territorial differentiation in particular is an important means of building tall inter-organizational hierarchies with convenient spans of control, and in this respect at least it seems to be as indispensable as a parameter of corporatist organizational design as the functional dimension of differentiation emphasized by Schmitter (1974: 93). A national federation such as the Central Association of German Building Trades (ZDB) can keep together and control 25 regional guild associations, but it could not possibly interact directly with 687 local guilds or 43,000 firms – at least not at the present 'state of the art' of organization technology. Regional guild associations do not have the capacity to manage direct relationships with the 1,708 firms that accrue to each on average, but they can handle their average 22 local guilds. The average chamber of artisans would find it difficult to administer and control the more than 152 guilds that belong to its domain; but it can supervise its six or seven county bureaus which, in turn, can control their 19 guilds. The DHKT, on the other hand, does not need separate regional federations since it has only 42 members, and the span of control of the BFH with its 51 members is of about the same size as that of the DHKT, making further organizational aggregation of trade interests among national federations unnecessary.

The 'Logic of Efficient Implementation' exerts pressures on associations to rationalize their structures, in response to changes in organizational technologies and in the logistic conditions of organizing. Again, the territorial dimension plays an important part. New communication technologies and higher spatial mobility of members make it possible, in artisanal interest associations just as in other political organizations, to push forward the point where diseconomies of scale begin to take effect. By enabling organizational units to interact directly with an increased number of constituents, changes in communication technology also widen the possible 'span of control' of higher over lower organizational levels and thereby facilitate centralization. One apparently trivial example – that has close parallels outside the artisanal associational system – is the widespread availability today of high-speed photocopying equipment which makes it unnecessary for regional guild associations to rely on the local guilds as intermediaries for transmitting information to the individual firm. In a number of cases, the enhanced technical capacity of regional guild associations to circumvent their local affiliates and address firms directly seems to have set in motion a process of slow functional attrition, not just of the guilds but also of the county artisan bureaus. This tendency is reinforced by higher mobility of the members themselves and by the simultaneous increase in the size, and the decline in the number, of artisanal firms. Developments like these are a constant source of tension and change in the associational system of artisans and affect its hierarchical structure and its pattern of territorial differentiation at least as much as, for example, changes in the structure of local government.

Mature corporatist systems such as the one under study are, and need to be, strongly shaped by the 'Logics' of 'Influence' and 'Efficient Implementation'. But in order to remain viable, they also have to respond to the two other Logics, and the pattern of territorial differentiation that we have found performs important functions for them as well. *Handwerk* firms are many, and the fact that most of them are small and that their trades are jointly listed in an Appendix to a particular piece of legislation is not necessarily sufficient for them to join the same interest organization. Territorial differentiation of organizational structures is an expedient way of breaking down a collectivity as large as *Handwerk* into sub-collectivities of manageable size that are small enough to satisfy the 'Logic of Membership'. Almost half a million firms cannot be directly organized into one organization; if this was tried, their large number and their enormous heterogeneity would inevitably result in low density and intensity of organization. Territorial differentiation admits into the organizational structure (local and regional) sub-identities that invite closer identification. It also provides an ideal basis for a pyramid-shaped inter-organizational structure – with narrow and 'segmented' organization of interests at the bottom and encompassing organization at the top – kept together by a multi-layered hierarchy. Whether or not territorial subunits are coextensive with the boundaries of localities or *Länder* is not essential for their function in inter-associational system building. In fact, the contribution of territorial differentiation to combining closeness to members with hierarchical integration of special interests into a common categoric interest seems so important that it might conceivably exist even in the absence of territorial differentiation of the state.

Territory is not the only social-structural parameter by which large groups can be subdivided for organizational purposes and by which inter-organizational spans of control can be kept manageable. Another axis of organizational differentiation that is present in economic interest groups is by economic activity – which is what Schmitter (1974: 93) refers to as 'functional differentiation'. However, in a complex economy activities tend to be so specialized that for any sizeable population of firms, the number of potential functional subdivisions, or subdivisions by 'trade', is, for all practical purposes, unlimited. The German artisanal sector, with its 500,000 firms grouped in 125 trades, provides an ideal example of the organizational design problems posed by large size and economic heterogeneity. In this case as in others, organizational differentiation by functional criteria only would result in long distances between members and organizational units (or system subunits), perhaps in suboptimal unit size, and certainly in under-representation of common as distinguished from sectional interests.

Since sub-identities formed by economic activity are likely to be more divisive and numerous than territorial sub-identities, territorial differentiation of organizational structures serves to 'channel' the formation of sub-identities in such a way as to make it easier for subunits to find common goals. It thus enables associational systems to meet a central requirement of the 'Logic of Goal Formation'. The contribution of territorial differentiation to system integration and to comprehensive goal formation is particularly evident in the two artisanal organizations, chambers and county bureaus, whose domains are exclusively demarcated by territory and which are of such crucial importance for the institutional identity of *Handwerk* as a whole. Moreover, territorial differentiation is essential for business associations that function as employers' associations since it reflects the territorial structure of (local) labor markets. Territorially based 'class', or industrial relations, interests, reinforced as they are by the presence of a common enemy, tend to be easier to 'discover' and to formulate comprehensively than joint 'functional' interests of a heterogeneous collectivity of economic actors. This is why in the organizational design of most systems of interest associability, the two axes of differentiation, functional and territorial, are used in a variety of complex combinations, with territorial differentiation serving as an important device in large and heterogeneous collectivities for the solution of the perennial problem of unity and variety – the creation of unity in the face of variety – while at the same time permitting for the expression of variety within unity.

Notes

* Research for this chapter was carried out as part of a project directed jointly by Claus Offe and the present author. Josef Hilbert, Jörg Rampelt and Helmi Südmersen participated as research assistants at different stages of the work.

1 The latter term is used by Doran (1984). Doran compares the industrial and associational structure of German *Handwerk* to that of the equivalent small firms in the United Kingdom. Readers who have no access to the German literature may want to take advantage of Doran's well-researched and highly perceptive study. In fact, there is no recent German publication on *Handwerk* that is nearly as enlightening – a clear case for comparative social science.

2 Similar structures are found in two other German-speaking countries, Austria and the German part of Switzerland, and in Denmark. Even in the GDR, the private *Handwerk* sector proved remarkably resilient against attempts at integrating it into the state sector. Some of its traditional institutions, like chambers of artisans, continued to exist at least on paper until unification.

3 The term 'sector' is not chosen arbitrarily. In spite of its high internal heterogeneity, *Handwerk* is generally regarded as a distinct branch of the German economy, and there is a strong 'sectoral consciousness' on the part of both individual artisans and their representatives.

4 Evidence of this can be found not least in the peculiar German terminology. An

artisanal trade is often referred to as a *Beruf* (the same word, by the way, that is used to translate the English 'profession'), and where the English language offers the concept of 'market access', German *Handwerksrecht* characteristically speaks of *Berufszulassung* (admission to, or qualification for, a vocation). An alternative term for an individual trade, or branch of industrial activity, that is used also outside Handwerk is *Fach* – the literal English translation of which is 'discipline' (and in fact the same word is used for subjects of teaching in school or at a university).

5 Running a small business in Germany, Doran (1984) comments, has essentially been turned into a profession.

6 National guild associations that are not affiliated to the BFH are too small to pay the (low) membership fee. Affiliation to the BFH may not be essential for trades with low trade union membership. Moreover, trades whose national federations are not in the BFH are nevertheless represented at the national peak level through the chambers system.

5

Co-determination: After Four Decades*

In 1951 the German Bundestag passed an Act providing for equal representation of capital and labor on the supervisory boards of coal and steel companies. Ever since, *Mitbestimmung* – or, in a somewhat clumsy English translation, co-determination – has been an inexhaustible subject of both political controversy and social science research, in Germany as well as abroad (Wilpert, 1975).

This chapter presents an account and assessment of the system of co-determination as it moves into the fourth decade of its existence. It pays particular attention to the changes co-determination underwent as a result of new legislation in the 1970s. While it will be inevitable to go into certain legal technicalities and to discuss some of the ideological connotations attached to co-determination, the focus of the chapter will be on its empirical consequences and its factual impact on the relations between labor and capital in the German economy. The chapter argues that supervisory board co-determination cannot be discussed separately from the co-determination rights of works councils under the Works Constitution Act and from trade union structure, and that the three are closely linked functionally as well as structurally, and have to be seen as elements of an integrated system of representation in the enterprise (see also Adams and Rummel, 1977). As to the consequences of co-determination, it is argued that it has significantly changed the way in which employers utilize labor as a factor of production, and this was accompanied by a takeover of managerial responsibilities by representatives of the workforce which, in turn, has contributed to creating and reinforcing a vested interest of workers in 'social partnership' and 'cooperation' in the enterprise.

The chapter proceeds in four steps. It first outlines the system of co-determination as it existed in the 1950s and 1960s; this section ends with a summary of the experience with coal and steel co-determination by the end of this period. In a second step, the paper summarizes the legislative changes introduced in the 1970s. The third part describes the system of representation in large companies outside coal and steel that emerged from the new legislation in the late 1970s and early 1980s. Finally, the chapter discusses the impact of co-determination on the status of labor as a factor of production in German companies.

Co-determination in the 1950s and 1960s

The concept of 'co-determination' refers to two different istitutional channels of employee representation in German industrial organizations: co-determination at the workplace (*betriebliche Mitbestimmung*) which is exercised through works councils, and co-determination in the enterprise (*Mitbestimmung auf Unternehmensebene*) which is exercised through workforce representatives on the supervisory board and, to an extent, the management board.[1] The first form of co-determination, which relates to manpower and employment matters, is provided for all establishments with more than five employees. The second, relating to the enterprise's general economic decisions, is limited to companies beyond a certain size and of specific legal forms. Co-determination was first introduced, shortly after the founding of the Federal Republic, through two major pieces of legislation: workplace co-determination through the Works Constitution Act of 1952, and enterprise-level co-determination through either the Works Constitution Act or the Co-determination Act of 1951, depending on the industry.

The main features of the German 'Works Constitution' have remained unchanged since 1952. They have often been described, and will only briefly be summarized here. (An English translation of the basic legislation on workplace and enterprise co-determination is given in Bundesminister für Arbeit und Sozialordnung, 1978.) Workers in establishments with a minimum of six employees have a legal right to elect a works council (*Betriebsrat*) as a representative of their interests in relation to the employer, and duly elected works councils are entitled to information, consultation and co-decision on a range of specified subjects. At the same time, works councils have a general obligation to cooperate with the employer for the benefit of the enterprise and not to engage 'in acts of industrial warfare'. The law permits all employees to vote and stand for election regardless of whether or not they are union members.

Concerning co-determination at the enterprise level, the Works Constitution Act of 1952 stipulated that in joint stock companies, companies with limited partners holding shares and limited liability companies with at least 500 employees one-third of the seats on the supervisory board had to be allocated to representatives of the workforce. These were to be elected by secret ballot by all employees, again regardless of whether voters or candidates belonged to a trade union. If the number of seats for workforce representatives exceeded two – which depended on the size of the board which, in turn, was determined by the shareholders – the additional seats could be filled by representatives who were not employed with the company. In practice, 'external' representatives, to the extent that there were any at all, were normally full-time union officials.

The Co-determination Act of 1951 differed from the Works Constitution Act in that it was exclusively concerned with supervisory board co-determination and was limited in scope to companies in the coal and steel industry with more than 1,000 employees. It is important to note that as far as workplace co-determination is concerned, the coal and steel industry is fully under the jurisdiction of the Works Constitution Act. The Co-determination Act provided for 'parity' on the supervisory board, that is, for an equal number of workforce and stockholder representatives. To prevent deadlock, the board had to coopt one 'additional member'. Workforce representatives were elected by an assembly of all works council members from the company's establishments. In the normal case in which the number of workforce representatives was five, two of these – who had to be employees of the company – were nominated by the works councilors. The other three were nominated:

> to the electoral body [that is, the assembly of works councillors] by the central organizations [of the trade unions represented in the various establishments of the undertaking] after prior consultation with the unions represented in the undertaking and with the works councils. The nomination rights of the central organizations shall be proportional to the strength of their representation in the establishments. (Section 6, 3)

One of the three had to be neither an employee of the company nor a full-time trade union official.

Another difference between the Co-determination Act and the Works Constitution Act was that, in the former, enterprise-level co-determination extended not only to the supervisory board but also to the management board. The Act made it obligatory for coal and steel companies to add a 'labor director' (*Arbeitsdirektor*) to their board of management. The labor director could not be appointed against the majority of the labor representatives on the supervisory board. The Act said nothing on the tasks of the labor director; it merely stated that he had to have the same rights as the other management board members, and that board members had to work together 'in closest collaboration'. Normally, the labor director was given responsibility for personnel matters and was placed at the head of a newly created manpower department.

'Parity' co-determination was one of the central issues of German politics throughout the 1950s and 1960s – so much so that to many it became synonymous with *Mitbestimmung* as such. In part, it may have been due to continuous, although fruitless, pressures by the unions for the extension of parity to industry as a whole that many observers have tended to under-rate the significance of workplace co-determination, and to overlook the fact that whatever differences there were between parity and the 'one-third formula' were qualified by the universal presence of works council co-determination. In any case, there was a tendency, especially in the 1950s, to discuss parity co-determination in rather fundamentalist terms – which is perhaps not surprising given the history of coal and steel co-determination – and it may be useful to remind oneself briefly of this context.

Initially, parity co-determination was seen by its proponents as a major element in the design of a democratic political order in Germany (Kerr, 1954). The reason it was first introduced in coal and steel by the allied occupation government was to prevent these industries once again becoming a basis of political and material support for German militarism and fascism. With increasing acceptance of postwar liberal democracy in Germany, with growing European integration and with declining economic and military importance of the two industries, this rationale soon became obsolete. The same did not hold for the union view of parity co-determination as an element of 'economic democracy' (*Wirtschaftsdemokratie*) presenting an alternative to capitalism on the one hand and state socialism on the other. Originally, *Wirtschaftsdemokratie* as a 'third way' implied joint decision-making by representatives of labor and capital not just at the enterprise level but also at the level of entire industries and the national economy (Naphtali, 1928). From this perspective coal and steel co-determination has always remained incomplete – just as it remained limited to merely one industry – although, at least in the early years, unions sometimes conceived of 'external' representation on supervisory boards as an instrument of some form of union-controlled industry-wide economic planning.

A third motif that was originally associated with parity co-determination was related to the topic of 'alienation' of workers in modern industrial organizations. Many of its early proponents hoped that co-determination would restore to workers a sense of involvement in their working situation and a feeling that they had an effective influence on decisions concerning their working life. In this respect, it was not the political development but rather empirical social research that brought about growing disenchantment. According to Adams and Rummel (1977: 11), who summarized the relevant literature (in particular Friedeburg et al., 1955; Pirker et al., 1955; and Popitz et al., 1957), 'surveys indicated that workers had an incomplete and inexplicit idea of what co-determination was or how it was supposed to function in practice'. By the early 1960s at the latest, it had become clear that as far as the everyday experience of workers on their jobs was concerned, there was no important difference between coal and steel on the one hand and the rest of industry on the other. Workers under parity co-determination were as much subject to hierarchical control as workers everywhere else, the organization of their work continued to be determined by impersonal mechanisms beyond their influence and understanding, and their attitudes towards their work did not differ in any perceptible way from that of workers in other industries.

That unions nevertheless continued to demand an extension of parity co-determination may have been in the belief that the shortcomings of co-determination in terms of fundamental, systemic change were due precisely to its incompleteness. At the same time, parity co-determination was increasingly seen under new perspectives. Whatever it had not achieved, it certainly had improved the position of the unions in the respective industries. Coal and steel, as in other countries, have always been union strongholds, but there was no doubt that parity co-determination had considerably reinforced this. Three aspects of this deserve mentioning.

First, while any formal job discrimination against non-members of trade unions is illegal in Germany, union control over the personnel department through the labor director makes it possible for unions to recruit union members in a manner very similar to a union shop. The density ratio of the German Miners' Union (IGBE) in the coal mining industry increased from 65 percent in 1960 to 83 percent in 1970, that is, in a period of general decline of union density, and to 92 percent in 1975 (Streeck, 1981a: 473). A detailed account of how this development was related to co-determination has been given elsewhere (Streeck, 1981a: 236ff.; Treu, 1979; on the steel industry, see Streeck, 1981a: 254, 268). In addition, and partly as a result of high density, industrial unions in industries under co-determination are more successful in works council elections than unions in other sectors. Between 1960 and 1975 about 93 percent of the works councilors elected in the coal mining industry were IGBE members – by far the highest score of the major DGB unions (Streeck, 1981a: 488). Eighty percent of the companies in coal and steel that were surveyed by Tegtmeier had a works council that was 100 percent unionized, as opposed to 38 percent in the other industries (1973: 124). Moreover, in 61 percent of the coal and steel companies, more than 10 works councilors were released full-time from their normal work, and this compares to 9 percent outside coal and steel (Tegtmeier, 1973: 285).

Secondly, the presence of full-time union officials on supervisory boards ensured close and continuous contacts between union headquarters and the trade union at the workplace. The establishment and the maintenance of such contacts is a perpetual problem for industrial unions, and the coal-and-steel type of co-determination offered considerable assistance in solving this problem. Outside coal and steel, union officials were, under certain conditions, free to stand for election as 'external' representatives. However, they had to compete with internal candidates, and it was not infrequent that workplace union officials successfully opposed the nomination of full-time officials. Eighty-five percent of the companies outside coal and steel that were surveyed by Tegtmeier had no external labor member on their supervisory board (1973: 272).

Thirdly, 'parity' co-determination considerably strengthened the position of the works council – which in coal and steel, more than anywhere else, had become a de facto union body – in relation to management. Since the internal labor representatives on the supervisory board were appointed by the works councils, they were all works councilors (Tegtmeier, 1973: 126). To them, co-determination on the supervisory board was primarily an extension and reinforcement of co-determination under the Works Constitution Act – the more so the more the original, grander ambitions associated with parity were becoming obsolete. Sitting on the supervisory board not only improved works councilors' access to information; it also gave them a say in the appointment of the company's top management, that is, their counterparts at the negotiating table in their role as works councilors. According to Tegtmeier (1973: 126ff.), the presence of the leading works councilors on the supervisory board resulted in more frequent and more intensive contacts between the works council and the management board, with the two sides discussing matters on the supervisory board agenda between them in advance of full board meetings, and the management trying to accommodate the position of the works council beforehand. In effect, this amounted to an extension of works council co-determination to a wide range of subjects not covered by the Works Constitution Act.

Summing up so far, while publicly the unions – as well as their ideological enemies to the right – continued to discuss parity co-determination in terms of a radical alternative to the existing economic and political order, in practice their interest had increasingly shifted to its positive functions for them within that order. In late 1966, when a 'Grand Coalition' government of Christian Democrats and Social Democrats took office, the unions saw this as an opportunity to spread the advantages of co-determination in coal and steel to the other industries. In response to their pressure, the government appointed an independent committee of investigation, chaired by Professor Kurt Biedenkopf, who was a member and later became the Secretary General of the CDU, to study empirically the economic and social consequences of parity co-determination in the coal and steel industry. The committee completed its work in early 1970. The gist of its report was that the positive functions of parity were not limited to the unions, and that there was no indication that parity was incompatible with, or detrimental to, the existing economic system. The following findings of the commission stand out as of particular importance in the present context.

(i) Co-determination on the supervisory board had not, as many had feared carried the confrontation between capital and labor into the decision-making bodies of the enterprise. Rather, it had fostered accommodation and cooperation. The commission characterized the prevailing pattern as 'integration in spite of the continued existence of different interests' (MBK [Mitbestimmungskommission], 1970: 61). Parity was found to exert a 'constraint towards cooperation' (MBK, 1970: 91). By far the majority of supervisory board decisions were taken unanimously (MBK, 1970: 62), and most of the motions put forward by the labor representatives were accepted (Tegtmeier, 1973: 88). In 72 percent of the companies concerned there had not been a single occasion between 1964 and 1968 in which the vote of the 'neutral' member was decisive; in 12 percent there had been one such occasion, and in 6 percent two or more (no answer: 10 percent; MBK, 1970: 225). In most of these cases the neutral member voted with the shareholders. There are indications that, at least sometimes, he did so with the tacit approval of the workers' representatives (MBK, 1970: 70).

(ii) Companies under parity co-determination were no less orientated towards profitability than other companies, and their ability to rationalize and increase productivity was unimpaired. 'The internal labour representatives, normally the works council chairmen, were interested in preserving and increasing the efficiency of their establishments. This attitude was clearly motivated by their interest in higher wages and safer employment' (MBK, 1970: 73). External representatives were found to share this attitude, not least because the high ability of employers to pay improved the position of the union in wage negotiations (MBK, 1970: 73). Rationalization measures proposed by the management to cut costs were not opposed 'provided that sufficient care was taken to protect the social status of the workers affected' (MBK, 1970: 73). Decision-making on new investment and rationalization took longer than in companies not under parity, especially if the management had failed to take the employment consequences of proposed measures into account. The Commission argued that the costs of a (slightly) retarded decision-making process might be outweighed by a higher preparedness of workers to accept the resulting decisions as justified and appropriate (MBK, 1970: 72). An adverse effect of parity co-determination on a company's ability to raise capital was not found (MBK, 1970: 97).

(iii) Attempts by trade unions and external labor representatives to introduce other criteria in company-level decision-making than profitability and efficiency, if made at all, met with the successful resistance of the internal board members. The Commission found among the latter what it characterized as 'a certain enterprise egoism' (MBK, 1970: 58). The influence of the external representatives was 'frequently overestimated' (MBK, 1970: 64). Efforts by trade unions to coordinate the behavior of labor representatives in different companies ('remote control') were found to be infrequent and to have always failed (MBK, 1970: 59). Tegtmeier, who is more explicit on this point, argues that an industry-wide co-determination strategy designed and coordinated by an industrial union would inevitably be opposed by the individual works councils and their delegates to the supervisory boards (1973: 180).

(iv) Parity co-determination contributed to the professionalization of management and increased its independence from stockholders. Through its regular contacts with the works council, and through preparatory meetings with the labor representatives in advance of meetings of the full supervisory board, management was normally able to secure in advance the agreement of half of the board members to its proposals (MBK, 1970: 63). Moreover, there were identical interests between management and labor representatives with regard to the use of profits, with both tending to favor reinvestment rather than higher dividends (MBK, 1970: 82). Concerning the selection of management boards members, the Commission found that labor representatives were as interested as shareholders in candidates with high professional qualifications. Unlike shareholders, labor members in addition emphasized leadership style and a candidate's ability and willingness to cooperate and to share information (MBK, 1970: 86ff). Given the specific challenges confronting management in modern large-scale enterprises, the Commission did not find this inappropriate.

(v) Companies under parity co-determination paid much more attention to manpower policy and manpower planning, and their policies in this area differed from those of companies outside coal and steel. Eighty-one percent of the coal and steel companies that were surveyed by the *Mitbestimmungskommission* reported that employment and social questions were among the four most frequent subjects on their supervisory board agenda; the respective percentage outside the two industries was 45 (Tegtmeier, 1973: 276). Moreover, 47 percent of companies outside coal and steel, and among these no less than 33 percent of those with a workforce of 10,000 or more, had no manpower department at the management board level (Tegtmeier, 1973: 280). Under parity co-determination, managements asking for their supervisory board's agreement to investment projects were inevitably requested to provide information on the employment consequences, and the assent of labor representatives was conditional upon the simultaneous introduction of measures to protect the interests of employees (MBK, 1970: 78). This made it necessary to develop new methods of middle- and long-term manpower planning, and to integrate such planning into the company's financial and technical decisions. As an example, Tegtmeier mentions a company that had set up a special team charged with studying any proposed investment measure as to its employment effects (1973: 167; see also the case accounts by Geisler, 1981, and Heese et al., 1981).

Manpower policy in coal and steel was the responsibility of the labor directors, most of whom were former works council chairmen or full-time union officials. Manpower departments worked in close cooperation with the works council and the external labor representatives, and this not only gave unions access to first-hand information but also continued substantive influence over manpower policy. Among other things, parity co-determination was found to have favored a substitution of internal mobility of labor for redundancies as a way of industrial adjustment (Tegtmeier, 1973: 159). Labor representatives on supervisory boards, and in particular the works councils with their additional strength gained from parity co-determination, were generally in a position, if not to prevent redundancies, to delay them in time and make them expensive. The results were considerable rigidities confronting companies' manpower policies – 'a limited variability in the use of labor as a factor of production' (Tegtmeier, 1973: 186) – which, in both steel and coal mining, led to 'time lags' in the adaptation of the workforce to declining demand (Tegtmeier, 1973: 171). While this – partial – uncoupling of employment from economic developments and uncertainties may have been advantageous from the viewpoint of social stability (Tegtmeier, 1973: 186), it burdened the enterprise with substantial short-term costs. The only way in which companies could hope to reduce or avoid such costs was by preventive measures to increase the *internal* mobility of labor – for example, by retraining workers early enough to enable them to operate new equipment. This required rather sophisticated methods of anticipatory manpower planning, in terms of both quantity and quality, comprising not just white-collar workers and middle management but virtually all workers in the enterprise. It was through the introduction of such methods, and through the positive attitude of unions and works councils towards technological change that was made possible by them, that the employment rigidities created by parity co-determination did not have economically negative consequences (Tegtmeier, 1973: 187).

The Reforms of the 1970s

In 1969 the government changed again, this time to a coalition of Social Democrats and Free Democrats. Among the central projects on the new government's agenda was new legislation on industrial relations. When the unions pressed their case for the general introduction of the coal and steel model of co-determination, they placed much emphasis on the findings of the *Mitbestimmungskommission* showing that parity was not incompatible with a market economy, did not interfere with efficiency and profitability, and had positive functions for social stability. However, because of the high symbolic significance of the composition of the supervisory board, the government decided to leave this problem for a possible second term and concentrate on a reform of workplace-level co-determination. In 1972 the Works Constitution Act of 1952 was repealed and replaced with a new Act. It is indicative of the interdependence of the two channels of co-determination that most of the changes introduced by the Works Constitution Act of 1972 in effect amounted to a generalization of important elements of the co-determination pattern in coal and steel: (1) the Act strengthened the organizational base of the works councils; (2) it reinforced the influence of works councils over management, particularly in the area of manpower policy and manpower planning; and (3) it institutionalized formally some of the links between works councils and trade unions.

(1) The Works Constitution Act of 1972 increased the number of seats on works councils, especially in large establishments. It also increased the number of works councilors who are by law released from normal work duties, and it made it easier for unions to initiate

the election of a works council in a plant where, normally because of employer resistance, none exists. Perhaps most importantly, the Act prescribed the formation of 'central works councils' in companies with more than one plant. Central works councils are composed of delegates of plant works councils, and they negotiate with management on matters concerning the company as a whole. In making central works councils obligatory, the 1972 Act responded to increasing economic concentration and centralization of management functions.

(2) As far as the substantive rights of works councils in relation to the employer are concerned, the Act entitled works councils to co-determination on all matters relating to *working time* unless regulated by law or industrial agreement. Moreover, it extended co-determination to the setting of *piece rates* and the *design of workplaces* and the *work environment*, and it made it obligatory for an employer to ask the works council in advance for its assent on 'any *engagement, grading, regrading* and *transfer*' of employees. Works councils were given a veto on a number of grounds laid down in the Act. Furthermore, the Act granted works councils an unqualified right to be consulted on an employer's '*manpower planning*'. It obliged the employer to inform the works council of his plans 'in full and in good time', and it gave the works council a legal right to demand that *vacancies* 'are *notified for internal competition* within the establishment before they are filled'. (For a synopsis of the differences between the co-determination rights of works councils under the Works Constitution Acts of 1952 and 1972, see Adams and Rummel, 1977: 9.)

(3) Concerning the relation between unions and works councils, the Act removed all legal obstacles for works councilors taking on union office and performing union functions. It also gave works councilors a right to attend trade union courses at the expense of the employer and with their full pay continued. The rights of full-time union officials to take part in works council meetings were considerably extended, and so were their rights to enter establishments with or without prior notification of the employer.

Immediately after it had won a new term in the autumn of 1972 the government began to prepare legislation for parity co-determination at the enterprise level in large companies outside coal and steel. It was agreed at the outset that the 1951 Co-determination Act was to remain in force, and that the new legislation was not to deal with the coal and steel industry. Moreover, it was to apply only to very large firms so that the one-third model of the old Works Constitution Act would remain in effect for middle-sized firms. In the end, the minimum size for a company to fall under the new legislation was set at 2,000 employees.

The Co-determination Act of 1976 was the result of protracted struggling within the coalition. During the legislative process it increasingly became a source of sometimes bitter conflict between the government and the unions. While the Social Democratic Party was in principle committed to a general extension of the coal and steel model, its coalition partner was not – and, under pressure from business, grew increasingly hostile to it. The final Act was a compromise that lay somewhere between the coal and steel model and the one-third formula of the Works Constitution Act. In particular, the Act:

(1) Increased the representation of employees to parity but required that one of the labor representatives had to come from the ranks of middle management. (Middle management was thus for the first time officially recognized as a separate group among the workforce, having special interests in need of collective representation.) In addition, the Act gave the sharholders' representatives the right to determine the chairman of the supervisory board, and it gave the chairman a casting vote in the case of a tie.

(2) Refused unions the right to appoint the labor representatives on the supervisory board directly, but did not make direct election by the workforce obligatory, as had been demanded by the Free Democrats. As a compromise, the Act provided for direct election in companies with up to 8,000 employees, and for indirect election by an electoral college (whose members had to be specifically elected for the occasion) in firms with more than 8,000 employees. It also made it possible for the electorate to change the voting procedure from direct to indirect and from indirect to direct, respectively, in a separate ballot in advance of the election.

(3) Set aside, in response to union demands, some of the labor seats on supervisory boards for representatives of trade unions. These seats could be, but did not have to be, filled with persons not employed with the company. Seats for union representatives were fewer in number than the seats for 'internal' representatives, and occupants could not be appointed by the unions but had to be elected by the same procedure as their 'internal' colleagues.

(4) Provided for a 'labor director' on the management board who is, however, appointed in the same way as the other management board members. As a concession to unions, the Act requires that all management board members are appointed by a two-thirds majority of the supervisory board. However, if no such majority can be found, appointments can be made by a simple majority, and the chairman may use this casting vote.

Due to the tremendous legal complexity of the Act (cf. Hartmann, 1975: 69f.), and in particular to the need for a special statute on voting procedures – on which the government was deadlocked for almost two years – the first elections of supervisory boards under the 1976 legislation could take place only in 1978. By this time the 600–50 firms that were expected to fall under the Act when it was passed (Unterhinninghofen, 1978: 662) were reduced to 484. (For a list of these firms see WSI-Mitteilungen, 1981.) The remainder had changed their legal status to one that was outside the purview of the Act, split up in formally separate firms, and had transferred part of their operations pro forma to foreign subsidiaries, etc. (*Manager Magazin*, 1982). Especially where it became necessary to vote first on the voting procedure, the time from the beginning of an election to its completion could be as long as one year (Unterhinninghofen, 1978: 665). The average time needed was 31 weeks. In large companies the election cost up to DM1 million (HBV, 1978). All in all, it took about two and a half years after the passing of the Act until the new supervisory boards were properly formed and could begin to take up their functions.

Immediately after the Co-determination Act of 1976 had passed into law, the Federal Association of German Employers' Associations (BDA) and a number of major companies challenged its constitutionality in the Federal Constitutional Court. Their suit was pending during the implementation of the Act and added to the general uncertainty and confusion. The central argument of the employers was that while on the surface the Act did not provide for parity on the supervisory board, in reality the casting vote of the chairman was rendered insignificant by a mutual reinforcement ('cumulation') of workplace and enterprise co-determination. The recent increase in the co-determination rights of works councils was said to have already led to 'parity' between labor and capital. If the increased co-determination rights under the 1976 Act were added to these rights – which in practice they would be, given the substantive overlap of the two forms of co-determination – the result was at least equivalent to parity. Parity, however, was unconstitutional because it amounted to expropriation without compensation. (Concerning coal and steel, the plaintiffs argued that the Co-determination Act of 1951 had been imposed by the occupation government and was therefore not supposed to be in agreement with the German constitution.) On 1 March 1979 the Court rejected the case of the employers and declared the Act constitutional. The verdict (published in Bundesminister für Arbeit, 1979) did not consider, as the plaintiffs had done, the possible or probable effects of the Act on the *actual behavior* of companies and their decision-making bodies. Rather, it restricted itself to reviewing the formal provisions of the Act. Having established that these did not formally introduce parity on the supervisory board, the Court saw no need to discuss the general problem of whether or not parity is constitutional.

A few months after the verdict the Federal Association of German Employers' Associations circulated a series of position papers which in effect advised companies to apply the new law as restrictively as possible. The papers offered legal justification for restricting the possibilities for labor representatives to meet in advance of supervisory board meetings, limiting the information the management has to give to the supervisory board, tightening secrecy rules and forming supervisory board committees with below-parity membership of labor representatives (*Mitbestimmungsgespräch*, 1979: 252–7). This move was preceded, and followed, by a number of firms – which could not altogether escape the jurisdiction of the 1976 Act – revising their by-laws and those of their supervisory boards so as to minimize the impact of the new legislation. In particular, firms established quorums for supervisory board decisions that favored the representatives of the stockholders; excluded external labor representatives from certain supervisory board committees; limited the decision-making powers of supervisory boards in favor of supervisory board committees, the management board and the assembly of stockholders, etc. (Föhr, 1977; Jürgens and Unterhinninghofen, 1978). The result was extensive litigation, with the most legally significant cases moving all the way up to the Federal Court. A first set of these cases was decided in February 1982. By and large, the Court upheld the position of the unions. As a general principle it pointed out that the Co-determination Act took precedence over the civil-law autonomy of joint-stock companies since co-determination was a matter of the public interest. Company by-laws designed to circumvent the 1976 Act were therefore void. In particular, the Court held that all members of supervisory boards had to have equal rights and responsibilities, and that any discrimination among them, other than provided for in the Act, was illegal (*Mitbestimmung*, 1982: 121).

With the decision of the Constitutional Court in 1978, the Co-determination Act of 1976 has become an established part of the structure of German industrial relations. In spite of the Act's numerous technical flaws and even absurdities (Unterhinninghofen, 1978: 657), it is unlikely that any government in the near and not-too-near future will undertake to open up this Pandora's box again. Given that the final version of the Act was adopted by the

Bundestag with unanimous vote, this holds even for a CDU/CSU government. While the unions continue to demand both technical changes – in particular, a simplification of election procedures – and the introduction of full parity; and while employers continue to apply the new law restrictively, there is no doubt that both unions and employers will have to live with the Act for quite a long time.

By the late 1970s 4.5 million of the 23 million employees in West Germany (19.6 percent) worked with the 484 companies covered by the Co-determination Act of 1976. One million (4.3 percent) were employed with firms for which the one-third formula of 1952 had remained in force, and about 600,000 (2.6 percent) worked in the coal and steel industry and fell under the parity model of 1951. All these (26.5 percent of the workforce) were in addition represented at the workplace level by works councils under the Works Constitution Act of 1972. Another 10.1 million (43.9 percent) worked in firms without co-determination at the enterprise level; their representation took place exclusively through works councils. A total of 3.4 million employees (14.8 percent) worked with public employers and were covered by the civil service equivalent of the Works Constitution Act, the Staff Representation Act of 1973, and 3.2 million (13.9 percent) fell outside the jurisdiction of the various co-determination laws and had no access to any institutionalized channel of co-determination (Niedenhoff, 1979: 20).

Co-determination after 1976: a New Company Constitution

To understand the significance of the legislation of the 1970s, it is useful to take a comprehensive look at the 'constitution' of large German companies as it had emerged by the early 1980s. By a company's 'constitution' we mean its system of interest representation in the widest sense, and the way it is connected into the organization's decision-making structure. The discussion will be limited to the almost 500 companies falling under both the Works Constitution Act of 1972 and Co-determination Act of 1976. It will pay particular attention to the differences and similarities between co-determination in these companies and in the coal and steel industry.

Generally speaking, the developments of the 1970s profoundly eroded the traditional legal distinction between workplace and enterprise co-determination. This distinction was from the beginning difficult to maintain. As Gaugler (1981: 836) points out: 'as soon as the co-determination rights of works councils touch upon questions of principal importance, these become subjects for the bodies at the enterprise level to decide'. Where works councils are strong their influence inevitably extends beyond industrial relations subjects in a narrow sense, and this is bound to affect the firm's general business policy. In fact, already in the 1950s and 1960s works councils used the instruments of the Works Constitution, works agreements in particular, to extend their co-determination and participation rights to economic decisions at the enterprise level. In a study on the influence of employees on enterprise policy in 82 German joint-stock companies, Witte (1980: 552) found that the strongest correlate of employee influence was the existence of 'internal formal agreements and established procedures' extending the range of co-determination. It is important to note that these agreements and procedures had grown out of the Works Constitution. Witte's data were collected before the implementation of the 1976 Co-determination Act, and there are indications that the spill-over of co-determination rights from workplace to enterprise was particularly strong after the Works Constitution Act of 1972 with its strengthening of workplace-level co-determination. The emergence after 1972 of what Witte (1982a: 169) aptly calls 'supra-legal co-determination' may explain why works councilors – unlike full-time union officials, bankers and managers – were found not to believe that the 1976 legislation added significantly to the influence of employees in the enterprise (Witte, 1982b).

The progressive factual integration of workplace and enterprise co-determination – which was not taken into consideration by the Constitutional Court in 1979 – emanates not only from the work-place. We have seen above that the erosion of the formal distinction between the two channels of co-determination has started in the coal and steel industry where enterprise-level co-determination was most advanced. With the obsolescence of the more general, political objectives of 'parity' co-determination, its institutions became inevitably subservient to interests emerging at, and tied to, the workplace. This is reflected not just in the composition of the workplace delegation on the supervisory board – that is, the strong presence of the works council and the marginal role of external union officials – but also in the themes that figure prominently in co-determination in the enterprise (see below). Here, too, the example of the coal and steel industry has been paradigmatic. On the other hand, the structural and functional integration of the two channels of co-determination not only enhances the representation of workplace-related interests in the enterprise but also, and at the same time, makes it possible for workplace co-determination to become part of the system of enterprise-level decision-making.

Turning to the more specific characteristics of the emerging new 'company constitution', the following points are of particular interest in the present context.

(1) More than ever, industrial unions use the works council system as the institutional framework and the major source of support for their activities at the workplace and in the enterprise. The tendency of unions at the workplace to act through the institutions offered by the Works Constitution was significantly advanced by the strengthening of works council rights in 1972. Especially in large establishments, works councils have, just as in coal and steel, become de facto union bodies (Streeck, 1982), and the proportion of works council seats won by industrial unions, in spite of various external or factional challenges, approaches that in the coal and steel industry. Like the distinction between workplace and enterprise co-determination, that between voluntary representation through trade unions and legally regulated representation through co-determination has become increasingly blurred since the early 1950s (Streeck, 1979). Union density ratios among workers have generally increased since the early 1970s, and this has been partly due to increased opportunities for unions to use works councils for recruitment purposes (Streeck, 1981a: 201–14). While there frequently are tensions between works councils and industrial unions – even where the majority of works councilors are union members – these are basically tensions between 'external' and 'internal' union organizations which are universal and independent of the legal institutions of co-determination (Adams and Rummel, 1977: 19).

(2) Central works councils are even more union-dominated than plant works councils. This is because of their indirect election which makes it possible to exclude competing minority groups from them. The importance of central works councils is increasing as a result of the growing centralization of manpower policy and manpower planning at the company level. With more and more works council functions being moved upwards to the central works council – which is in spite of the fact that the legislators wanted to prevent central works councils becoming 'super works councils' – the chairman of the latter, who is always a member of the industrial union and normally holds important union offices, is increasingly becoming the central figure in a company's system of representation.

(3) The facilities available to works councils in large companies frequently exceed the legal minimum (which is already fairly high, especially since 1972). For example, the number of works councilors who are full-time is often higher than prescribed by the law; works councilors frequently have access to chauffeured business cars and company planes; and some works councils employ, at the

expense of the company, their own expert staff of professional lawyers and economists. Also, co-determination rights of works councils in practice extend further than legally prescribed. Works councils, and central works councils in particular, are being consulted earlier and on a broader range of subjects than is required under the law, and employers seek the consensus of the works council even if legally they do not have to. In part, this is because the Works Constitution Act of 1972 has given works councils considerable additional powers which they can use to obstruct decisions if the management does not cooperate on subjects that are formally not under co-determination. (According to a manager of a large German enterprise: 'Without the works council, nothing goes; with the works council, everything goes.'). In this respect the Works Constitution Act of 1972 has clearly reduced the distance between coal and steel and the rest of industry, with the additional co-determination rights being exercised not through supervisory board representation but through the works council directly.

(4) Almost all of the 'internal' workforce representatives on supervisory boards are works councilors, and the chairman of the central works council fails only in very exceptional cases to sit on the supervisory board. For example, an inspection of the lists of supervisory board members in the automobile and construction industry has not yielded a single example of an internal workforce representative who was not a works council member. Here we have one of the clearest indications that the legal separation between 'representation of workers on the supervisory board (enterprise constitution) and representation through the works council (works constitution) is not empirically tenable' (Witte, 1982a: 170). In this respect the situation in the companies under the 1976 Act is almost the same as in coal and steel, and the special election procedure that was designed to favor 'independent' candidates has made almost no difference (see IGCPK, 1978: 687).

Works councilors sitting on supervisory boards have greatly improved access to information, and this holds regardless of whether there is parity on the supervisory board or not. In law, members of supervisory boards are entitled to any information that management may have. Any two supervisory board members can, upon request, inspect any document in the possession of management. The prevailing legal doctrine is summarized in the formula: 'Whatever the management knows, the supervisory board may also know' (Nagel, 1981). Although much of the information given to supervisory board members can be declared confidential, a works councilor bargaining with management in his capacity as works councilor can hardly be expected to forget what he has learned as supervisory board member. For this 'cumulation' of co-determination rights to take place, works councilors need in principle no more than the 'minority rights' they had already in advance of the 1976 legislation. The latter has in addition entitled labor members to the post of vice-chairman of the supervisory board (see below) and to membership in important board committees, and this has further improved their possibilities of getting information. Moreover, information requests have now become more difficult to vote down, and the fact that labor representatives have some, however limited, influence over the appointment and reappointment of management board members may have a positive effect on the latter's preparedness to cooperate with them, especially where stockholders tend to be internally divided.

(5) Seats for trade union representatives in the 1978 election were almost completely won by DGB unions who had nominated only external candidates; the least favorable results were recorded in the retail, banking and insurance sector (57.3 percent), in the wood-working industry (75.0 percent) and in chemicals (81.4 percent) (*Gewerkschaftliche Monatshefte*, 1978: 762). This lends support to the demand of the DGB for direct appointment of union representatives by the unions organizing a company's workforce. Under the present law any organized group represented in the company, even if its membership is limited to this company, can enter candidates for 'union' seats, and unions can nominate internal as well as external candidates. Some unions came under pressure from their workplace organizations to nominate candidates from among the workforce, but such pressures were generally not successful (IGCPK, 1978: 685).

In spite of the reassuring experience in coal and steel, employers continue to suspect trade unions of using their external representatives for 'remote control' of co-determination companies. This subject played an important role in the public debate over the Act. One of the central concerns of stockholders and managements after the new supervisory boards had been formed was to prevent union concertation of supervisory board co-determination. This was attempted by tightening up secrecy rules and trying to exclude external labor representatives from sensitive information. In particular, companies refused to appoint external representatives to important committees, or tried to prevent their election to the post of vice-chairman, often by offering their support for the post to the chairman of the central works council.

On the other hand, there is considerable impressionistic evidence that unions have long abandoned any plans for what has been referred to as 'macro-economic counter-management'. For the unions as organizations, the principal advantage of external representation is that is provides them with another institutionalized link to the works council system, especially the central works council, and to the union workplace organization in large firms. In this respect the Co-determination Act of 1976 serves similar functions to the Works Constitution Act of 1972. Central works councils pose a difficult organizational problem for industrial unions since, unlike local works councils, contacts with them cannot be maintained through district offices (Streeck, 1981b: 164). For important central works councils, unions have therefore appointed special liaison officers located at the national headquarters. But these often had difficulties getting sufficient access to, and information on, the companies to which they were assigned. With the Co-determination Act of 1976, unions could have them elected onto companies' supervisory boards, and this gave them a formal status in their companies and, at least on paper, unlimited rights to information. Moreover, it made their access independent of the goodwill of the works councils they were supposed to advise. This is essential since works councils often share their management's concern that distribution of secret information to 'outsiders' may impair the company's competitive position.

(6) Just as in coal and steel, it seems that majority votes on supervisory boards were not frequent in the first four years of the 1976 model, and most decisions were made unanimously. The most common exception seems to have been appointments to the management board (see below). It appears that the chairman was generally reluctant to use his casting vote, and efforts were made by management and shareholders to reach a compromise with the labor representatives before a matter was placed on the supervisory board agenda. According to Witte (1982a: 171), 'a confrontation in formal voting is viewed as a scandal and gives rise to accusations that the meeting was insufficiently prepared'. In part, this may have been because management and shareholders were afraid of damaging their relationship with the works council. On the other hand, little is known yet on the role and the voting behavior of middle management representatives.

While it may not have made much difference in terms of effective voting strength, the Co-determination Act of 1976 guarantees labor the post of at least one supervisory board vice-chairman. The chairman and the vice-chairman of large supervisory boards form a kind of executive committee of the board. Among other things, they prepare the agenda of board meetings and discuss it with the management. One important advantage of the new law for the representatives of the workforce is that they can no longer be excluded from these discussions and in this respect the 1976 Act has created the same conditions as the Co-determination Act of 1951. The same holds, although to a lesser degree, for the membership of workforce representatives on important supervisory board committees.

(7) Concerning the substantive scope of the jurisdiction of supervisory boards, is that workforce representatives have consistently pursued two objectives: to push problems of manpower management and manpower planning on the supervisory board agenda, and to strengthen the role of the supervisory board in the company's decision-making structure on the whole. Although there is considerable variation between companies, it seems that the effort to change the agenda of supervisory boards was more successful, and in this respect there should by now be not much difference to the coal and steel industry. As to the decision-making authority of supervisory boards, union attempts to bring management decisions under supervisory board jurisdiction, and to bind the management by specific supervisory board instructions, were countered by initiatives of the shareholders to reduce the authority of the supervisory board to the legal minimum (see above). Nothing is as yet known on the actual practice, but it seems that, at the very least, manpower policy is now more than before treated as a regular subject of enterprise-level decision-making, and managements find it less easy than in the past to avoid making commitments in this area vis-a-vis the supervisory board.

(8) Differences between individual companies are probably greatest with respect to the status of the labor director. The official position of German business is that the labor director is just one member of the management board among others, and that the union has to play no particular part in this appointment. A number of firms went so far as to appoint their incumbent personnel manager labor director before the new supervisory boards were formed. This was later declared illegal by the courts. Others appointed their labor director with the casting vote of the supervisory board chairman or with the vote of the middle management representative against a candidate proposed by the union (an example for the latter category is Bayer Leverkusen; *Manager Magazin*, 1982).

There are also counter-examples, however. Extreme cases are companies that appointed a full-time trade union official, the chairman of their central works council or another trade union nominee. In an article in May 1982, the *Frankfurter Allgemeine Zeitung* listed 33 companies that fall into this category. Fifteen of these are fully (Deutsche Bundesbahn) or partly (Volkswagen AG) in public ownership; 14 others are dominated by coal or steel companies which are under the 1951 model of co-determination; and 4, among them a shipyard and an aerospace company, are heavily dependent upon state purchases and subsidies.

Labor directors in companies of this kind are in practice not different from labor directors in coal and steel. But even where the labor director was appointed against outright union resistance – the majority of cases should lie somewhere between the extremes, with more or less intensive consultations between the two sides preceding the appointment – the introduction of the institution of labor director has in several respects made a difference. In particular, the following should be noted.

1   It has elevated the function of manpower policy and manpower planning to the level of the company as a whole and of the management board.
2   It has thus made it easier for the labor side to make corporate manpower planning an issue for the supervisory board.
3   It has created a vested interest inside management in an extension of the role of manpower planning and manpower policy. Here the interests of the labor director and his department parallel those of the works council, and labor directors may sometimes feel tempted to draw on the support of the works council in their attempts to increase their influence within management.
4   It has provided the chairman of the central works council with a direct contact inside management on the company level.
5   It has institutionalized a boundary-spanning role between management and labor whose incumbent – especially where labor is well-organized – depends for his effectiveness on a good working relationship with the works council (Zander, 1981: 318).

The typical labor director under the 1976 legislation is certainly not a union nominee. On the other hand, labor directors in the coal and steel industry have often been criticized by left-wing trade unionists for identifying too closely with management and the company, and works councils and unions have always accepted that the labor director has a managerial and not a trade union function to perform (MBK, 1970: 88). Moreover, research has shown that coal and steel labor directors have become increasingly professionalized and that today their formal qualifications hardly differ from those of other leading managers (Spie and Bahlmann, 1978: 308).

**The Impact of Co-determination on the German
Political Economy**

Co-determination, as is generally agreed, has not given rise to a new economic order. By the late 1960s there was nothing that could be said against it from the viewpoint of an efficient management of a capitalist economy, and in this respect the *Mitbestimmungskommission* had no trouble giving even parity representation on the supervisory board 'a clean bill of health' (Hartmann, 1975: 56). The 1970s showed that much of what had been associated with parity co-determination could be transferred to other industries by way of the Works Constitution, with the highly politicized issue of parity remaining on the sidelines. However, it would be mistaken to conclude that co-determination has made no difference. In fact, it has had a deep and lasting impact on the German political economy and has significantly changed the relations between capital and labor in German society.

At the heart of the changes brought about by co-determination is the fact that it has subjected enterprises to specific, institutionalized constraints limiting and regulating their options as buyers of labor in the labor market. Put in a nutshell, co-determination, and in particular parity co-determination, has contributed to making labor as a factor of production less variable and more fixed than it traditionally was in capitalist enterprises. The first and most spectacular empirical expression of this was the partial uncoupling in coal and steel companies of the size of the labor force from changes in product demand, and the delayed adaptation of employment to economic fluctuations. Co-determination has imposed organizational rigidities on employers that have in effect reduced the dependence of employment on the product market and that have turned labor, within limits, from a dependent into an independent, or even constant, factor. For many practical purposes labor in co-determined enterprises is almost as difficult and costly to dispose of as fixed capital. In this sense the status of capital and labor as factors of production has been made more similar by co-determination, and this may be exactly what 'parity' in economic terms is all about.

Co-determination, of course, is not the only factor that has created rigidities for enterprises as employers of manpower. That employment has become less 'fluid' than in the past is an experience that has been made outside the coal and steel industry and in countries other than Germany. Developments that have contributed to this include employment protection legislation, growing union pressures and union power, changing qualificational requirements, public and political pressure on large enterprises to provide 'jobs', etc. Co-determination has partly preceded these developments, especially in coal and steel, and partly added to them. It has also made the new rigidities more resistant against economic crises and unemployment. Nevertheless, the constraints that co-determination has imposed on the enterprise are not unique and have appeared, with varying degrees of intensity, in quite different institutional environments.

What, then, is specific about co-determination? Unlike the other factors that have limited the variability of employment, co-determination has not merely posed a problem for enterprises but has also offered a solution. While on the one hand co-determination has contributed to growing organizational rigidities, on the other hand, and at the same time, it has provided the organizational instruments to cope with such rigidities without major losses in efficiency. Co-determination has changed not just the status of labor, but also the structure and performance of management, and it has in this way equipped enterprises with a capacity for efficient manpower use in spite of labor having become a much more fixed organizational resource. Parity co-determination in coal and steel has played an important historical role in this since it had already confronted managements with the challenge of reduced labor variability at a time when generally variability was still relatively high. Later, when the same problems began to confront other industries, the experience in coal and steel was available for diffusion, and this may be one explanation why German enterprises, although confronted with constraints on their manpower use which are similar to, or tighter than, their foreign competitors, seem to possess a higher ability to prevent these adversely affecting their economic performance.

Co-determination has changed management in basically two ways. First, it has upgraded manpower management in terms of both its formal organizational status and its methods and instruments. From the perspective of the enterprise as an organization, this appears as a successful adaptive response to the decline in labor variability (which was in itself partly caused by co-determination). The more manpower and employment began to take on a weight of their own, the more dysfunctional organizational arrangements were bound to become under which manpower management was expected merely to react to, and execute, decisions made by other departments. On the other hand, the assumption of a more active role by the manpower department required profound changes in managerial structures. The legal introduction of the labor director greatly facilitated such changes. The elevation of the manpower function to the management board level equipped it with the necessary authority not only to adopt a more long-term perspective of employment and manpower use, but also to enforce it gradually on the other managerial functions such as production, finance and sales. That the first labor directors were outsiders to traditional management was inevitable since the manpower department was at that time not considered attractive by capable and ambitious managers. Moreover, only outsiders could be expected to develop the independence and the activism necessary to challenge established organizational practices, and the preparedness to see through the inevitable organizational conflict. For this, outside backing was helpful if not essential, and here parity on the supervisory board has undoubtedly performed an important function.

This aspect of the impact of co-determination on management can be put in more general terms. Management in co-determined enterprises is exposed to constant pressures to provide information and to give reasons for its decisions. This has forced it to consider decisions more thoroughly, to take more factors into account, to make underlying assumptions more explicit, and to learn to communicate more freely within the organization in general and with the workforce in particular (Tegtmeier, 1973: 148, 198–9). As the *Mitbestimmungskommission* has pointed out, this has both delayed and improved decisions, with the latter usually compensating for the former (MBK, 1970: 72, 78). These observations apply not just to manpower management and labor relations, where, according to Adams and Rummel (1977: 14), 'union and works council pressure combined with the existence of labour directors has produced more rational, objective and equitable patterns of administration', and where 'the historical pattern in Germany of arbitrary and capricious paternalistic management has been substantially modified'. More generally, co-determination has brought about a modernization of managerial structures and practices, making management put more emphasis on objective data, on a free flow of information within the organization, and on discussion, consensus and co-operation (Neuloh, 1960). An important element in this seems to be the positive effect of co-determination on the independence of management from stockholders. For example, Witte's empirical research showed that in companies in which the influence of the labor representatives on the supervisory board is high, the influence of professional management is also high; influence of shareholders, on the other hand, is negatively correlated with management influence (Witte, 1981: 281; 1982a: 173).

The second major change co-determination has caused in management is that it has transferred, or devolved, part of the managerial function from management proper to the representatives of the workforce, in particular the works council. Management under co-determination is essentially co-management, especially but not exclusively in the manpower area where it is based on a close relationship between the personnel department and the works council. This, too, reflects the increased fixity of labor as a production factor. The more similar the status of labor in the enterprise becomes to that of capital, the more impossible it becomes to manage the enterprise efficiently without participation and assistance of organized labor, and the less governable the enterprise becomes for capital acting on its own. This lies at the bottom of what Tegtmeier describes as a 'constraint towards co-operation' that he sees institutionalized in co-determination (1973: 148). Again, the historical role of parity in the coal and steel industry seems to have been that it created this constraint quasi-artificially at a time when the structural factors making cooperation imperative were not yet far enough developed.

That a cooperative manpower policy can be a functional necessity for enterprises faced with rapid economic and technological change had already been recognized by the *Mitbestimmungskommission*. As the Commission pointed out as early as 1970, there are 'constraints towards co-operation that arise from the nature of the enterprise and that increasingly add to the respective constraints emerging from parity on the supervisory board'. These developments were said to have led in many companies outside coal and steel to the same kind of cooperation as under parity. 'All those questioned [by the Commission] have unanimously agreed that without intensive cooperation between management and the representatives of the workforce, the running of a modern enterprise is impossible' (MBK, 1970: 95). This may have been somewhat premature at the time – and perhaps was politically motivated in that it seemed to show that for cooperation to take place parity was not really necessary. However, it certainly became increasingly realistic after 1972 and, to an extent, 1976. At this time the combination of additional works council rights, strengthened union power, employment protection legislation, growing pressures for industrial adaptation and restructuring, increasing public concern over unemployment, together with the new institution of the labor director, accelerated the diffusion of techniques and procedures of manpower management that had been developed in the 1950s and 1960s under parity co-determination. The new, 'softer' approach to manpower policy that is increasingly being taken in large German companies – and which is ideal – typically exemplified by the 'middle line employment policy' introduced at Volkswagen in 1976 (Streeck, 1984a) – is based on the following principles.

(1) Integration of manpower and employment policy with production and investment planning to identify as accurately as possible future short-term and medium-term manpower needs and manpower constraints.

(2) Restriction of new recruitment to such categories and numbers of entrants that, on present estimates, can be given continuous employment. Seasonal or cyclical peaks are worked off by overtime. Whenever possible, extended delivery terms, or similar devices, are preferred over new employment which later may have to be redundant.

(3) Reduction of labor input by short-time work or, for a medium- or long-term period, by natural wastage. Forced dismissals are avoided at high costs – for example temporary labor shortages as a result of early, anticipatory recruitment bans, or even the 'stretching' of investment programs to fit them to the 'natural' development of the workforce. The structure and the dynamics of the existing workforce are increasingly becoming an (additional) factor influencing decisions on investment and production. 'Employment guarantees' for those presently employed, in the form of an informal undertaking by the management to the works council or the supervisory board, or as an element of the corporate image, seem to have become more frequent with growing sophistication of manpower managerial instruments.

(4) Accomplishment of changes in the structure of the workforce by mobilizing, and jointly administering, the internal labor market. Central for this is a commitment by labor and its representatives to continuous retraining and redeployment in accordance with the requirements of technological change, and a legal obligation for the employer to offer vacant positions to the existing workforce first, before turning to the external labor market. Acceptance by the workforce of rapid technological change, flexible work organization and high internal mobility is required to ensure the competitive edge and the economic success of the enterprise on which, in the last instance, the realization of the employment guarantee depends. In this sense manpower policy is part and parcel of a collaborative 'productivity coalition' which, in providing for higher efficiency than other forms of industrial relations, both supports and is supported by the traditional German pattern of export-led economic growth.[2]

The constitution of the co-determined enterprise cannot adequately be understood in terms of an adversary relationship between management as the source of authoritative decisions, and the works council as the representative of a group interest trying to influence such decisions. Rather, the essence of co-determination is the existence of a 'joint and integrated decision-making process'

(Tegtmeier, 1973: 150) in which the contributions made by both sides are in practice indistinguishable, and in which the works council not only shares in what used to be managerial prerogatives, but also accepts responsibility for the implementation and enforcement of decisions made under its participation. This constellation has frequently been described as 'integration' or 'cooptation' of labor, or organized labor, in management; with the same justification, however, it can be seen as 'colonization' of management, and in particular manpower management, by the representatives of the workforce. The most adequate metaphor would probably be that of a *mutual incorporation of capital and labor* by which labor internalizes the interests of capital just as capital internalizes those of labor, with the result that works council and management become subsystems of an integrated, internally differentiated system of industrial government which increasingly supersedes the traditional pluralist-adversarial system of industrial relations (similar to Tegtmeier, 1973: 187).

How is it possible that the interests of capital and labor should merge into a single, overriding interest of the (common?) enterprise? Workforce representatives under co-determination can win more stable employment for their constituents, and they can make the management take the social needs of workers into account as a central, and sometimes even co-equal, criterion of decision-making. But the more secure the status of workers as employees of a particular enterprise becomes, the more their interests come to include the economic well-being of this enterprise. The works council is ideally suited as an institution to represent the emerging enterprise-specific interests of a stable, safely entrenched workforce: its constituency is coterminous with only one enterprise, and since works councils are elected at large, they have no special obligations to individual groups within this constituency. While the former permits, and in fact demands, an identification with the competitive needs of the enterprise as an economic unit in the market, the latter makes it possible to cooperate in efforts to remedy the economically dysfunctional consequences of stabilized employment, and to help compensate external manpower rigidities by internal mobility and flexibility.

From the perspective of both management and unions, co-determination as it has developed since it was first enacted represents a highly ambivalent phenomenon. While it is true that co-determination offers a way of coping with organizational rigidities in the utilization of labor, at the same time it has added to these. Moreover, managing a co-determined enterprise is more demanding as it requires more communication, more sophisticated use of information and more encompassing long-term planning. Not least, a co-determined manpower policy is costly since it may involve extended delivery terms in times of peak demand, stockbuilding during demand slumps, internalization of training costs, and even the postponement or modification of investment plans to fit the constraints of the existing manpower structure. These short-term costs may well be offset by long-term gains deriving from fewer disruptions, swifter introduction of new technology, and higher quality. But this is not always certain, and foreign competitors may sometimes be advantaged by their greater ability to exploit short-term changes in the market price and the market power of labor.

Above all, co-determination carries with it considerable costs in managerial discretion and managerial prerogatives. The price for labor not obstructing internal mobility and technological change is the cooptation of its representatives into the structure of entrepreneurial decision-making – if only to create confidence that compromises will be honored in the future, that commitments will be kept and that long-term investments will be rewarded. Integration, that is, cuts both ways, and if it is to be effective with regard to labor, it must bind capital as well. This is why co-determination, for all its advantages, is seen by capital as a thoroughly mixed blessing. For example, Zander warns against appointing a union nominee as labor director 'in the hope of facilitating impending severe rationalization measures by keeping the unions quiet' (1981: 316). Especially the labor director appears to many as a dangerous bridgehead of labor invading the capitalist heartland. Furthermore, enterprise-specific interests of workers, once developed and institutionalized, tend to extend beyond employment and manpower questions in a narrow sense. With the interests of labor in the enterprise becoming as vested and 'fixed' as those of capital, labor representatives will inevitably demand to be involved, in the same way as the representatives of stockholders, in decisions on prices, products, marketing strategies, etc. For an enterprise that depends on its workforce taking a 'responsible' attitude and identifying themselves with its long-term future, this is only functional. Nevertheless, it runs counter to traditional concepts of management, and it increases the ambivalence of business towards co-determination as an institution.[3]

Both the short-term economic costs and the long-term costs in authority and status make the advantages of co-determination expensive for the capitalist class, and this explains the otherwise incomprehensible resistance of business to any extension of co-determination rights. It must not be forgotten that in taking the 1976 Act to the Constitutional Court, German employers knew that they were provoking the withdrawal of the unions from the Concerted Action (cf. the statement of the DGB in *Mitbestimmungsgespräch*, 1977: 108) – an event that they were prepared to accept although the Act had not even provided for parity.

To understand why organized labor should feel ambivalent about co-determination, it is necessary to look at the impact of co-determination on the way in which collective interests of workers are formed and articulated. That co-determination has made labor less variable as a factor of production is just another way of saying that it has reduced the role of the (external) labor market as a mechanism of allocation in favor of the status individuals have as members of a specific organization. Co-determination has proven an effective mechanism to bring about an accommodation of interests at the level of the individual enterprise resulting in a commitment of labor, in the form in which it is organized at the workplace, to competitiveness, productivity and profitability. The dilemma for the unions is that while they cannot want to restore the external labor market to its controlling position, the line of conflict along which they are organized, which is one between social classes, may be gradually pushed into the background by cleavages between consensually organized production units at the product market, and between workers who have acquired organizational status and those who have not. How internal accommodation in co-determined enterprises may undermine the influence of industrial unions is indicated by the failure of efforts to use co-determination for central control and concertation and by the precarious position of external labor representatives, with or without direct union appointment, in relation to the works councils.

What makes the situation so difficult for the unions is that the problems created for them by co-determination arise precisely from its achievements. Co-determined manpower policy has increased the employment security of workers who are already employed. At the same time, it is based on the understanding that new workers are taken on only if they can be guaranteed the same degree of security. The result may be workers in expanding enterprises working overtime in a period of rising unemployment (for an example, see Streeck, 1984a: Chap. 7), and extreme disadvantagement of workers who have lost their jobs or, like young people, enter the labor market for the first time (see Adams and Rummel, 1977: 16). A co-determined manpower policy in large companies makes it possible for a crisis of employment to develop in the economy as a whole without making itself felt inside the major places of employment – except perhaps for a slow decline in the number of jobs as a result of vacancies not being filled. Co-determined workplaces may thus become insulated from rising conflicts over an increasing disadvantagement of sizeable sections of the population, and wherever else these conflicts may express themselves, they may not show at the workplace.

Co-determination, then, seems to carry with it a trend towards 'closure' – something already observed by Tegtmeier (1973: 205) – and towards offloading the costs of internal accommodation to the outside world. This can take many different forms, from the costs of 'social plans' being transferred to the social security system (Spieker, 1977: 358), to successful joint pressures for public subsidies (Tegmeier, 1973: 204), up to unemployment in countries with a less competitive institutional structure. Internal accommodation in a social system generally increases the danger for its environment of being exploited, and reduces the chances of successful external intervention. The latter concerns not only the unions but also the state, especially its employment policy. As long as production units are internally divided along general lines of social conflict, they lay themselves open to, and in fact are in need of, external imposition of general rules of behavior, and there is room for solidarity of workers across enterprise boundaries. Co-determination, among other things, offers an institutionalized opportunity for enterprise-specific interests of workers to be articulated *and satisfied*, and thus tends to reinforce the segmentation of labor along the boundaries of production units and their internal labor markets – that is, along the same lines as capital. For trade unions, and perhaps for government as well, the problem of co-determination in coming years will be to prevent a gradual replacement of industrial unionism by company unionism, and to ensure that the shift of loyalties from class to enterprise will leave room for other, more encompassing social alignments and responsibilities.

Notes

* This chapter was first published in 1984. See Preface.

1 German companies have by law two boards: a management board consisting of professional managers who run the company's day-to-day business, and a supervisory board consisting of elected representatives of stockholders and workers whose major tasks are the appointment and dismissal of the management board and the supervision of its activities. The by-laws of the company may in addition provide that certain decisions of the management board require the prior assent of the supervisory board.

2 Using data from 82 major joint-stock companies before the taking effect of the 1976 Co-determination Act, Witte has related the relative influence of management, shareholders and employees on enterprise decisions to six different 'outcomes': the yearly rate of profit, the net cashflow, increase or decline in the value of stock, the size of the dividend, the frequency of forced dismissals, and the size of wages and

fringe benefits (1981: 295). The results are a fascinating confirmation of the 'productivity coalition' hypothesis, even if one takes them with a grain of salt for methodological reasons. Where the influence of the workforce is strong, dismissals tend to be infrequent, and wages and fringe benefits are high. The same is the case in companies with a relatively independent management (management independence and employee influence are correlated), and the reverse is true in companies with strong shareholders. This much one might have expected. A less obvious finding is that employee influence correlates strongly and positively with increases in the value of stock and with the size of dividend, and also, albeit not significantly, with profits and net cash flow. Shareholder influence, on the other hand, shows no significant correlation with either of these four outcomes, and in three cases the sign of the correlation is not even positive but negative. In other words, companies under strong co-determination perform better than companies with strong shareholders, not only in terms of the interests of the workforce but also in terms of important shareholder interests! Witte reports that these correlations remain stable even when they are controlled for firm size (number of employees) and general economic situation (gross cash flow).

3 A case in point was the unofficial strike at Volkswagen Wolfsburg in the spring of 1982. Shortly after the yearly wage negotiation, and a few weeks after the takeover of a new general manager, Volkswagen raised its prices. This was publicly criticized by the works council and the union, which hinted that there had been an understanding with the old management that prices would not be raised. The reason for the objections of the workers' representatives was that they expected higher prices to depress sales and thus undermine employment security. To back up the protests of their leaders, workers went on a one-day strike.

Successful Adjustment to Turbulent Markets: the German Automobile Industry in the 1970s and 1980s*

By the mid-1970s, a number of factors had come together to make the future of the West German automobile industry look extremely gloomy. The domestic market had for successive years been showing signs of saturation. The first oil shock in 1973 had brought energy shortages and high fuel prices, and the ensuing general economic crisis was bound to depress further the demand for new cars. After the revaluation of the Deutschmark in 1969 which had made German automobiles more expensive in foreign markets, the breakdown of the Bretton Woods agreement in 1972 added further uncertainties for an industry which was heavily dependent on exports, especially to the United States. Moreover, a new concern with environmental problems had arisen and was likely to make the auto industry a target of extensive regulation. By far the largest German producer, Volkswagen, had failed to replace its outdated mass production model, the 'Beetle', with a more modern design. As if all this had not yet been enough, the Japanese, with their superior production system and with products of unmatched price and quality that were uniquely matched to changed consumer preferences, were entering the industry's domestic and foreign markets, and lurking over the horizon were the newly developing countries with their huge supply of cheap labor. Not least, a rise in worker militancy after 1969 had added substantially to the industry's wage bill, and a new trade union strategy to overcome the Taylorist organization of work in mass manufacturing had led to a successful strike in 1971 for 'humanization of working life' which imposed hitherto unknown limitations on managerial prerogative.

A decade later, the pessimistic predictions of inevitable decline of one of the key industries of the West German economy have become bizarre exhibits in the museum of economic history. Today, the automobile industry, together perhaps with the chemical and machine tools industries, has become the favorite example of those who continue to believe that West Germany can remain a major economic and industrial power. The number of automobiles sold in

West Germany was much higher in 1986 than it was in 1971, the peak year before the crisis (2.83 million as compared to 2.15 million), and the same applies to the number of cars produced (4.31 million in 1986 as compared to 3.70 million in 1971). West German producers still hold a share of 67.6 percent in their domestic market (1986), and their export share has increased steadily since 1978 (48.9 percent) to no less than 61.6 percent in 1986. The energy problem has turned out to be far less dramatic than expected, and it was considerably eased by technical innovations which cut average fuel consumption of new cars by 23 percent between 1978 and 1985. Japanese competition was countered with a wave of product and process innovations in what had been seen by many as a mature industry with little potential for technical change. Perhaps most importantly, after a decade of vigorous rationalization, domestic employment in the West German auto industry has not declined but increased, reaching 717,200 in 1985 as compared to 609,000 in 1973, the year with the highest employment before the crisis. VW, the sick giant of the early 1970s, has rebounded to become again the largest producer in Europe. Of the old industrial countries, the West German auto industry is clearly the winner of the restructuring period of the 1970s and 1980s, producing today 38 percent of all European automobiles as compared to 32 in 1973, and having become the only serious European competitor of the Japanese.

The spectacular performance of West German automobile manufacturers in the extremely competitive world markets of the 1980s was associated with a peculiar product strategy. German automobile production always had a strong specialist element. Daimler-Benz, BMW and Porsche do not produce a full range of models but concentrate on a comparatively secure niche in the world market for expensive high-quality and high-performance cars. Their market was largely unaffected by the crisis and has as yet remained unchallenged by the Japanese. Just like the two Swedish manufacturers, Volvo and Saab – who also expanded considerably during the restructuring period – the German specialist producers kept to their traditional strategy of low-volume, high-margin production, cutting out smaller models and increasing steadily the value-added per unit.

Unlike Sweden, however, specialist production cannot alone account for the industry's success as the bulk of German automobile production remains in the volume range. On the other hand, it had been argued that the very distinction between specialist and volume production had been eroded in the 1970s. While for a long time the 'conventional wisdom' in the industry was 'Be a GM or a BMW, but nothing in between' (Altshuler et al., 1984: 139), the success of the

Japanese manufacturers in the small and medium-sized mass market was in large part due to the fact that they introduced in this market segment a level of quality and a number of features that had previously been confined to large, specialist cars. To this, and to the unmatchable price competitiveness of the Japanese, German mass manufacturers responded by moving upmarket – by improving product design and product quality; offering a broader range of options and model specifications to meet better the individual customer's preferences and thereby relieve the pressure of price competition; and generally increasing the value-added per car, which largely offset the negative employment consequences of the simultaneous introduction of micro-electronic production equipment. Most notable in this respect was VW, which moved away from the 'Beetle monoculture' in 1974 and introduced a completely new model range – among others, a car like the Golf GTI (1976) which combined the features of a mass market automobile with those of a specialist car – while at the same time not only extending its separate upmarket AUDI line but also using AUDI technology for design cross-fertilization. In many ways, this was a 'Swedish' product strategy adopted by what had been a picture-book mass manufacturer, with marketing methods abroad which successfully exploited national stereotypes of German quality manufacturing and with a pricing policy of high margins especially in foreign countries.[1]

It was above all this product and process strategy of an upmarket move within the mass market segment – with high product variety, flexible specifications, a strong emphasis on quality engineering and manufacturing – that brought commercial success in the face of increased competition, and which sustained high and growing employment in spite of more efficient production technologies. In effect, what happened in the German automobile industry in the 1970s was a restructuring of mass production in the mould of specialist production, with important elements of the latter being blended into the former, and with small batch production of highly specific model variations becoming enveloped in large batch production of basic models (for a more general discussion, see Sorge and Streeck, 1988). This strategy may well have been inspired by the strong specialist tradition in the German automobile industry, and it was almost symmetrically reciprocated by the two leading specialist producers, BMW and Daimler-Benz, which in the same period gradually extended their model range into the family car market, applying quality manufacturing methods to mass production. The culmination of this development was the introduction in the early 1980s of the first Daimler-Benz compact, the 190, which increased the company's turnover on passenger cars to no less than half of total VW turnover; raised its market share in West Germany above that of Ford; and made for a yearly output of Daimler-Benz cars far in excess of, for example, the British 'mass manufacturer', BL.[2] This configuration of high-volume specialist production, based on superior product design and rigorous quality standards, is now generally regarded as the most likely success formula for automobile production in old industrial, high-wage countries. It also fits in astonishingly well with the traditional pattern of German manufacturing which has always drawn its strength from high product quality and customized design (Cox and Kriegbaum, 1980). Moreover, it seems to be of importance far beyond the automobile industry itself, potentially providing a model of restructuring and adjustment for other old industries such as steel and textiles which need to find new profitable markets sheltered from price competition (Piore and Sabel, 1984).

The present chapter discusses how the restructuring of the industry in the 1970s and 1980s towards a product strategy of high-volume diversified quality production was accomplished. In particular, it tries to identify the political, historical and institutional resources on which German automobile manufacturers could draw in this remarkable episode of successful industrial adjustment. To do this, the chapter will start with a brief description of the structure of the West German auto industry. It will then look at both adjustment problems and the potential of the industry to respond to them successfully at two separate levels: the shopfloor and the individual enterprise, and the national political system.

The Industrial Organization of Automobile Manufacturing in West Germany

There are five major automobile manufacturers in West Germany: Volkswagen (VW) with AUDI, Opel (the German subsidiary of General Motors), Daimler-Benz, Ford and BMW. The largest producer is VW with a workforce, at the end of 1985, of 160,000 (22 percent of the industry as a whole), an output of 1.7 million passenger cars (42 percent) and a turnover of DM 48,531 million (29 percent). The second largest number of passenger cars is produced by Opel, the German subsidiary of General Motors, followed by Daimler-Benz, Ford and BMW.

Concentration is lower in the German auto industry than in any other leading producer country except Japan. Going by what in the 1960s and 1970s was received opinion in industrial economics, the industry's highly decentralized structure would appear to be in urgent need of rationalization and integration. However, although the pattern of industrial organization seems to correspond to an early stage of the product cycle, it has been stable for a number of years and there are no indications of impending change. This contrasts strongly to the United Kingdom where a variety of independent producers were merged in the 1960s and 1970s into one national car manufacturer to achieve higher economies of scale (Wilks, 1984). Today, it is increasingly recognized – not least in view of the Japanese case – that the presence of a large number of independent firms may in fact be a source of strength, making the vital domestic market an exercise ground for competition abroad and preserving a variety of designs and engineering philosophies which seems to be conducive to success in turbulent and diversified world markets (Altshuler et al., 1984).

Domestic competition is vigorous, both among German producers and between them and foreign manufacturers.[3] For reasons that will be discussed later, German manufacturers enjoy little protection in their home market. Nevertheless, they have together managed to hold on to a market share of 67.6 percent in 1986. Of this, 28.6 percent were held by VW (including AUDI), followed by Opel (13.3 percent), Daimler-Benz (10.7 percent), Ford (9.4 percent) and BMW (5.2 percent). The fragmentation of their highly contested home market forces German producers to expand into exports as their domestic sales potential does not normally permit for sufficient economies of scale. In this sense, German-built cars are by economic necessity always 'world cars' (or, better, 'Europa cars'). The demanding German market also requires producers to offer a broad range of models, and in 1986 the 10 most often sold models accounted for only 56 percent of all German-built cars sold in West Germany.

German producers represent a wide variety of manufacturing traditions and histories. Mass manufacturing methods were introduced by the two American multi-nationals, GM and Ford, which set up German subsidiaries in 1925 (Ford in Berlin) and 1929 (GM taking over Adam Opel AG in Rüsselsheim). However, they met with sustained skepticism and resistance on the part of established small, craft-style manufacturers. The Nazis, having failed in their attempt to make the industry join together for the mass production of a 'people's car' (Volkswagen), built their own automobile factory on a green-field site which was later to be called Wolfsburg. The company, owned by a subsidiary of the *Arbeitsfront* (the Nazi ersatz of the trade unions), bought its production equipment completely from Ford. For his contribution to the modernization of German industry, Henry Ford in 1939 received the highest civilian German decoration, the *Schwarzer Adlerorden*, from a grateful *Führer*. When shortly thereafter the war began, the new plant was used exclusively to build transportation for the army.

After the war and the division of the country, a North–South divide emerged between North German mass production (VW, Ford, Opel) and South German specialty production (BMW, Daimler-Benz, Audi, NSU, Porsche and others) – especially after the collapse in 1963 of the Bremen company, Borgward, whose production strategy resembled that of the South Germans. Regional differences correspond to differences in manufacturing philosophies, although these are of course difficult to pin down, with the South Germans having always had a ('small and beautiful') image of technological creativity and engineering perfectionism. The regional divide was crossed only twice, by two significant events: the take-over of AUDI (1964) and NSU (1969) by VW which ultimately enabled the parent company to accomplish its critical model change in the first half of the 1970s (the new models were based on designs that had been developed at NSU)[4]; and the location in Bremen of the new Daimler-Benz plant for the ('mass') production of the 190 compact which started in 1984.

Ownership patterns vary strongly among German manufacturers. Opel and Ford are owned fully by their American parent companies and are to different degrees integrated in their worldwide operations. VW was held in trust after the war by the Federal Government and the *Land* of Lower Saxony. In 1960, 60 percent of the shares was sold in small allotments to private owners ('people's shares'), with the Federal Republic and Lower Saxony each keeping 20 percent of the capital. At present, the Kohl government is committed to privatizing its remaining shares. A large part of Daimler-Benz capital (about 39 percent) was for a long time in the hands of the Flick industrial dynasty. After a family quarrel in 1975, they decided to sell most of their Daimler-Benz shares, amounting to 29 percent of the company's total stock. Among the would-be buyers was the Shah of Iran. Under pressure from the Federal Government, which had to be shielded from the public to avoid foreign policy complications, the shares were sold to the Deutsche Bank which held them for a number of years and then placed them on the market. However, to prevent ownership becoming too dispersed, the bank did not sell the shares directly but set up a special holding company which today [1986] owns 25.2 percent of the Daimler-Benz capital. Shares in the holding were sold to the public, one half to institutional investors and the rest to small shareholders. Deutsche Bank itself owns another 28.1 percent of Daimler-Benz shares whereas 14 percent have been owned since

1974 by the state of Kuwait. The Flick family in 1986 sold its remaining 10 percent of Daimler-Benz stock, again to the Deutsche Bank, which distributed it in small tranches. As a result, 32.7 percent is now held by about 160,000 small share owners. BMW is still largely owned, at a suspected share of more than 50 percent, by the Quandt family, who also have interests in the automobile supply sector (holding in particular a majority share in Varta) and who up to 1974 held the 14 percent share in Daimler-Benz which then went to the Emir of Kuwait. Porsche is owned by the numerous descendants of the legendary Ferdinand Porsche who, among other things, designed the Volkswagen Beetle.

As is generally the case in German industry, the influence of the banks on the automobile sector, especially on the four German-owned companies, is strong. Bank representatives sit on all five supervisory boards, either as shareholders or on account of their proxy votes for shares they have in deposit. Each manufacturer has a long-term working relationship with one bank which serves as *Hausbank*.[5] Little is known about the way the banks exercise their influence, but in the VW crisis of 1974 the Deutsche Bank was crucial in getting reorganization under way by threatening, in a supervisory board meeting, to withhold further credit and let the company go to the receiver (Streeck, 1984a).

Germany has a strong and technically advanced automobile supply industry, as exemplified by firms like Varta, VDO and, in particular, an industrial giant like Bosch. German auto manufacturers buy most of their supplies in Germany, although suppliers are subject to the same industrial wage agreement as assemblers. In 1986 domestic sourcing accounted for 64.9 percent of total supply purchases of German assemblers, including the two American multi-nationals.[6] One reason for this is certainly the traditional obsession of German manufacturers with product quality. Domestic sourcing also offers opportunities for close cooperation between assemblers and suppliers not just in quality control but also in research and development – one example being the longstanding alliance between Daimler-Benz and Bosch (both located in Stuttgart) which resulted among other things in the development of a sophisticated ABS device. Domestic sourcing also makes for short supply lines, and in this respect the German manufacturers were always closer to the 'Kanban' than to the 'world car' philosophy. In fact, recent efforts to introduce a zero-stock purchasing policy went remarkably smoothly. The South German manufacturers, especially, rely extensively on local networks of small craft (*Handwerk*) firms for specialized supplies,[7] which is one explanation why in Baden-Württemberg, a regional economy largely dominated by

Daimler-Benz, unemployment is lower than anywhere else in Germany (Maier, 1987; Sabel et al., 1987).

Regardless of their strong domestic supply base, German auto assemblers are highly vertically integrated, and this is one major difference compared to their Japanese competitors. In 1986 inhouse value-added accounted on average for 40 percent of total production value, as compared to 30 percent in France, 33 percent in Italy and 35 percent in the United Kingdom. This was in spite of the presence of the two American producers which are closely integrated into their companies' worldwide production networks. The apparent preference for 'making' over 'buying' seems in part to be accounted for by pressures from the works councils for high and stable employment (see below). Also, German manufacturers seem to be less interested than most of their international competitors in joint ventures with other companies, except where they are the dominating party and in particular control the engineering element. In fact, none of the major international cooperative arrangements in the industry in recent years include a German manufacturer. Related to this is a preference for large integrated plants, with the biggest German plant, VW Wolfsburg, employing no less than 65,000 people.

Pressures and Resources for Adjustment

The Shopfloor and the Enterprise

Nowhere else has the German industrial relations system performed better than in the automobile industry, and no industry has in the past contributed more to the evolution of the system.[8] Most of the important innovations in German industrial relations originated in this industry and then spread to other branches and sectors. Especially in the 1970s and 1980s, the industry's labor relations were a model case for the ability of German enterprise and shopfloor institutional settings to process and absorb rapid economic and technical change. Indeed their flexibility and contribution to manufacturing performance were such that they were able to bear the brunt of an unprecedented adjustment process without at any time requiring external political intervention. This was not because of trade union weakness; if there is a stronghold of trade unionism in Germany, this is the big auto manufacturers. But trade union strength in the industry is organized in a highly governable pattern of institutions at the point of production (Maitland, 1983) which in the 1970s and 1980s revealed a remarkable 'elective affinity' to the new production methods and product strategies that enabled the industry to compete so successfully – so much so that one feels tempted to speculate whether and how the industry's strategic choices may have been conditioned in part by its labor relations system (Streeck, 1987a).

One remarkable aspect of the industry's performance is its increasingly important role as a source of employment. It has already been indicated that automobile employment in the mid-1980s was well above the level before the 'first oil shock'. But what is perhaps even more astonishing is that much of the increase took place in the 1980s, which was a period of steeply rising unemployment and declining employment. In 1985, the West German automobile industry (passenger cars and trucks) employed 717,200 workers, that is, 3.2 percent of the total national workforce and 7.8 percent of the workforce in manufacturing. Of these, about 245,000 were engaged in the production of automobile components. This was clearly above the level of 1981 when automobile manufacturing employed 670,400 workers equivalent to 2.9 percent of total employment and 6.6 percent of manufacturing employment (220,000 of these produced components). The 1980s thus continued a trend that had already been visible in the late 1970s when the automobile industry was found to be one of the few industrial sectors in West Germany to generate employment growth inside an overall declining manufacturing sector (Streeck and Hoff, 1983).

Absolute and relative employment gains were achieved by an industry which is, by domestic standards, highly unionized. In an economy with an overall union density of 40.5 percent in 1986, roughly 70 percent of the automobile workforce (excluding the car repair shops) were members of IG Metall, in 1984. Membership in other unions is negligible. IG Metall is an industrial union with as many as 2.7 million members (1986) which organizes both blue- and white-collar workers in the entire metal-working sector. Union membership among workers of the big assemblers is even higher and can be estimated to range between 80 and 95 percent, in spite of the fact that the closed shop is illegal in Germany. However, other forms of union security do exist, notably check-off arrangements and participation of union representatives in the hiring of new workers which often amounts to a de facto 'union shop'.

The road vehicles industry is covered by industrial agreements on wages and other, 'qualitative' matters that are negotiated for the entire metal-working sector between IG Metall and the employers' association, Gesamtmetall. Again, the car repair shops are excepted as they are part of the artisanal sector which has a separate employers' association; workers in car repair shops, however, are also represented by IG Metall, although union membership is low in this area. Another special case is VW, which, due to its history of public ownership, never joined an employers' association and negotiates a special industrial agreement with IG Metall. In principle, however, VW agreements follow the general outlines of the metal-working agreement.

As a result of informal but effective intersectoral coordination of collective bargaining in Germany, inter-industry wage spread is low by international comparison (Marsden, 1981: 41). This holds all the more for the different branches of the metal-working industry which are covered by the same encompassing wage agreement. Wage drift in individual plants or enterprises is limited by institutional factors. Enterprise-level workforce representatives are barred under co-determination law from negotiating on wages, and industrial unions guard jealously their wage bargaining and strike monopoly. Nevertheless, some wage drift exists and wages at the big car assemblers should be 20 to 25 percent higher than stipulated by the metal industry agreement. About the same difference exists between the VW agreement and the industrial agreement.[9] In terms of its position in the national wage structure, the auto industry is doing well, with wages in road vehicle building in 1986 amounting to about 120 percent of average wages in the West German economy (Krupp, 1984). German automobile wages are also high by international standards; total labor costs per hour in 1986 amounted to about 87 percent of US labor costs, and 115 percent of labor costs in Japan.[10] Wages in the German automobile industry are also clearly higher than in other Western European countries, amounting to 141 percent of French, 139 percent of Italian and 186 percent of British labor costs (calculations based on communication from the VDA, 1985). High and sticky labor costs are an important factor forcing German automobile manufacturers to orientate themselves towards non-price competitive markets.

Being covered by the general agreement for the metal industry has advantages as well as disadvantages for German auto manufacturers. While it does not protect them from high labor costs, the legal enforceability of agreements during their currency – which is normally about one year – precludes short-term opportunistic wage militancy, especially by sectional groups in the labor force in periods of prosperity. By preventing competitive bargaining, settlements at the sectoral level enhance predictability and provide for a stable, governable wage structure. The resulting stability of shopfloor labor relations contributes to high productivity which, in turn, may make up for high labor costs – as witnessed by the fact that Ford's West German plants had throughout the 1970s lower unit costs than the British plants, with identical models and technology. Coverage by the general industrial agreement also means that firms with above average performance can make high profits before wages are adjusted; to the extent that such profits are reinvested this is not necessarily in contradiction with union objectives. It means also, however, that loss-making firms cannot expect to get short-term wage concessions. For example, VW, although not even included in the metal industry agreement, had to concede a wage increase in 1974 of 11.0 percent – which was about the level of the metal industry in general – even though the company was operating on the brink of bankruptcy (Streeck, 1984a).

Inside the encompassing bargaining unit of the metal sector, the auto industry performs something of a pilot role for the union. Strikes by IG Metall in pursuit of an industrial agreement are always selective, and since the 1960s they have regularly included the auto industry, especially in a prosperous area in Northern Baden-Württemberg which is economically dominated by Daimler-Benz. The three largest and by far the most important strikes of the 1970s and 1980s were called here, resulting in regional 'pilot' settlements that were then transferred by the parties to the entire country and later gradually diffused throughout the economy: the strike for improvements in working conditions and work organization ('humanization of working life') in 1971; the strike for 'protection against rationalization' in 1978 (Streeck, 1981b); and the strike for reduction of working hours in 1984. Each settlement represented a breakthrough for the trade union movement and a major innovation in industrial relations. Although the conflicts that preceded them were long and bitter, and always involved a large number of workers being locked out, each time relations were repaired afterwards, and in spite of its role as a testing ground and battlefield for trade union policy the auto industry has remained a paragon of a style of industrial relations that has aptly been described as 'cooperative conflict resolution' (Jacobs et al. 1978).

If industrial unionism is one cornerstone of the industry's industrial relations system, co-determination – the 'peculiar institution' of German labor relations – is the other.[11] Workers in Germany are represented under the Works Constitution Act (last amended in 1972) by works councils which are elected every three years by an establishment's entire workforce. Works councils have legal rights to information, consultation and co-decision-making on a wide range of subjects. They may negotiate works agreements with the employer that are an equivalent to industrial agreements at the enterprise level but must not deviate from an industrial agreement where one exists. Works councils are not permitted to call strikes, however; they always have to take recourse to arbitration or mediation. In large firms, there is also elected workforce and trade union representation on the supervisory board, which outside the coal and steel industry, however, falls short of the 50 percent of the votes demanded by the unions.

Works councils in the large auto assembly firms are well resourced and generally have more influence on more subjects than given to them by the law. In 1985 the works council at VW Wolfsburg had 65 members who were all released from their normal duties and practically served as full-time union representatives. Works council influence differs between firms, the two opposite extremes being probably VW and Ford, but generally the situation is well described by a General Motors manager who after a stint at Opel Rüsselsheim concluded: 'Without the works council, nothing goes; with the works council, everything goes' (interview with the author).

Leading works council members are usually also elected to the supervisory board where they represent the workforce together with full-time union officials. The structure of influence at the supervisory board level differs markedly between German- and American-owned firms; whereas at Opel and Ford the shareholder representatives are all delegates from the American parent company, in the German firms the shareholder side is less monolithic. Workforce influence on the supervisory board is clearly strongest at VW, with the President of IG Metall serving traditionally as Vice-President of the VW supervisory board, much to the dismay of small shareholders. VW also as a rule reserves one seat on the management board, that of the personnel director, to a trade union nominee, following the practice in the coal and steel industry.

Co-determination and industrial unionism complement each other in a complex pattern of interaction. More than 80 percent of elected works councilors are trade unionists, and leaving aside a few cases of factional strife and local discontent this has been so for decades. Works councils have become the center of trade union organization at the workplace, in the auto industry even more so than elsewhere. Moreover, all external workforce representatives on supervisory boards are IG Metall full-time officials, and leading works councilors hold important trade union offices; for example, the chairman of central VW works council is as a matter of routine elected to the IG Metall national executive. Works councils perform vital functions for trade unions in the provision of union security. The legal no-strike rule under co-determination also serves to protect the strike monopoly of industrial unions, and works councils are charged by law with supervising the implementation of industrial agreements. There is furthermore the possibility for industrial agreements to delegate specific subjects to works councils and employers for regulation by works agreement, and this has been increasingly made use of in recent years in response to the growing complexity of industrial relations issues. The result has been an imperceptible but nevertheless significant decentralization of the industrial relations system which has increased its flexibility. Again, this trend has been particularly strong in the automobile industry.

Co-determination, with its peculiar rules, has become the institutional core of what is best described as a firmly established 'productivity coalition' between management and labor at the point of production. Prototypically in the automobile industry, co-determination has provided the basis for a trade union policy of cooperative productivism which is not adequately captured by the often-used concept of 'enterprise patriotism' (*Betriebspatriotismus*) as it is generally supported by the full-time union officials sitting on the industry's supervisory boards and giving advice to works councils. The tendency of works councils in Germany to identify with the economic fate of their firm – due to their being elected as representatives of an enterprise's entire workforce – is reinforced in the auto industry by a keen sense, shared by the external union, of exposure to a volatile and competitive world market. As a consequence, hardly anywhere is there a greater willingness than among automobile trade unionists to think through and accept the consequences of labor-management cooperation. Together with the opportunities offered by the framework of industrial unionism and co-determination, this gave rise in the 1970s and 1980s to an interactive configuration of policies and institutional structures which appear to have formed a 'virtuous circle' ideally matched to, and indeed almost making inevitable, an industrial strategy of upmarket restructuring (for more detailed discussion, see Streeck, 1987a). This configuration includes the following elements.

(1) *The emergence of internal labor markets.* Employment in the German auto industry has always been comparatively stable, with firms such as Daimler-Benz and BMW having for long operated an informal policy, as part of their 'corporate culture', not to dismiss workers for economic reasons. But employment stability increased further in the critical second half of the 1970s when it declined in all other countries (Streeck and Hoff, 1983). This reflects the effect of industrial agreements on 'protection against rationalization' and of works council influence as well as the co-determination legislation of 1972 and 1976. For example, VW conceded a far-reaching employment guarantee in 1976 in return for works council and union agreement to production in the United States. Works councils also generally oppose fixed-term contracts – which had in the past

been given primarily to foreign workers – to rule out any opportunity for management to use hiring and firing to adjust employment. In compensation for the growing ('external') rigidity of employment, works councils in the 1970s cooperated in improving internal labor market flexibility and supported the introduction of medium- and long-term manpower planning, in which they became closely involved (Hoff, 1984). The trend towards internal labor markets was reinforced by industrial agreements making it obligatory for employers to offer new jobs first to the existing workforce. In 1978 a landmark agreement was signed at VW on a new payment system which simplified the wage structure and introduced broader job descriptions, thereby facilitating internal mobility (Brumlop, 1986; Brumlop and Jürgens, 1986). The growing fixity of employment made it necessary for managements to devise manpower, production, product and marketing strategies capable of sustaining a, for all practical purposes, constant workforce. At the same time, growing sophistication of internal labor market management, with works councils serving as effective co-managers, afforded the kind of internal flexibility required for diversified high-quality production.

(2) *A large-scale training and retraining effort*. German manufacturing industries have always employed a comparatively large proportion of skilled workers who have formed a human resource base compatible with 'paternalistic' policies of stable employment. This tradition was reinforced in the automobile industry during the restructuring phase by a strong commitment of unions and works councils to training as a way of maintaining employment in internal labor markets and reducing youth unemployment. In the second half of the 1970s, the number of apprentices in the German automobile industry increased sharply while in other countries apprenticeship programs were cut (Streeck and Hoff, 1983). This is attributable to the 'neo-corporatist' German vocational training system which provides trade unions and employers' associations with institutionalized opportunities to influence individual employers' training decisions. Overskilling contributed to the emergence of internal labor markets in that new recruitment was often limited to apprentices who, in the absence of skilled vacancies, were for the time being assigned to production jobs. It also added to firms' human capital stock, increasing their capacity to absorb technological change and giving them in this respect a competitive edge over foreign producers. Investment in retraining and further training was also expanded, for technological reasons as well as to facilitate redeployment. Offering displaced workers retraining is also obligatory for employers under rationalization protection

agreements and works agreements on new technology. This general policy of upskilling seems to explain more than any other factor the decline in the number of foreign workers which is paralleled by an overall decline in unskilled employment. The automobile industry, both employers and works councils, played a leading role in the adaptation of the metal industry vocational training scheme to new technology (Streeck et al., 1987).

(3) *A long-term investment perspective on the part of both firms and workers' representatives.* Strong worker representation under co-determination has several times been found to coincide with high reinvestment of profits, with professional management and works councils sometimes conspiring against shareholders (Tegtmeier, 1973; Witte, 1981). It has also been shown that German firms in world market-exposed sectors tend to have long-term profit expectations and performance standards, and high 'intangible' investment in marketing and research which pays only over a longer period (Cox and Kriegbaum, 1980). This fits with a characteristic conservative attitude towards technology which places more emphasis on perfection than on being the first in the market. Moreover, the share of the total receipts of a German automobile firm that is paid out in wages is lower than for example in British automobile firms, although wages are much higher, both being due to higher long-term investment which sustains a high real wage level (Cox and Kriegbaum, 1980). The emphasis on production as opposed to distribution, as institutionalized in both the finance and the industrial relations system, corresponds to a pattern of high value-added manufacturing, which in turn is conditional upon high skills and cultivation of a continuously employed workforce. This constellation is very much present in the German automobile industry where it is protected by the system of industry-wide wage bargaining and by works councils who under co-determination can afford to wait, just as prudent investors on the capital side, for long-term restructuring projects to bear fruit.

(4) *De-Taylorization of work organization.* Since the 1960s IG Metall has actively pursued programs for a 'humanization of working life' aimed, among other things, at broader job contents and a reintegration of conception and execution. This it could do since, as an industrial union, it is not pledged to the special interests of either skilled or unskilled workers. Such initiatives were also facilitated by the large supply of broad skills generated by the apprenticeship system. In the restructuring period of the 1970s and 1980s, broad job descriptions proved a crucial asset for redeployment in internal labor markets, and the presence of young skilled workers in production jobs – which resulted from excess training

and internalization of labor markets – put further pressure on the existing division of labor. Indeed the automobile industry was found to be one of the strongholds of the 'new production concepts' described by Kern and Schumann (1984), which combine a commitment to diversified high-quality production with more integrated job contents. Traditional trade union policies for a less Taylorized organization of work have thus converged with the requirements of quality-competitive, high value-added production.

(5) *Rapid absorption of technical change*. German unions, being industrial unions, have never needed to impose restrictive job demarcations. This, together with wage maintenance and retraining under 'protection against rationalization' agreements, as well as steady employment under co-determination and internal labor market human resource management, has made for a highly flexible shopfloor capable of absorbing technical change without disruption. The skilling offensive of the 1970s, the influx of highly skilled apprentices and the gradual erosion of the distinction between direct and indirect work under 'humanization of working life' projects have further prepared the ground for the new microelectronic technologies. Employment protection also ensured that new technologies were not used for classical rationalization involving workforce cuts, but rather had to be put to the purpose of diversified quality production. Today, the German auto industry is among the leaders in production technology, especially in automation of final assembly, which used to be a mainstay of unskilled labor. The automated final assembly of the Golf at Volkswagen Wolfsburg (Halle 54) was introduced with works council and union support although on paper it eliminated about 1,000 jobs. In fact, employment increased due to growing production volume.

This configuration, which coped so well with the challenges of the 1970s and early 1980s, still appears to be both stable and well-adapted to current industrial adjustment problems. Not that there were no pressures for change. But change of some kind there always was, and indeed it was precisely the capacity of the German industrial relations system to evolve gradually in response to a changing environment which in the past accounted for its successful performance. One important area in which existing arrangements may by now have reached their limits, calling for a major overhaul of the institutional structure at the workplace, is quality assurance. In 1987, quality problems for the first time affected Daimler-Benz, where during the year more than 200 new model variations were introduced, resulting apparently in an unprecedented number of faulty cars reaching the customers. At Volkswagen, both the need to extend warranty periods and the high costs of rectification – with the number of faulty cars exceeding by far that in Japanese factories – caused considerable concern not just among the management but also with the works council. In both cases, it appears that product diversification had been driven to a level where even under German conditions it ceased to be easily compatible with product quality – the second and equally indispensable element of the 'diversified quality production' strategy. By the mid-1980s, it thus seemed to have become necessary for German auto manufacturers to update their traditional methods of quality assurance by new, special measures.

Most of these, however, are not likely to cause dramatic deviations from existing patterns of shopfloor cooperation and industrial relations. The most 'natural' response in the German manufacturing environment to problems of this kind is intensified training and further training, combined with new, more integrated forms of work organization that make it possible to utilize higher and more polyvalent skills. After the reform of initial vocational training in the metal industry which is now being gradually implemented, increased attention is presently being paid by both management and workforce representatives to further training. Although there is some disagreement over the exact terms, both sides are committed to what they tellingly call a 'qualification offensive', involving considerable human resource investment aimed at safeguarding the international competitiveness of German manufacturers. A first, comprehensive works agreement on the subject was signed at Volkswagen in early 1987. IG Metall, in a national policy document, has even gone as far as to suggest using further cuts in working hours for training at the workplace, as a way of combining redistribution of work with improving the industry's skill base.

Also, while it took a long time for the quality circle movement to hit the German auto industry, it now has forcefully arrived, and with it various managerial initiatives for more substantial decentralization of the organization of work ('team working' or 'group work'). For a number of years, quality circles and group work were regarded by many in the industry as a foreign fad, useful at best for firms and countries with a history of excessively Taylorist work organization and large skill deficits. The prevailing belief was that the traditional organization of the German shopfloor, in combination with the important role played by the *Meister* (the highly skilled German equivalent of the foreman), provided for sufficient quality and flexibility. Now this has changed, and there is growing interest among management, not just at the subsidiaries of the two American multi-nationals, in new, 'Japanese' forms of work organization.

Whether the objectives pursued with team working and quality circles will eventually be accommodated in a modified 'German' pattern, or whether there will have to be more fundamental change, is difficult to say; in any case, it may not be the most important problem. This might well turn out to be the compatibility of quality circles, and team working in particular, with the present system of co-determination and the veto powers of works councils vis-a-vis management. Here, most works councils and IG Metall believed for a long time that delegation of co-decision rights from management to small groups of workers serves primarily the purpose of undermining co-determination and workers' trade union loyalties. However, in 1986 the new leadership of the VW central works council signed a works agreement on the introduction of quality circles which gave the works council a measure of influence on their operation, and IG Metall, not least in response to changing works council attitudes, is now beginning to take a much less adverse position. Uncertain as the outcome is, going by its tradition one can expect the union to try everything possible to avoid having to choose between becoming an obstacle to improved competitiveness, and resigning its industrial power and influence; and going by the traditions of the employers in the sector, it appears likely that after some hesitation they will find it advisable to help the union avoid this choice.

The National Polity

The post-war German state has no strong tradition of 'industrial policy' or 'selective intervention' (Webber, 1986). Nor is there much public ownership in the manufacturing sector, and where the Federal Government does hold shares in manufacturing companies it does not use this as an instrument of economic or employment policy. The powerful Federal Ministry of Economic Affairs has throughout its history held on to a German version of liberal supply-side policy under which the principal responsibility of the government is to safeguard the functioning of the market, among other things through free international trade and promotion of domestic competition. The privatization of the majority of VW shares in 1960 was in line with this philosophy, and in fact having been re-elected the present government intends to sell off its remaining VW stock.

Public (minority) ownership in VW has made much less of a difference to the way in which the company is run than is often assumed. Apart from the strong position of the union and the co-determination bodies, VW was always required to operate like a private enterprise, and it has never received significant public subsidies.[12] This was true even in 1974 when the company was about to falter. At the peak of the crisis, the leadership of IG Metall and the works council went to see the Social-Democratic Minister of

Finance to ask for financial support, only to be told that the Federal Government had not one Deutschmark to spare for automobiles that nobody was willing to buy. This attitude had the full support of the Chancellor of the day, Helmut Schmidt, who on various occasions had committed himself publicly to what he called a 'private sector solution' (which in the end was extremely successful). All the government did was to prepare a range of regional labor market measures to relieve possible mass unemployment (Streeck, 1984a).

The government's lack of enthusiasm on industrial policy is clearly not shared by the union. In its 'Automobile Policy Paper' (IG Metall, 1984; 1985), IG Metall reiterated its long-standing proposal for a tripartite 'industry council' to oversee and guide private investment in the industry in order to prevent over-capacity. However, this demand – which is of course anathema to the employers – had gone unheeded already under the Social-Liberal government, and the present government has rejected a parallel proposal even for the ailing steel industry. Given that the automobile industry, with its outstanding performance, seems to provide such excellent confirmation for the government's free market philosophy, the union's demand for an institutionalized sectoral policy stands no chance of acceptance.

In a sense, this may not be totally against IG Metall's interest. As a union which organizes the entire metal-working sector, IG Metall has found it difficult enough to assume the role of 'sectoral mastermind' for the steel industry, where it plays a special role due to a particular form of co-determination. Assuming the same responsibility for more subsectors of the industry may very likely be just too much for a trade union. There are, after all, good reasons why IG Metall is organized on a unitary basis without special divisions for individual industries (the exception again being steel, Streeck, 1984a): a divisional organization, as would be required to formulate specific industrial strategies, would easily set free too many centrifugal forces. In the past, IG Metall has accomplished the maintenance of solidarity among its 2.7 million members by focusing on their common interests in the labor market, and involving itself as little as possible in the much more diverse interests of their firms and industries in the product market. Interestingly, the same holds true for the employers' association, Gesamtmetall, which also represents the entire metal industry. While there is a trade association of the automobile industry, the VDA, this is a weak organization because it is not simultaneously an employers' association; because its internal politics are dominated by five large, prosperous, independent companies who fiercely believe that they can well take care of themselves; and because of the split among its ranks between German- and American-owned firms which makes a joint strategy very difficult to formulate.

The unwillingness of the government to intervene in sectoral restructuring and the weakness of both the union and the trade association as agents of industrial policy has placed the burden of adjustment exclusively on the individual enterprise and the shop-floor. Their flexible performance depends in large measure on the capacity of the industrial relations system for 'cooperative conflict resolution' (Jacobs et al., 1978) – which, in turn, is enhanced by a legal and political framework facilitating and encouraging 'social partnership'. In many ways, then, *liberal economic policy* in Germany, in the auto industry and beyond, is viable and successful because it is underpinned, and its potential deficits are compensated, by *neo-corporatist social policy* – just as *abstention from direct intervention in industrial strategy* on the part of the government is made possible by *procedural intervention in industrial relations*. It is this mixture of three elements – government unwillingness to fend off adjustment pressures; a lack of capacity of the trade union and the trade association to act as lobbies for protective selective intervention; and a legally based industrial relations system safe-guarding governability of the workplace by imposing obligations and responsibilities on both 'sides of industry' – that seems to have been needed for successful performance in turbulent markets.

Not only has the German automobile industry not had the benefit – or, if one looks at the United Kingdom, the liability (Wilks, 1984) – of selective government intervention on its behalf; it has not even received financial support for research and development, which goes almost exclusively to sectors such as telecommunications, micro-electronics, nuclear energy and the aerospace industry.[13] Just as other export-oriented manufacturing sectors, the auto industry has been one beneficiary among many of global economic, fiscal and monetary policies that were and are tuned to the need for the German economy to remain competitive in world markets. It has also been favored by the pervasive political consensus during most of West Germany's history that both public investment and regulatory policies should promote, or at least not undermine, industrial performance. The latter at least is now being forcefully challenged by the 'new politics', and it is especially in three policy areas that the automobile industry and its traditional hold over government policy have come under attack.[14]

First, Germany, just as other industrialized countries, has a strong 'road lobby' consisting of the automobile associations with their large membership, the construction industry and the automobile industry. Owing at least in part to their activities, West Germany in the mid-1980s had one of the most extensive and expensive road systems, its backbone being a network of 8,200 kilometers (4,970 miles) of large super highways, or *Autobahnen*. Support for road-building was for a long time bipartisan. When in 1966 the Social Democrats joined the Federal Government, they appointed the leader of the construction workers' union, the IGBSE, as Minister of Transportation. During his tenure the government committed itself to a national *Autobahn* program which was to give each citizen, wherever in the country he or she might live, access to an *Autobahn* in a range of no more than 10 kilometers.

This ambitious project had later to be revised due to lack of funds. In addition, however, there was also increasing resistance in local communities against new roads being built in a country as small and densely populated as the Federal Republic. Since the Social-Liberal government improved the rights of citizens to have public building projects reviewed in the courts, *Autobahn* construction has become difficult, and only very few new projects are presently under way. Hardly any major road project, *Autobahn* or not, today proceeds without lengthy litigation, and frequently the courts uphold claims that projected roads are unnecessary and damaging to the environment. Moreover, the Green Party demands that a significant number of existing roads be scrapped to restore the natural environment, and to some extent this became government policy in the state of Hesse when the Greens were in coalition with the Social Democrats.

The industry that is hardest hit by this is, of course, construction, which, for this reason as well as others, has for years now been going through a phase of painful contraction. For the automobile industry, the expansion of the road network has in the past been helpful first because it made car ownership attractive, and later because it relieved its growing disutilities for the individual user. This holds in particular for the congested inner cities where parking prohibitions or a total ban on private car traffic were avoided, or at least postponed, by improvement of the road system and the construction of new parking facilities. (The same effect, incidentally, was caused by the replacement in several large cities of street cars with subway systems.) Today this solution has become less and less politically viable, and a collective preference is developing for stricter regulation of private automobile use to prevent further depletion of the natural or urban environment.

It is hard to see, however, how the declining acceptance of public construction projects could seriously damage the industry's domestic sales prospects. The relationship between the size of the road network and the number of cars has for some time been deteriorating. In 1970, there were 13.9 million passenger cars in a road network of 408,000 kilometers, which amounts to 34 cars per kilometer. In 1985, the number of passenger cars had increased to 25.8 million, whereas the road system had grown to only 472,000 kilometers – which made for 55 passenger cars per kilometer. In spite of this, it is expected that in the year 2000 the number of automobiles will have grown to between 29.5 and 30.6 million (Shell, 1985). Similarly, pedestrian zones spread in the inner cities during the 1970s without the automobile industry having been visibly affected. West Germany also has, by comparative standards, extensive mass transit systems and a large and well-functioning railway – neither of which has stopped the growth of the private automobile fleet. Bicycle ownership has dramatically increased in recent years, especially among young urban people, but most of them also own cars, often more than one per family. While in the past the expansion of private motorization may have been conditional on the simultaneous expansion of the road system, today this connection seems no longer to exist.

Secondly, West German *Autobahnen* have no general speed limit and this has for some time been a highly emotional and divisive issue in domestic politics. (There are of course frequent specific speed limits and it is a punishable offense not to adjust one's speed to driving conditions.) A general speed limit of 100 kilometers (60 miles) per hour was first proposed by the Social Democrats after the 1972 election and later became one of the central themes of the Greens. While the demand remained the same, the reasons that were given for it changed over time – from the high number of accidents which was emphasized in the early 1970s; to energy conservation which figured prominently in the years immediately after 1973; to, in the 1980s, the environmental hazards of fast driving as exemplified by, in particular, the *Waldsterben* ('the dying of the forest'). The industry has always forcefully objected to a general speed limit, and the proposal is not popular with the majority of the electorate in a country where so much of social life is subject to effectively enforced legal regulation. The present government clearly sides with the opposition to a general speed limit, and to close the issue it conducted a large-scale test in 1985 which appears to have shown no significant energy savings, only a minor decline in pollution, and a low level of compliance (VdTÜV, 1986).

There are complex reasons behind the industry's resistance to a general *Autobahn* speed limit. Publicly, the industry claims that the high engineering standards of German cars, which contribute importantly to their world market competitiveness, derive from the pressure to make cars capable of continuous high speed performance, at 160 kilometers per hour (100 mph) and more for many successive hours. This is questioned by the proponents of a speed limit, who cannot see why German manufacturers should give up their competitive advantage just because of stricter driving regulations on the German *Autobahn*. Indeed, more important for the industry may be the image abroad of German cars being capable of relentless racing at unheard-of speeds. It may also be true that the preference of German consumers for German cars has to do with a belief that foreign cars are not quite up to the kind of performance possible, and indeed almost required, on *Autobahnen*. If fast driving was banned, German consumers might no longer be willing to buy the expensive upmarket models in which German producers specialize. In this sense, the absence of an *Autobahn* speed limit may amount to something like free advertisement in foreign markets and a non-tariff trade barrier in the domestic market at the same time. This may explain why the European Community presses the Germans to introduce a speed limit as a precondition of joint action to reduce exhaust emissions.

In any case, the industry has prevailed on the subject and no general speed limit is in sight barring a red–green coalition government in Bonn. In part, the successful defense of 'free driving for free citizens' (the road lobby's slogan in the early 1970s) was possible because the industry managed to invalidate some of the arguments of its opponents. The number of road accidents in relation to driving performance has been declining sharply since the early 1970s, due among other things to improved safety features and regardless of cars having become much faster on average. *Autobahn* accidents in particular are infrequent.[15] Moreover, fuel consumption per car has strongly declined after the two oil shocks, due to improved engine and body design. And when the proponents of the speed limit shifted their argument to the *Waldsterben* in the 1980s, the industry was once again able, after some fumbling on the way, to take the momentum out of their attack through technical improvements that offered, at least for a time, an alternative to restrictive behavioral regulation.

Finally, environmental protection has always been a problem for the German automobile industry since it became a political issue, and the industry and its association, the VDA, have proven remarkably inept in dealing with it. When in the early 1970s the Social-Liberal government took measures to reduce the lead content of gasoline, the industry began an aggressive publicity campaign to convince the voters that less lead would result in lasting damage to their beloved automobile engines. After a law had been passed in 1971 setting the maximum lead content to 0.4 grams per liter of gasoline, the government in 1975 proposed to lower the lead content further to 0.15 grams. Why the industry fought this bill so violently is far from clear, even with hindsight; a benevolent interpretation would be that the campaign was intended to deter once and for all any attempt at environmental regulation of the kind that was giving such a hard time to American producers in the 1970s. In any case, the law was passed and took force in 1976. No engine breakdowns were reported, German automobile production continued to soar, and the industry had lost much of its credibility with both the public and the government.

The same pattern repeated itself in the 1980s, only this time on a larger scale. When the new conservative government took over, it felt it had to do something about the *Waldsterben*. The problem was perceived as a national catastrophe even by many voters in the conservative camp, and visible and dramatic action was felt to be required, preferably of the 'blood, sweat and tears' type involving some degree of opportunity for sacrifice by citizens who were feeling guilty about what their prosperity was doing to the trees. Since a speed limit was seen as too much of a sacrifice, though, the government in the summer of 1984 came up with the idea to make catalytic converters meeting US pollution standards obligatory for all new cars, allowing only for a very short transition period until the end of 1985.

Initially, this was violently opposed by the industry, which seems to have been afraid that the measure would further increase the Japanese price advantage especially with smaller cars (the Japanese having had longer experience with converter technology and better economies of scale in their large domestic and American markets). Later the technological problems of gearing catalytic converters to high speed *Autobahn* driving took front stage. Mutual accusations of bad faith between the Minister of the Interior, one of the most conservative government members, and the industry made almost daily copy, and the theme of the impending decline of profits and employment in one of the core sectors of German industry was reiterated once and again. When it became clear that the government would not back down – and, one supposes, after the engineers had finally been able to communicate to their superiors that the technical problems were after all solvable – the industry in late 1985 made a turnaround, which hardly restored its credibility, and came out in favor of the catalytic converter provided the requirement would apply also to imported cars.

At this stage, opposition arose from West Germany's partners in the European Community, which regarded the intended German measures as a non-tariff trade barrier and announced legal action in the European Court. This may have been because other European producers felt less confident than the Germans that they could master the converter technology, or just because they preferred to put their scarcer — research and development money to other, more potentially profitable purposes. As the discussions in the Council of Ministers proceeded, it became clear in early 1985, to the government's considerable embarrassment, that unilateral German action was not only legally impossible but, more importantly, might impair the willingness of West Germany's partners in the Community to continue to absorb the giant trade surplus of the German automobile industry.

The issue was resolved in a typically 'European' way. Agreement was reached in June 1985 on a complicated set of common European pollution standards to come into force during the 1980s and 1990s, as well as on additional, national action by the German government. The latter consists essentially of tax relief for the purchase of new cars which meet the European standards ahead of time. It was at this point that the German automobile industry began to discover that it had never really been against the catalytic converter. Meanwhile, it has learned to live exceedingly well with the new law, which not only gives it another technological edge – on catalytic converters – but also provides it with a new way of selling more expensive cars – which is by making catalytic converters, and the tax relief that goes with them, available only for models with many other extras. Moreover, since diesel engines get the same tax break, the European regulation also favors those German producers who are leaders in diesel technology, especially Daimler-Benz and VW.[16]

The automobile, and the 'automotive system' as a whole, is one of the favorite targets of the 'green', post-industrial left. But it is also a favorite toy of people in the mainstream of German society, and these are still the vast majority. In the war of faith between its opponents and supporters – which is fought with the usual German rudeness and *Gründlichkeit* – the latter have clearly prevailed, and the automobile industry has weathered the storm undamaged. Compared to the chemical and the nuclear energy industries, its problems with the 'new politics' are minor – although the industry still has to learn to respond to political intervention by other means than predictions of impending doom and decline which have too often been disproved to be believable. The cultural challenge to the habits of the automotive society has been successfully met by technical improvements – higher fuel economy, more effective safety features and better pollution control – which have, if anything, further reinforced those habits. As a side effect, technical progress in response to domestic political threats has increased the industry's international competitiveness.[17]

Notes

* Part of the research for this chapter was done in collaboration with Andreas Hoff. Winnetou Sosa provided competent research assistance. This chapter was first published in 1986. See Preface.

1 A famous AUDI advertisement on British television ends with an off-screen voice saying: '*Vorsprung durch Technik*, as they say in Germany, France, Italy, Spain, etc. etc.' The German words are not translated.

2 In 1985, BL built 465,100 and Daimler-Benz 537,910 passenger cars.

3 Competition among the German manufacturers has even increased in recent years as a result of the restructuring process. For example, just as Daimler-Benz moved into the traditional BMW market by developing the 190, BMW now challenges Daimler-Benz with its 7 series. Moreover, AUDI – and thus VW – today operates in a market segment where it competes with both Daimler-Benz and BMW.

4 AUDI, now merged with NSU, has up to the present day resisted its full integration into Volkswagen and maintains a degree of independence which is only grudgingly granted by central VW management.

5 In 1985, the supervisory boards of the German auto manufacturers included representatives of the following banks: VW: Deutsche Bank, Dresdner Bank; AUDI: Bayerische Vereinsbank, Commerzbank; Daimler-Benz: Deutsche Bank, Commerzbank; Ford: Commerzbank; BMW: Dresdner Bank; Porsche: Landesgirokasse, Landessparkasse.

6 It seems that in the late 1970s even more components were produced in Germany. Our calculations yield a domestic sourcing ratio of 72.7 percent for 1979. However, statistics are poor on this subject, and further inquiry is needed.

7 On *Handwerk* see Chapter 4 in this volume.

8 For more detail on automobile industrial relations in West Germany, see Streeck (1984a).

9 However, there is no wage drift at VW since wages are determined by company agreement.

10 Exchange rates obviously play an important part in such calculations. Applying the DM–Dollar rate of February 1987, German labor costs come out as equivalent to 103 percent of US labor costs. Under the exchange rates of 1980, German labor costs were as high as 186 percent of Japanese labor costs in that year.

11 For a detailed account of co-determination see Chapter 5, this volume.

12 Grants and tax concessions per employee in the automobile industry amounted to DM 480 in 1981, as compared to DM 37,840 in the railways, DM 23,830 in coalmining, and DM 14,660 in the aerospace industry, the three most favored sectors. The machine tools industry received DM 1,190. A comparable amount to automobiles was received by the textile and clothing industry which was supported at a level of DM 400 per employee (Webber, 1986).

13 Among the large firms that were given financial support for research and development projects from the Federal Ministry of Research and Technology between 1972 and 1982, VW ranks 16th and Daimler-Benz 18th. The two firms

received 1.0 and 0.9 percent, respectively, of the Ministry's total payments. The three largest recipients alone (Siemens, Brown Boveri & Cie and MBB) accounted for 56.1 percent of total grants (Webber, 1986).

14 The following discussion is limited to problems that beset the automobile industry specifically. There are other challenges by the 'new politics' which affect industry as a whole, and in fact most large organizations and institutions in West Germany. For example, in a recent wave of renewed interest in the Nazi past, both Daimler-Benz and VW were confronted with questions and charges relating to their employment of forced labor and KZ inmates during the war. Among other things, it turned out that Ferdinand Porsche, the designer of the original Volkswagen Beetle, seems to have been much more closely involved in the barbaric use of prison labor at VW than had for long been believed. Large German firms, in the automobile industry and beyond, are only slowly getting used to the fact that whoever scratches on the surface of decades of postwar West German accomplishment, is likely to find something of this kind, and that such scratching will continue especially if attempts are made to prevent it. Both Volkswagen and Daimler have made first moves to open their archives to independent historians; but it is certain that many more such steps will be demanded of them.

15 The number of people killed in road accidents has steadily declined in recent years, from 14,614 in 1974 to 8,400 in 1985. There were 669 deaths in 1985 (8.0 percent) resulting from accidents on *Autobahnen*. A total of 69 percent of all registered traffic accidents occurred in inner cities; only 4.4 percent happened on *Autobahnen* (*Statistisches Jahrbuch der Bundesrepublik Deutschland*). While the *Autobahn* network in Germany takes about 27 percent of total traffic volume (France 15, UK 12 percent), *Autobahn* traffic accounts for only 5.2 percent of all casualties (France 2.5, UK 2.2 percent; European Conference of Ministers of Transport 1987, 42). Using for comparison the three indicators of deaths per million population, per million cars and per million motor vehicles, Austria, Belgium, Switzerland and France in 1984 led Germany on all three; Spain and Ireland ranked higher on two; and Denmark and the United States ranked higher on one. Fewer deaths on all three dimensions were recorded in Finland, Italy, Norway, the Netherlands, Sweden and the United Kingdom (European Conference of Ministers of Transport, 1987: 28). Countries ranking low on all three indicators seem to be those with little or no transit traffic. Unfortunately, there are no cross-nationally comparable data on traffic performance, making it impossible to relate accidents, casualties and deaths to the total volume of vehicle or passenger kilometers.

16 Rising concern about the environment affects the automobile industry in other ways as well, but this experience it shares with all of manufacturing industry. For example, in 1987 the Federal Constitutional Court struck down plans by Daimler-Benz to build a new, large test track in a rural area in Baden-Württemberg. Opposition to the track had been widespread, and local farmers successfully resisted expropriation of their land by the State Government on behalf of the company.

17 Unless otherwise indicated, the quantitative data in this chapter have been drawn from the following sources: VDA, *Tatsachen und Zahlen aus der Kraftver-kehrswirtschaft*, consecutive editions; VDA, *Das Auto International in Zahlen*, consecutive editions; telephone communications from staff members of the VDA and of Daimler-Benz and Porsche; Automobil-Datenbank des WZB (Lutz Atzert); Karl H. Pitz, no date: Beschäftigungsrisiken in der Autoindustrie: Nationale und internationale Lösungsansätze aus gewerkschaftlicher Sicht, Frankfurt: typewritten manuscript; Business Reports of VW, AUDI, Daimler-Benz, Opel, Ford, BMW,

Porsche, consecutive editions; various reports in *Handelsblatt* and *Manager Magazin*; *Statistische Mitteilungen des Kraftfahrt-Bundesamtes*, consecutive editions; *Fachserie 4 des Statistischen Bundesamtes, Produzierendes Gewerbe*, Reihe 4.2.2., 1982; *Monatsberichte der Deutschen Bank*, various editions; *VDA Pressedienst*.

7

From National Corporatism to Transnational Pluralism: Organized Interests in the Single European Market
(with Philippe C. Schmitter)

Whatever the differences between the various versions of the theory, or 'pre-theory' (Haas, 1970), of European regional integration, organized interest groups were always assigned a prominent place.[1] Especially in the 'neo-functionalist' image of 'Europe's would-be polity' (Lindberg and Scheingold, 1970) and of the way towards it, supra-national interest group formation was expected to serve, in an important and indispensable sense, as a substitute for popular identification with the emerging new political community above and beyond the nation-state (on the following see in particular Haas, 1958: 318–89). Most observers and, in fact, participants in the integration process fully expected that the citizens of Europe would for a long time continue to adhere to traditional, national passions and identities. They knew that if the united Europe had to wait until its citizens began to feel as 'Europeans' – rather than as Frenchmen, Germans, Italians, etc. – it would not in any foreseeable future come about, and Europe as a political entity would in their lifetime never be more than a small bureaucracy in Brussels with very fragile support in national politics.

One reason why there nevertheless appeared to be hope was that things were believed to be different with the professional leaders of organized interest groups. Unlike the voters, they were seen as likely to orientate themselves, rationally and calculatedly, to where the action was – that is, under the presumed logic of the neo-functionalist spill-over process,[2] to 'Brussels'. Indeed, in attitude and outlook, interest group officials and European civil servants could easily appear as birds of the same feather: both appointed rather than elected, both experts and technocrats, both susceptible to a cosmopolitan orientation and lifestyle, both professionally interested in the smooth management of complex interdependencies, and likely to be distinctly disinterested in the traditional rituals and symbolisms of nationhood. Just as civil servants like Jean

Monnet had been persuading, cajoling, manipulating, the elected politicians and the administrative machineries of national states into emergent supra-nationalism, so the *Geschäftsführer* of business associations and trade unions were expected to enlighten their elected leaders that their interests had migrated to a new place and that the offices and decisions of their representatives had to follow suit.

In fact, the relationship between European bureaucrats and the full-time managers of collective interests that was envisaged by integration theory was even more intimate. As pointed out, interest groups were believed to have a much better, much sharper, much more intense perception of the effects of spill-over on the situs and locus of decisions than the average voter, and as a result were expected to make their appearance at the supra-national level earlier than their less insightful fellow-citizens. But more importantly perhaps, the move of organized interests onto the European scene was expected to be further accelerated by European bureaucrats who, in their search for a constituency, would be more than willing to promote interest organization on a scale coterminous with their supra-national jurisdiction. Indeed, in the perception of early integration theory, especially its neo-functionalist version, there was hardly anything in which 'Brussels' could be more interested than in cultivating an environment, around the Commission in particular, of powerful interest organizations negotiating with Community officials and each other – as an ersatz for the elusive pan-European citizen humming a pan-European supra-national anthem when facing the Berlaymont office building.

Attracting a growing number of supra-national lobbyists into the Community's decision-making process was seen as offering important pay-offs especially for the Commission. Cooperation with organized interests would not only provide civil servants with an indispensable input of detailed factual information in complex decisions; it also and above all was to bring about the socialization of powerful forces in European civil society into a world view compatible with that of European bureaucrats and with the requirements of continued spill-over. Having been drawn into the ambit of the Commission, a multitude of political players would learn from experience that management from the top, from the center, from Brussels, was more efficient and effective than national policy-making. When returning to their national capitals, they – it was hoped and in fact predicted – would again become a lobby: this time not of their interest group vis-a-vis Brussels, but of Brussels vis-a-vis their national leaders, including their governments. By fostering a transnational system of organized interest representation, the

Community, and the Commission in particular, would thus contribute to its own growth as a policy arena and executive body, and lift itself out of the parochial entanglements of national politics and intergovernmental non-decision-making into a safely anchored new world of supra-national political management.

In many ways, the status provided for organized interests in the future European polity bore strong resemblance to a model of interest politics that some time later came to be known to students of politics as 'neo-corporatism'. As in the latter, the integrated European polity was to be one that was primarily concerned with governing a 'mixed economy', according to rules of technical and professional expertise whose prudent application was to help avoid social conflict and disruption. There also was to be a shift away from the territorial-electoral-parliamentary realm of politics, towards powerful mechanisms of functional representation of producer groups, and there was an emphasis on close linkage between state and society through privileged participation of organized interests in policy, and through mutually supportive organizational arrangements between the machineries of government on the one hand and of large, centralized interest organizations on the other. Above all, there was the idea of the future European political economy being kept together by a combination of technocratic professionalism, shared between all major players regardless of divergent, specific interests, and a web of dense and durable, bi-, tri- and multilateral bargaining relationships, involving public and private bodies alike, that was seen as contributing to order, if not through shared values and interests, then through common strategic imperatives of self-restraint and compromise reflecting and respecting the complexity of a modern society and economy.

But while motivated speculation about the politics of a unified Europe prepared the ground for the (re-) discovery of (neo-) corporatism as a concept (see Schmitter, 1974, 1988a, 1989), it was not at the European level that modern corporatism as a reality was finally found. When in the early 1970s students of European integration, in despair over their subject, searching for new themes (Haas, 1976), turned their energies to comparative politics, they recognized at the level of European nation-states something that looked conspicuously like what integration theory had long had in mind for Europe as whole. At the time, European nation-states were almost universally turning to centralized bargaining between firmly institutionalized class and sectoral interest groups – facilitated, moderated and supplemented by the government – as a reaction, first, to the turmoil of 1968 and 1969, and as a recourse, second, against the dislocations of the economic crises after 1973, and especially the threat of inflation in societies with a strong labor movement whose governments were afraid of reneging on the postwar Keynesian welfare state commitment to politically guaranteed full employment. In turning to 'neo-corporatist concertation', as it came to be called, national governments appeared to be doing precisely what integration theorists had been counseling the European Community and the European Commission: in order to integrate their political systems, they were relying more and more on deals with interest groups, as distinct from electoral and parliamentary participation; they were sometimes bypassing, and generally downgrading, their parliaments as places of political decision-making; they attempted to govern through compromises with and between organized interests; and they were generating obligations of special interests to the collective good, not through legislation passed by parliamentary majority, but through collective bargaining in all possible forms and manners (Lehmbruch, 1979a).

The Failure of Euro-corporatism

Not that there was nothing like that at all at the European level. But compared to the paradigmatic national political systems of the time, interest representation around and within the Community was always much more 'pluralist' than corporatist: more organizationally fragmented; less hierarchically integrated; more internally competitive; and with a lot less control vested in peak associations over their affiliates, or in associations over their members. Union and business association officials who were transferred to Brussels in the 1970s more often than not perceived this as a falling from grace at home and as an – usually well-paid – elimination from the excitement of domestic power games and succession struggles – rather than as accession to the new center of political power. By the mid-1970s at the latest it had become clear that, belying the predictions of integration theory, the Brussels system of functional representation had failed to develop into a corporatist engine of supra-nationalism.

The history of organized supra-national interests in Europe is short. Prior to the formation of the European Economic Community (EEC) in 1958, European class, sectoral and professional interest groups had only vague memories of collective action across national lines, and very little of it had been successful. Around the turn of the century, industry cartels among business firms, 'proletarian internationalism' between trade unions, and some cooperative ventures involving professional groups emerged, but the First World War seems to have put an end to most of this activity. After

1945, the insistence of the United States under the Marshall Plan that European countries act in concert on matters of postwar reconstruction laid a new foundation. But there is little evidence, until the stimulus of the Treaty of Rome, that national interest associations were prepared to establish permanent European-level organizations.[3]

Immediately after 1958, European peak associations began to form, especially for the representation of broadly encompassing industrial, commercial and agricultural business interests: UNICE for industry (1958); COPA for agriculture (1958); a permanent conference for chambers of commerce (1958); UNACEE for craft industries (1958); COGECA for agricultural cooperatives (1959); BFEC for banking (1960); GCECEE for savings banks (1963). Workers and consumers took much longer to build their peak associations: both the ETUC and BEUC were established only in 1973. SEPLIS, representing the liberal, intellectual and social professions, was created in 1975. By then, roughly the time of the first enlargement to include Great Britain, Ireland and Denmark, all of the major functional groups were present. Affiliated to their broadly encompassing European peak organizations were exclusively national associations, most of which continued to command far greater resources than their nominally superior *Spitzenverband*, and all of which reserved the right to act on their own on matters of particular importance to them. For example, demonstrating their continued autonomy, the national associations of industrialists for each member state opened their own offices in Brussels. None of the European peak associations of this first wave had individuals or firms as direct members.[4]

Meanwhile, a myriad of more specialized, sectoral associations were also being formed. Some of these did have direct membership, but then they were rarely affiliated (and never subordinated) to the European peak associations. By 1985, the number of interest associations registered in Brussels had reached 654, according to a census carried out by the Commission (Repertoire des Organisations Professionelles, various editions). Associations of business interests vastly outnumbered those of labor, with 20 unions and 79 professional associations facing 332 associations from industry, 139 from commerce, 6 representing craft and artisanal interests, and 5 associations of small and medium-sized enterprises. This mirrors a similar situation at the national level where business interests also prefer to work through a greater number and variety of specialized intermediaries than workers (Chapter 3, this volume).

The Commission seems to have deliberately encouraged the formation of these associations[5] and very quickly established a procedure for recognizing their special European status. This implied privileged access to its deliberations (Lindberg and Scheingold, 1970: 173; Sargent, 1985: 236–7), even if recognition was typically not limited to only one organization per category. Each of the Commission's Directorates-General soon surrounded itself with a vast number of standing, advisory and management committees, most of which were based on functional rather than territorial principles of representation.[6] Apparently, in the early stages, the Commission attempted to confine lobbying to certified European associations, but this was subsequently relaxed to permit an increasing volume of direct contacts with national interest representatives (Caporoso, 1974: 23–52).

Advisory committees and expert groups mushroomed in subsequent years. The Commission itself has never employed very many officials,[7] and has depended heavily on consultation with interest representatives, national government employees and experts for drafting its directives and monitoring compliance with them. By the time the Single European Act was signed in 1985, the number of consultative bodies had grown to about 700, and it has almost doubled since, to 1,336 in 1988 (Grote, 1989). Interest representatives are well-remunerated for attending meetings in Brussels, and indeed these payments might be interpreted as a subsidy for the development of an 'appropriately structured' system of interest intermediation related and obligated to the European Community.

The corporatist capstone of the emerging system of Europe-wide functional representation might have been the Economic and Social Committee (ESC). This body was inserted in the Treaty of Rome and persists to the present day. Its 189 members (as of 1985) represent three 'grand categories' of interest: employers, workers and 'others', that is, agriculture, transport, shopkeepers, artisans, consumers, environmental groups, etc. Committee members do not, however, represent European interest associations; rather, they are nominated as individuals by member governments and appointed by the Council of Ministers (that is, *not* the supranational Commission) to four-year terms. While the ESC likes to think of itself as the 'other European Assembly' – a sort of functional shadow to the territorially based European Parliament – there is general agreement that it has, in fact, accomplished very little (Lodge and Herman, 1990; Nugent, 1989).[8] In particular, it was never able to serve as a privileged access point for organized interests to European-level decision-making, and therefore failed completely in providing focus and structure to the growing pluralist system of European interest associations. It also proved entirely unsuitable to accommodate labor's ritual demands for a 'Social

Europe' and prevent the 'common market' from remaining exactly that: a customs union committed to liberalism and free trade.[9]

For a few years after 1968, this seemed to be about to change. With the accession to power of social-democratic parties in major member countries, and with national political elites still suffering from the shocks of their respective *autunni caldi*, the first Paris summit of the heads of states and governments inaugurated an ambitious program to extend the domain of the European Community to a wide range of social policies. Subsequently, for a short, intensive period between the early and the late 1970s, it seemed that labor was about to capture the same or similar substantive concessions and institutional privileges at the European level as it was picking up simultaneously in individual countries.[10] If at all, it was then that labor leaders, in the way predicted by early integration theorists like Ernst Haas, began to take 'Europe' seriously as a political arena in which to launch strategic initiatives.[11] Characteristically, at that point the ESC was set aside as too cumbersome and insufficiently *paritaire* to bear the burden of leading the Community into the era of 'social partnership'. Instead, the Ministers of Social Affairs and, later, of Economic and Financial Affairs decided to convoke a series of 'Tripartite Conferences' bringing together the European peak associations and national representatives of capital and labor with officials of national governments and the Commission. These met six times until 1978 – often in highly publicized settings – to discuss a wide range of macro-economic and social policies. Their agenda paralleled that of the national concertation efforts of the same period: full employment, inflation, wage restraint, fiscal policy, worker training, productivity measures. A Standing Committee on Employment with tripartite representation was established, and there was even a plan for creating a set of sectoral councils wherein capital, labor and state officials were expected to come up with proposals for governing the steel, shipbuilding, textiles, aerospace and telecommunications industries.

All this effort came to naught in 1978 when the strongest proponent of Euro-corporatism, the European Trade Union Confederation (ETUC), withdrew its support under complaints about lack of progress, and was also confronted with rising dissent within its ranks. Especially after the defeat in the councils of Europe of the draft European company statute that was in essence to expand co-determination from Germany to companies incorporated in Community law, and later with the slow and painful demise of the draft directive on consultation and information in multi-national enterprises (the so-called 'Vredeling Directive'), there was not much left that would have justified the enormous effort and political capital labor had invested in the building of a corporatist 'Social Dimension' for the Community.[12] By the early 1980s, all that remained of Euro-corporatism was the Standing Committee on Employment and a few specialized working groups that continued to recycle the by-now tattered idea of concertation.

Why was it that a centralized pattern of interest politics did not emerge at the European level when it was so common in national polities? Rather than in neo-functionalist terms, the answer to the puzzle of the stagnant record of European interest politics has to be given in a language that recognizes the significance of conflict and power and does not submerge politics in the technicalities of managing sectoral spill-overs. In particular, our argument emphasizes the importance for the growth of a centralized, publicly institutionalized interest politics of highly developed organizational and political capacities of *labor* during a polity's formative period – adding to whatever incentives *capital* may have on its own to get organized, as well as contributing to the emergence of an active, interventionist, non-liberal *state* which may then, in turn, institutionalize labor as well as capital as principal participants in a centralized structure of political bargaining. That latter relation, we believe, is in itself crucial for the (further) growth of labor's political capacity, as is the availability of partners for mutually centralizing cross-class alliances on the side of capital. In a nutshell, our point is that in the uniting supra-national Europe, it was not only the case that labor was and continues to be *under-organized*, but there also was never a real possibility of a mutually organizing *interaction effect*, a *Wechselwirkung*, between labor and the two other major players in the political economy, capital and the state.

As to labor itself, there is no doubt that as a European actor labor is afflicted by *specific disabilities* that were not usually present at the national level and that do not in the same way affect business. Business, for example, finds it easier than labor to overcome the problems posed by different national languages (at least nine in the Europe of the Twelve). It also is much less hampered by ideological divisions between different political orientations such as, most prominently on the labor side, between communists and social democracts. More importantly, however, the low organizational capacities of labor at the European Community level also reflect the wide regional disparities in Europe, and the resulting divisions of interest between national labor movements (Alexander, 1989; Campbell, 1989; Visser, 1989). The vast divergence in union concerns and strategies to which this gives rise are reflected, among other things, in the traditionally low significance for their affiliates of European sectoral and intersectoral union confederations. While for unions from advanced economies a joint European strategy is unlikely to offer improvements over what they have already gained on their own, to unions from weaker countries common demands tend to appear unrealistically ambitious and far remote from their everyday practical concerns. Moreover, to unions in rich countries common labor standards, even if they are intended to do no more than set a floor, may appear to threaten their own, higher standards. Still and at the same time, they may *exceed* the marginal productivity of the workforces of less wealthy countries, thereby undermining their ability to take advantage of increased capital mobility and attract foreign investment (Padoa-Schioppa, 1988). While it is *also* true that common standards may help unions in weaker economies to make more progress than they otherwise would, and while they may make it easier for more affluent working classes to defend their employment against capital migration, bringing the different interests together and finding a compromise acceptable for both sides is far from simple. Indeed, uniting national union movements behind European programs and policies always required great political effort and skill. Even where these were successfully applied, the joint platforms that were in the end adopted often had to be left deliberately vague and rarely were more than symbolic in character (Cressey, 1989).[13]

As a consequence of fundamental national differences, European union officials always had to face tendencies among their constituents either to seek national solutions for their problems and ignore the supra-national level altogether, or to pursue their 'European' interests through intergovernmental channels, using their access to home governments to work either through the national embassy in Brussels lobbying the Commission or, more likely, through the Council of Ministers (for a case study, see Teague, 1989a). Frequently such initiatives were coordinated with the respective national peak associations of employers, resulting in trilateral national coalitions pursuing joint objectives in competition with other countries and thereby effectively cutting out, or starving off, the European system of functional representation.

On the other hand, labor fragmentation had originally been a condition in many countries whose labor movements later proved able to propel themselves into a trajectory of growing unification and centralization. Indeed we believe that the specific disabilities of European labor are often over-rated in comparison to two other factors *that would have frustrated progress towards comprehensive organization of labor and towards corporatist modes of interest intermediation and concertation even in the best of circumstances.*

First, there is the complete absence, on the side of *business*, of significant factions with an active interest in centralized negotiations with labor. While European capital is strongly represented in Brussels by lobbyists for individual firms, as well as through sectoral and subsectoral trade associations, the interests that these defend are primarily those of enterprises and industries demanding protection and/or (de-) regulation of their *product markets*. Although sometimes the same channels are also used to address social policy and labor market concerns – for example in the 1970s, to defeat the European Community directives on workforce participation and consultation – this is not their principal purpose. In fact, many of the *producer interests* firms and trade associations pursue in Brussels are by and large, and more or less tacitly, shared by their workforces, with business interests often functioning in effect as vertical associations representing important firm-specific or sectoral interests of labor as well as of capital.[14]

By comparison, the interests of firms *as employers* are typically not directed at extracting favorable policies from Community bodies. European business has from the beginning refused to contribute to a transfer of social policy matters from the national arenas to (tripartite political bargaining in) Brussels. While firms and their associations are always available to European officials for formal and informal consultations, binding decisions are opposed, usually with reference to the widely different conditions in member states and the economic need for 'flexibility'. It is important to note in this context that getting its will and keeping supra-nationalism and tripartism from growing did not require major organizational efforts from business. To protect the Brussels body politic from contagion by the neo-corporatist disease that befell European nation-states in the 1970s, all business had to do was refuse its European peak associations the competence to enter into binding obligations on behalf of their national constituents. A trilateral polity can exist and grow only if all three sides are sufficiently centralized to take part in it. By not delegating authority upwards to the European level, employers were and still are able to confine institutions like the Social Dialogue to a strictly non-binding, consultative status.[15] The growing frustration of European unions in the late 1970s with the minuscule results of long and complicated discussions in Brussels, and increasingly with the European Community as such, was in large part due to the *political strength business was able to draw from its organizational weakness.*[16]

Nowhere else is the neo-functionalist image of interest groups centralizing their organizations and activities at European level and thereby pushing regional integration forward as far from reality as in the case of European business associations. The implicit assumption in much of neo-functionalist writing is that in a set of interdependent economies a centralized pursuit of group interests is always and unproblematically the superior alternative to traditional, national or subnational strategies. The evidence shows, however, that there may indeed be policy arenas, such as social policy and industrial relations, where *different levels of regulation favor different social interests*, and where groups that are favored by decentralized regulation or by the unfettered operation of 'market forces' find it easy to *prevent centralization of regulatory capacity simply by refusing to build the organizations necessary for them to be able to make binding commitments at the central level*. The result is growing interdependence between national economies due to progressing market integration without proportionate growth of regulatory institutions – with the consequence of *integration and deregulation becoming one and the same*.

The second factor is the presence inside the European Community's quasi-state, or *non-state*, of a strong *centrifugal center*, in the form of the Council of Ministers, that stopped in its tracks any attempt by supra-national bodies, especially the Commission and the Parliament, to cultivate a strong constituency of organized interests that would in turn have enhanced the status of supra-national Community institutions as an incipient sovereign government. No comparable barrier to central state formation and state growth has ever been present in a traditional nation-state. It should be noted that 'intergovernmentalism', as it came to be called, had the same discouraging impact on the organization of business as it had on labor, with opposite consequences for the realization of the respective interests. This is because under the unanimity principle of decision-making, which is the hallmark of intergovernmentalism, a European interest group that wants to *prevent* a specific decision needs just one national government willing to veto that decision in the Council, frustrating even the most sophisticated lobbying efforts vis-a-vis the Commission. Where such a veto is not cast on ideological or interest-political grounds, a class like business, whose interest was and is essentially not in *shaping* but in *preventing* a centralized European social policy, could always hope to find allies in national governments concerned about their *sovereignty*.[17] Intergovernmentalism thus made both encompassing organization and centralized negotiations with labor largely dispensable for European business, whose social policy interests, under the specific configuration of markets, national states and supra-national institutions that is the European Community, tend to be realized, as it were, by default.

Much of the corporatist debate of the 1970s was on the question of whether a strong state is a precondition for strong associations, or whether strong associations can develop without, and may even substitute for, a strong state. Based on national observations and cross-national comparison, what seemed to emerge as a tentative consensus assigned a prominent place to the indispensable contribution of public power even in cases of 'societal corporatism' (Cawson, 1985; Grant, 1985). The European Community has never been permitted to develop the organizational design capacities necessary to reshape powerful interest organizations rooted in civil society. Whatever capacity it may have in this respect is vastly inferior to that of the Community's nation-states, from which it is derived in the first place. Moreover, the policy-making process in the Community is too fragmented and dispersed to place a high premium on interest organizational centralization at the European level. In the history of the Community up to the present time, intergovernmentalism and the veto powers of individual nations have always been strong enough to preempt or modify centrally made decisions. Organized interests thus have had no other choice, even if they have been otherwise inclined, than to maintain a strong national base and to cultivate established national channels of influence. This, as has been pointed out, holds in particular for groups and in policy arenas *where the interest is more in non-decisions than in decisions.* As long as the Community – that is, its non-intergovernmental institutions such as the Parliament and the Commission – cannot autonomously determine the range of policy issues that come under its jurisdiction, its ability to influence the structure of organized group interests will remain low indeed.

Corporatism, the Nation-state, and the Deregulation of European Economies

There are, however, more, and equally important and vexing, relationships between corporatism, nationalism, supra-nationalism and the distribution of power in the political economy. The heyday of corporatism in the 1970s was a period of distinctly *national* responses to the catastrophic de-institutionalization of the capitalist world economy that started in the late 1960s, and the ensuing, rapidly rising domestic and international disorder. Apart from the United States, where the absence of a European-style resurgence of labor militancy in 1968 (see the book by Crouch and Pizzorno, 1978) had set the stage for a strategy of economic recovery through de-unionization and deregulation, governments almost everywhere experimented with centrally negotiated 'social contracts' of all sorts, as a home-made replacement, or functional equivalent, for the now defunct set of international institutions that had in the past provided at least some form of stability for and among competing capitalist nations – by, for example, imposing and enforcing external 'balance of payments constraints' that helped national governments keep domestic 'discipline'. To an important degree, corporatist concertation in the 1970s must be understood as a sometimes desperate turn to domestic political and institutional resources in a search for solutions to what really were international problems – a turn that reflected the almost complete absence on the eve of the crisis, in spite of three decades of international institution-building, of technically viable and politically legitimate mechanisms of international cooperation (McCracken et al., 1977).

Member states of the European Community also and in particular had recourse to corporatism, or attempted corporatism, in the early 1970s. Indeed if the Community was mentioned in Europe, at all during that period, it was to point out how useless it had proven as an instrument for tasks like the restoration of a stable monetary environment; for working out a common energy policy with the United States and, perhaps, OPEC; or for fighting inflation and unemployment. The 'dark age' of the European Community was above all a time when European national elites seemed to believe as a matter of course that the supra-national European institutions they had set up in the 1950s and 1960s, embedded in a relatively stable world order, could not serve as a suitable tool for the restoration of that order, and that therefore everybody had to find their own, national solutions.[18]

National corporatism, we have maintained, was adopted as an alternative to an international response, including a European one. At the same time, the use of domestic concertation on a large scale was bound to make international concertation even more difficult, and thus contributed further to bringing the process of European integration, including the building of a European-level system of interest politics, to a halt. This was not only because emerging national corporatisms diverted the attention of policy-makers and association officials away from 'Brussels' and back to national capitals, or because attempts at international cooperation would have added further complexity to the domestic bargaining process, thus reducing elites' degrees of freedom and making compromise more difficult. It was also, and more importantly, because different countries turned out to be differently well equipped institutionally for corporatist concertation. While corporatism worked in some places, it dismally failed in others, and in yet others it worked for a while but created accumulated problems that later came home to roost. The economic performance of different capitalist economies thus became more divergent than ever in the 1970s, and as the history of European integration testifies, divergent performance is all but conducive to countries giving up a share of their sovereignty – the weak ones being afraid of becoming subservient to the strong ones, and the strong ones seeing no need and being afraid of diluting their national success.

Second, it almost follows from the above that the resurgence of European integration, as signified by the Single European Act and the Internal Market project, was more than just incidentally related to the demise of national corporatisms in the early 1980s. If anything, it had been the rapid decline of their 'effective sovereignty' (Hoffmann, 1989) that had undermined the capacity of national states in the developed capitalist world to sustain the kind of social contracts that they had entered into in response to the crisis. The neo-corporatist exercises of the 1970s had in large part been attempts to shore up the systems of economic and social policy-making that had been put in place under the postwar settlement (Gourevitch, 1986), and prolong their life beyond that of the international environment in which they had originally been embedded. Ultimately, it turned out, this was not possible. The changes in the international position of the United States that had exhausted its capacity to act as a benevolent hegemon had gradually given rise in the 1970s to a domestic move away from the New Deal compromise to a political economy that sought competitiveness through deregulation and de-unionization and abandoned the social-democratic principle that wages and social conditions were to be taken out of competition. After the final defeat of the Labor Law Reform Act in 1978, the Federal Reserve could feel free to respond to the second oil crisis with a dramatic increase in interest rates, ending inflation at the price of de-industrialization and causing a further, probably irreversible decline in union organization. In the early 1980s, with effectively deregulated, worldwide integrated capital markets, the destruction of American trade unions paid off handsomely in that it gave the United States the 'flexible' markets and the 'confidence' of financial investors required to underwrite an expansionist fiscal policy that has been ironically characterized as 'Keynesianism in one country'.

From the perspective of other capitalist countries, that term would appear to have carried a particularly ominous connotation. As the French socialist government after 1981 was soon to find out under the watchful eyes of other political elites, the dynamics of the international political economy after the second oil shock were governed by the old Roman imperial maxim, *quod licet Jovi non licet bovi*. Keynesianism had ceased to be universally available; it had become limited not just to one, but to *only* one, country. Being so much larger than everybody else and, as a consequence, so much less internationalized; having broken its unions; being still in control of the de facto world currency while no longer accepting the responsibilities of world banker; and for all these and other reasons being able to attract and maintain the confidence of what is euphemistically called 'the financial markets', in spite of gigantic and growing deficits in its budget and foreign trade – the United States could effectively and successfully apply fiscal stimulus, whereas the others could do so only at the expense of their capital running away and holders of financial assets dropping their currencies at their doorsteps.

The important point here is that some sort of effective Keynesian-expansionist capacity seems indispensable for the kind of corporatist concertation and social contract bargaining that was to stabilize non-American capitalisms in the 1970s. As much as these systems may otherwise have differed, under the rules of corporatist bargaining a state that cannot with any reasonable prospect of success promise to apply its fiscal and monetary policy tools to alleviate unemployment cannot possibly hope to gain concessions from unions or to influence settlements between unions and employers by, for example, offering to improve the terms of the bargain through a corresponding economic policy (Regini, 1986). To put the use of its sovereignty up for negotiation, a state needs to have sovereignty in the first place. As the effective sovereignty and, subsequently, the Keynesian capacity of European nation-states faded, so did corporatism – and with it the social-democratic project of politically guaranteed full employment.

Of course, not all of the causes for the demise of sovereignty and, therefore, national corporatism originated in the de-institutionalization of the international economy or in the internal politics of the United States and the deflationary bias it introduced in the world capitalist system. A more general explanation lies in the growing interpenetration of capitalist economies which has now increased the external contribution to a typical West European country's national accounts to a level where it can no longer be treated as a mere addition to a primarily domestic economy. As the French have learned, and everybody else learned from the French, interdependence does not make it impossible to create jobs by Keynesian stimulus; but unless a country has the size, the currency and the social system of the United States, chances are that many of those jobs will emerge outside the territory whose government has increased the national debt to create them. Given the absence of international institutions to manage such interdependence, governments in the early 1980s felt hard pressed, or saw a golden opportunity, depending on their political complexion, to withdraw the political full employment promise of the postwar period and yield control over the restoration of prosperity and employment in their internationalized national economies to 'the market', including a deregulated labor market – thereby in effect accepting the increasingly demanding conditions placed by capital holders on industrial investment and conceding what Burnham once called 'domestic sovereignty' to what is referred to in the jargon of international capitalism as 'market forces'.

It is true that the decay of national corporatisms in the late 1970s and in the 1980s was also rooted in domestic developments, like qualitative changes in social structures, in the economy and in domestic political systems that had, imperceptibly at first, eaten away at corporatism's structural and perhaps cultural foundations. While this is not the place to review these trends in any detail, three will be briefly discussed, adding to the reasons why a restoration of neo-corporatism, at either national or supra-national level, has become unlikely now and in the future.

(1) *Increasing differentiation of social structures and collective interests in advanced capitalist societies.* Neo-corporatism assumed an underlying social structure that could be plausibly conceived as polarized in two large producer classes, 'capital' and 'labor'. With hindsight, that assumption appears to have been already highly counterfactual when Western European countries in the late 1960s were increasingly moving towards neo-corporatist forms of governance. However, for a while the *corporatist working hypothesis of a bipolar organization of societal cleavages and identities*, although from the beginning no more than a *heroic simplification* of a much more complex reality, could be kept alive with the help of the powerful institutional reinforcements that both business and labor as organized actors had received from their beleaguered governments. Underneath the organizational and institutional structures, however, social change continued and perhaps even accelerated. In addition to strengthening the institutional position of labor movements, 1968 was also the birthdate of a new, highly educated and politically outspoken *middle class* that increasingly found its specific concerns insufficiently represented in the post-1968, class-political institutional set-up. Subsequently during the 1970s and 1980s the substantive content of interest conflicts and the focus of policy attention shifted away from class-based lines of cleavage towards a panoply of discrete issues focusing on consumer protection, quality of life, gender, environmental, ethical and other problems, each

with their respective movements. As is well known, in most countries this weakened the capacity of social-democratic parties to govern or, alternatively, undermined the alliance between social democracy and the union movement. Neither was conducive to corporatist governance.

(2) *Market instability and volatility, and pressures on firms to increase the 'flexibility' of their product ranges, technologies and social organization.* New production technologies based on microelectronics and cutting across traditional job classifications and professional categories have created possibilities for flexible production in relatively small units. In one sense, these processes increased the need for active assent on the part of workers – and, therefore, the need for employers to bargain with them over the quality as well as the quantity of their contribution. But, in another sense, this is occurring in highly differentiated settings that are not easy to cover by a standard contract and difficult for intermediaries to control. Indeed both unions and employers' associations are today finding themselves increasingly shut out of an expanding range of workplace-specific deliberations and bargaining between their respective local constituents.

(3) *Changing roles and structures of interest associations.* In the new social and market environment, negotiations aimed at establishing standard national solutions for the regulation of the employment relationship appear of decreasing relevance, and at times may even be counterproductive, when what is demanded are policies tailored to improving the productivity and international competitiveness of specific sectors and individual enterprises. As a result, the role of intermediary institutions, especially trade unions and employers' associations, changed from the point of view of members and interlocutors, both of whom are searching for more differentiated mechanisms of representation. While decentralization may have taken very different courses in different countries, what it inevitably had in common was a weakening of the center – and it is there that corporatist bargains are traditionally struck.

Moreover, the shift of employment from traditional manufacturing to the services and, in some cases, to public employment in a number of countries changed the character of unions, in that unions from the public and private service sector became the largest units in national confederations. This seems to have weakened the organizational discipline that was traditionally maintained by unionized manual workers, especially from the metal-working sector (Crouch, 1988). These unions, whose industries were exposed to world market competition, have in the past typically been willing to observe wage restraint in exchange for political concessions. Their sectors have often been hard hit by de-industrialization, and such workers as remained after successful restructuring – if they joined unions at all – were employed in more scattered sites with much more individuated tasks. The very categories upon which macro-corporatist compromises were built thus became disaggregated and dispersed, and as a result centralized negotiations on wages, benefits and working conditions came under severe pressures. In some cases (for example, Sweden), the system only survived by shifting to a sectoral level.

Deregulation thus spread – from the United States to Britain, the country with the most open capital markets, and from there to the European Continent – meeting with declining resistance in changing domestic political economies. What it involved was a more or less forceful, and more or less successful, attack on the accumulated 'rigidities' that over three decades of 'mixed economy' had installed. In many cases, this included the dismantling, or at least the disregard, of structures of collective bargaining and domestic compromise that already under the late Keynesian regime had increasingly been perceived as obstructing industrial adjustment. Where dismantling got stuck, the proven inability of governments to deliver on employment, and their growing unwillingness to try, together with the insistence of unions on concessions and institutional monopolies that capital and governments felt they no longer needed to provide, created the atmosphere of 'Euro-pessimism' and 'Euro-malaise', not to mention 'Euro-sclerosis', that was so pervasive in Europe during the first half of the 1980s. The Internal Market project emerged at this time and in this context.

The Relaunching of the European Community: Cutting the Currency of National Power Resources

If one wants a shorthand explanation for the renewed momentum of European integration in the mid-1980s,[19] one would probably account for it as the result of an alignment between two broad interests: that of large European firms struggling to overcome perceived competitive disadvantages in relation to Japanese and US capital, and that of state elites seeking to restore at least part of the political sovereignty they had gradually lost at the national level as a result of growing international interdependence. Unlike in the crisis years of the 1970s, European large firms seem to have resolved at some point in the early 1980s that using their clout in national political arenas to get protection from foreign competition through subsidies, technical standards serving as non-tariff trade barriers, or privileged access to public procurement contracts had become counterproductive given the increased size of production runs and investments required for world market competitiveness. Instead of trying to benefit from the economic nationalism that had made European integration grind to a halt in the 1970s business throughout Europe seemed to have become willing in the 1980s to join forces with political elites which, under the impact of their economies' poor performance, and with worldwide policy coordination with the United States and Japan out of reach, found themselves under pressure to seek a *supra-national pooling of eroded national sovereignties over economic policy*, to recapture collective autonomy in relation to the United States and to begin to organize a competitive response to the Japanese challenge.

The main concession governments seem to have made in return for business giving up previous claims for national protection was that the future European political economy was to be significantly less subject to institutional regulation – *national or supra-national* – than it would have been in the harmonization-minded *and* social-democratic 1970s when employers found themselves forced to struggle against a Community Directive that would have made German-style co-determination obligatory for all large European firms. In the 1992 compromise the project of European integration became finally and formally bound up with a deregulation project. While 1992 is all about sovereignty, it is about sovereignty vis-a-vis Europe's external environment, *not* its domestic economy. Indeed, part and parcel of the pooling of sovereignties (Keohane and Hoffmann, 1989) under the Single European Act, and of the political deals that made it possible, is a redefinition of the relationship between the Community's 'domestic' institutions and 'the market', under which the latter stands to gain unprecedented freedom from intervention by the former. The mechanism to acomplish this, and a powerful reassurance for business that supra-national sovereignty will indeed be used exclusively for the *external reassertion of*, as opposed to *internal intervention in*, the European economy, is 'negative integration' through preemption of national regulatory regimes, without a simultaneous supra-national restoration of regulatory capacity. The adoption of 'mutual recognition' as a novel method of defining and governing the Internal Market – a method that for all practical purposes amounts to a subtle form of deregulation (Hoffmann, 1989; Streeck, forthcoming) – can only be fully explained in this light.[20]

Seen from a national perspective, 1992 amounts to a formal devaluation of vast political resources that have come to be organized in and around the nation-state. Declining effective sovereignty had long been chopping away at the value of investments in national political power that had been accumulated and cultivated for more than a century; this, after all, was why corporatism was eventually becoming untenable. The 1992 principle of mutual recognition may well be understood in analogy to the cut of a collapsed currency – an inevitable but nevertheless painful adjustment to reality, with significant distributional side-effects in that currency holders are more severely affected than owners of real estate or productive capital. In present-day European nation-states, with the successive layers of political, industrial and social rights that have been built into them in the domestic struggles of the nineteenth and twentieth centuries, it is clearly labor that is in the former and capital that is in the latter position. *While mutual recognition and the resulting inter-regime competition devalue nationally institutionalized power resources, they leave property rights untouched, or even increase their value.* As neo-corporatism has always been conditional on a measure of political strength of organized labor, the prospects for its restoration in the post-1992 European nation-states are therefore dim.

This is not to say that everything that has in the analyses of the 1970s and 1980s come to be associated with corporatist modes of governance will disappear in Europe. Pragmatic sectoral partnerships between state agencies and groups of business firms, oscillating, as it were, between agency capture and *Selbstverwaltung* (self government), are likely to continue, to the extent that they are comfortably embedded in national policy styles and as long as they do not run afoul of European Community competition law – which they well may. Especially if they have from the beginning been labor-exclusive 'private interest governments' as we have called them elsewhere (Streeck and Schmitter, 1985), they may remain viable for some time, due to the savings on transaction costs they entail and regardless of the weakening of their sponsors in national state and legal systems. Multi-employer collective bargaining arrangements between trade unions and employers' associations, where they already exist, may not disappear either – at least, again, for the time being. But corporatism as a national-level accord between encompassingly organized socio-economic classes and the state, by which an entire national economy is comprehensively governed, would seem to be a matter of the past.

Towards a New European Interest Politics

The character of the emerging European polity has puzzled writers on European integration from its beginnings. As it became clear that 'regional integration' was an exclusively European phenomenon – the number of cases being no higher than one – the question became irrepressible of what the 'dependent variable' was that integration theory expected to explain (Haas, 1975); towards what 'final state', if at all, the integration process was moving; and what 'the nature of the beast' was that students of European integration, like in the parable of the blind men and the elephant, were trying to grasp (Puchala, 1972).

Unlike in the early, 'motivated' theorizing (until de Gaulle rehabilitated realism, both with and without a capital R), today hardly anybody[21] expects that the supra-national European polity of the future will be a replication of the European nation-state of the past. Wherever else students of European politics may disagree, and they like to disagree a lot, as a minimum it now seems to be accepted that the political system of the post-1992 European Community will be fundamentally and by a quantum leap *more complex* than anything that has preceded it. For example, while Europe as a whole will undoubtedly exist as a unified political entity of some as yet undetermined sort, the *nation-states* that now constitute the European Community will not disappear in that entity but will coexist with it (Puchala, 1972). Nor will Europe be simply an institutionalized system of *international, or inter-governmental, relations*; yet at the same time such relations will continue to play an important part in Europe, alongside and in interaction with others (Keohane and Hoffmann, 1989). And similarly, Europe will have *supra-national institutions* contributing to the governance of what will be a domestic Western European polity; but these will have to share authority with national, as well as with a dense web of international and trans-national, institutions which, too, will be constitutive elements of the emerging political system of Western Europe (Schmitter, 1989).

Europe's future polity, that is to say, will be composed of traditional domestic relations *within countries*, traditional inter-national relations *between countries*, less traditional transnational relations between both individuals and organizations across national boundaries, and entirely non-traditional supra-national relations *between European-level public institutions*, on the one hand, and, on the other, a *European civil society* consisting of domestic, inter-national, and transnational forces and relations and including both nation-states and, in manifold national and cross-national combi-nations, their constituents. The possible dynamics of this unique, and uniquely complex, system of governance are as yet only poorly understood, and there is very little theory, if any at all, to guide such understanding. This applies not least to the literature on *state formation* and the role of *class conflict* in it. While there always were more and other actors involved in the shaping of state structures than socio-economic classes – for example, regional, ethnic, and cultural communities and interest groups – in the case of European integration classes, as well as other forces in civil society, have to compete for control over the newly emerging central level of governance with a qualitatively different set of players: a number of already existing, sovereign (or, better and increasingly, 'semi-sovereign') nation-states. One reason why the latter's continued presence inside the European polity makes a difference is that the international boundaries between them constitute powerful, additional lines of cross-cutting cleavage inside classes and interest groups that stand in the way of their fast and effective polity-wide organization. Moreover, unlike in the nineteenth century when the system of European nation-states was formed, social structures today appear too differentiated, and political problems too variegated, to be easily organizable along bipolar class lines – a condition that, while it is gradually yet fundamentally transforming the political make-up of established nation-states, can be expected to exert a much more powerful, formative influence on the only now emerging polity of the integrated European Community.

There is, furthermore, a growing suspicion that conventional models of the growth of the *modern European welfare state* may not be applicable to the European Community. For some time to come whatever will occupy the place of the supra-national Single European State governing the Single European Market, will likely resemble a *pre-New Deal liberal state*, with, in Marshall's (1964) terms, the following characteristics.

1   A high level of *civil rights* enabling citizens freely to engage in contractual relationships inside and across national borders, accompanied by well-protected *human rights* to equal treatment before the law, freedom of movement, etc. Here the European Court of Justice is of crucial importance, and also the Council of Europe, although it is not, of course, a European Community institution.

2   A low level of *political rights*, with the European Parliament continuing to play only a minor role in the system of European institutions. This holds in spite of the fact that the Parliament's direct election and its new powers under the Single European Act have vastly improved its status over what it was in the mid-1970s.

3   An even lower level of *social rights*, these being essentially limited to a set of European-wide health and safety standards.[22] Historically, intervention on health and safety matters repre-

sents the earliest stage in the history of the modern welfare state. Present efforts to attach a 'Social Dimension' to the Internal Market by starting with a set of generally binding health and safety standards are aimed at replicating the familiar national trajectory of welfare state development. But in the face of the retarded advancement of European-level political rights, there is little reason to expect such efforts to be particularly successful, given in addition:

4 An almost complete absence of a European system of *industrial citizenship* that would give workers and unions rights to representation in industry as a functional domain at the European level, separate from the territorial domain of electoral politics. The closest the European Community will come to being a source of industrial citizenship – that is, to creating and safeguarding European-wide institutions of industrial relations and collective bargaining – is in providing for some form of labor participation under a European company statute. But whatever this will in the end entail, it is likely to pale into insignificance when compared to some of the national systems of union rights that were part of the post-world war national settlements.

The emerging shape of the European supra-national non-state – or even 'post-Hobbesian' state (Schmitter, 1989) – does not bode well for a reappearance of neo-corporatism above the disorganizing nation-state. In the following, we will try to trace some of the implications of what we think we know about the future contours of the European polity, for the structure and function of organized interests at the two newly emerging, additional levels of policy-making and interest articulation in Europe: the subnational or regional, and the supra-national level. Together with the member states, regional and supra-national political entities share in the diffuse and fragmented sovereignty of the Community, blending into a highly interdependent but incompletely unified, loosely coupled and diverse institutional complex – the new type of state that is the European Community – that confronts an at least equally diverse civil society acting in what after 1992 will be an integrated market.

Interest Politics at Sub-national Level

At the core of the 1992 process is the abolition of national boundaries between the markets of the 12 member states of the European Community (Bieber et al., 1988; Calingaert, 1988). As a result, the 12 formerly national economies will turn into *regional subunits* of a larger economic entity – a *region* being defined as a *territorial society without sovereignty over its borders.* Also, the existing regional subunits of European nations, being no longer fenced in by common, national economic boundaries, will themselves become subunits in their own right of the larger, integrated European economy. This transformation of national into regional economies, and of subnational regions into subunits of a supranational economy, amounts to a *regionalization of Europe* as well as, at the same time, a *Europeanization of its regions.*

The potential importance of the regional level for the developing politics of Europe, is underlined by the rich literature on *industrial districts* (for example, Brusco, 1982; Sabel, 1989). Its common theme is that of a strong, positive contribution of a dense, social-institutional infrastructure to the vitality of regional economies – like Baden-Württemberg in Germany or parts of the 'Third Italy' – that engage in 'high value-added', 'flexibly specialized' (Piore and Sabel, 1984), or 'diversified quality' (Sorge and Streeck, 1988) modes of production. In many of these prosperous and world market-competitive areas, interest associations, and apparently often including unions, seem to play an indispensable part in the negotiation of distributional compromises, the building of growth and productivity coalitions, the formation of public–private interfaces, the provision of a protective institutional exoskeleton for small, innovative firms, the generation of collective factor inputs and the creation of institutions that allow for non-zero-sum cooperation among firms, as well as between capital and labor at the workplace and beyond.

Recent developments seem to indicate that the former regional subunits of European national economies may be about to become independent actors on the European Community stage.[23] A number of European regions, most prominent among them Catalonia, Lombardia and Baden-Württemberg, have set up permanent offices in Brussels that bear conspicuous resemblance to embassies. Moreover, their heads of government have met several times to discuss strategy and form coalitions concerning their interests vis-a-vis the European Community. If this trend was to continue, regions would join nations, classes, sectors and firms as participants in European interest politics, adding another category of players and further complexities to a scene that is already highly complex and pluralistic.

Europeanization of regional interests, and especially inter-regional political competition for Community resources, is far from being universally welcomed.[24] For one thing, while it would improve the position of the Commission, it would also and ipso facto tend to weaken further what is left of sovereignty at the national level – which is why national governments have been found actively to resent the formation of direct connections between Brussels and 'their' subnational territories. Also, if regions are admitted to European politics, regional subunits of *federal* states, having independent powers of legislation, taxation, budgeting, etc., will likely have an advantage over regions in more centralized countries; see the absence from the above list of, say, the Midlands.

An important question with respect to the possible emergence of a regional level of European interest politics concerns the sources and conditions of labor-inclusiveness of regional regimes – especially whether regional power resources of labor can be generated *endogenously* inside the region, or need to be mobilized *exogenously* using national power resources under the protection of a sovereign border. Regions, as has been pointed out, are societies that lack control over their borders. As European nation-states turn into regions of an integrated market economy, nationally legislated labor market regimes are likely to lose much of their force, and the same holds for protective barriers against cross-border competition; this, after all, is what the expected deregulatory effect of 1992 is all about. The survival and growth of regional labor-inclusive institutions inside the integrated Internal Market, and with it perhaps that of regionally based non-price-competitive production, would then have to depend on non-national, regionally indigenous forces – or would require that functional equivalents for national-level supports be found at the supra-national level to balance the decline in national political capacities that is associated with 1992.

Much of the literature on regional political economies seems to take the position that the composition and survival of their regimes is indeed, and always was, largely independent from national institutions. Typically, the institutional infrastructure of economically successful European regions is described as based in *local* cultures, traditions and politics that, by implication, would be unlikely to be destabilized by an attenuation of national sovereignty. However, apart from the fact that culture and tradition may rapidly lose vitality in the modernizing, internationalizing post-1992 European economy, a case could be made that, certainly as far as the presence of unions and of a tripartite power balance in regional economies is concerned, this severely underestimates the role played in the past by *national* power resources (Korpi, 1978), like labor law creating or supporting various overt or covert mechanisms of union security, or protective monetary and trade policies.

Regions, not being states, are by definition unable to insert *coercive power* in the voluntary contractual and communitarian relations between their citizens. Their social organization is that of a civil society largely undistorted, as it were, by public intervention. In particular, regions would seem to lack the capacity to provide the kind of public support that has generally been found to be required to transform unstable, voluntaristic, pluralistic unions into institutionally 'mature' ones that are capable of looking, in corporatist fashion, beyond the individual enterprise or occupational group to the sector, the country or, for that matter, the region *as a whole*. Regionally based unionism in the European Community would have to do without external sources of associational monopoly, without authoritative stabilization of bargaining arenas, and without recourse to a public sphere balancing the manifold advantages employers enjoy in the marketplace. It is not easy to see how the disabling effects on union movements of the erosion of institutional supports at national level should be counterbalanced by unions turning to the regional level where such supports have never existed.

In any case, even if it was somehow possible to create stable tripartite systems of regional governance, referring to this as 'regional corporatism' may be highly misleading. Corporatism requires encompassing organizations that internalize a significant part of the externalities of a group's collective action and interests, and allow for hierarchical coordination between different levels of interest aggregation and group activity. Neither condition would be met in a Europe of regional tripartisms. If national-level corporatisms have been undermined by growing international interdependence beyond the control of the parties at the bargaining table, regional arrangements are even more affected by the shrinking effective size of modern polities. The tyranny of external effects, as it has been called, clearly is on the advance at the national level; but it certainly is incomparably more severe in the much smaller action space of a subnational region – especially after the demise of national regulations that in the past have taken a core set of social and constitutional conditions out of interregional competition.

Moreover, in moving their organizational center of gravity towards the region, as most of the industrial district literature more or less explicitly advises them to do, unions would write off any aspiration they may have had for playing a role in the political management of interregional externalities. Regionalized unions would inevitably be partners, junior or not, of regional capital trying to survive in interregional free market competition. Such unions would have to cease trying to act as agents of interregional redistribution. While the *mezzogiorno* policy of Italian unions in the

1970s, which relied on the movement's centralized, national power to demand regional development programs for the empoverished South of the country, may not have been particularly successful, a regionally decentralized union movement would have been unable to agree on any such policy in the first place. Today, regionalized unionism would for the same reasons be incapable of a political, as opposed to market-driven, response to the deep interdependence of regional economies with the larger European and global economic context – a condition that has become more profound than ever and that, incidentally, fundamentally distinguishes today's regional economies from those of the past.

It is conceivable that political control over economic interdependence is presently beyond recapture, and that union organizational domains may for a long time or forever be bound to be significantly narrower than whatever the relevant 'market' may be. But decentralization of unions and industrial relations towards regional arenas will clearly not remedy this condition, and to the extent that it ratifies the, possibly inevitable, fragmentation of organized interests, it actually amounts to the very opposite of corporatism. The emergence of regional arenas of interest politics seems to advance not the organization of labor or, for that matter, of capital, but rather its *disorganization*. In the 1992 environment in particular, new opportunities for interest articulation at regional level would appear to increase actors' range of *choice* between political channels widely beyond what would be compatible with the orderly world of corporatism. In addition to the enterprise, the sector, the nation and perhaps Europe as a whole, struggling factions inside interest associations, including unions, would have yet another option for pursuing sectional interests separately and on their own, in coalition with other categories of, equally fragmented, interests or with ambitious local governments. By undermining associational monopoly and inter-associational hierarchy, the fragmentation of interests and the pluralist proliferation of political opportunities that is entailed in the 'regionalization of Europe' adds to the decomposition of national-level corporatisms, as well as to the obstacles to its supra-national resurrection.

Interest Politics at Supra-national Level
Tripartism never really worked in Brussels, and where it was tried it was always too encapsulated and marginal to come in any way close to a neo-corporatist model of governance.[25] There is no reason to believe that this will change. The negative integration mode of the 1992 process – the move away from harmonization to mutual recognition – ensures that the eroded domestic sovereignty of

nation-states will only partly, if at all, be recreated at the Community level. Unlike older, more naïve images of regional integration, allowance has to be made today for the possibility that national political arenas, themes and regulatory instruments that are rendered obsolete by integration are not always and necessarily reconstructed at the level of the emerging supra-national polity. Rather than being moved upward, they may as well dissipate in a larger, less orderly or less mature institutional complex, and may thereby, more or less intentionally, be turned over to, or replaced by, the voluntarism of market and civil society. Where this happens, it deprives what might aspire to become a European federal government of a range of subject matter and decisional discretion that it otherwise could use, and indeed would need, to build the mutual give-and-take in and between interest groups and public bodies that is the indispensable basis for stable neo-corporatist exchange.

A case of limited state capacity at the European level reducing the incentives for comprehensive organization of economic interests is the absence of a *European Central Bank* (Holm, forthcoming). Historically, tripartite corporatist bargaining has typically involved the government's use not only of fiscal but also of monetary policy instruments. The need to be represented in bargaining over monetary policy was an important reason for socio-economic interests, for employers in particular, to get organized. However, the European System of Central Banks, provided it will some day come into being, will be carefully shielded from political pressures, not least by its diffuse and decentralized internal structure. Moreover, a European central bank is likely for a long time to continue to be subject to strongly institutionalized, deflationary, 'monetarist' preferences (Delors Committee, 1989) – if only because the European Community as an imperfectly unified actor in the world economy will need time to get used to the reflationary possibilities offered by a large economy with a currency that could in principle compete for the role of world money.

Another important ingredient of 1970s-style neo-corporatism – *centralized collective bargaining between capital and labor* – is entirely missing at the European level, and nothing is in sight that would indicate its impending appearance. In national industrial relations systems, centralized collective bargaining was often advanced by encompassing employers' associations forcing unions to unify their policies and organizational structures (Swenson, 1989). No such support will be forthcoming at the European level in the foreseeable future (Baun, 1990), not least because the inter-regional mobility of capital will, perhaps indefinitely now, exceed that of labor, and because centralization would deprive capital of the strategic advantages of competition-driven industrial relations at regional or enterprise level.

The same applies to the other historical source of external facilitation, government intervention. Europe-wide institutions are entirely devoid of any capacity to provide for carry-over from unionized to non-unionized firms or regions, thereby protecting employers in the former from competition by the latter. The celebrated 'Social Dialogue', also referred to as the 'Val Duchesse' talks, strongly confirms the fundamental deficiencies of the European Community as a would-be agent of social concertation. Started by Delors in 1985 in an effort to overcome the stagnation in European tripartism and, clearly, to redress the balance of the international-cum-constitutional bargain that had produced the Internal Market project, it nevertheless represents a significant retreat from earlier attempts at social policy associated with the Fifth Directive and the Vredeling proposal. Indeed Northrup et al. regard Val Duchesse as marking the Community's transition from what they call attempted 'Euro-Corporatism' to 'economic liberalism', in that its ground rules reflect a general tendency 'to subordinate legislation and direct government intervention through regulation to "informal dialogue"' (1988, 530). Up to now, the only outcome of the Val Duchesse exercise are two joint working groups set up by ETUC and UNICE to address questions of macroeconomic policy and the social aspects of new technology (Northrup et al., 1988; Teague and Grahl, 1989).

The emergence of European-level collective bargaining is further impeded by *mutual incompatibility of existing national industrial relations systems*. While in some countries collective agreements are negotiated at the *enterprise* level, in others they are concluded for all firms that belong to a specific *sector* on a given national or subnational *territory*. The latter, in addition to requiring the presence of strong employers' associations and, preferably, state-sponsored extension mechanisms making agreements binding on non-affiliated firms, depends crucially on the large and more prosperous firms being included in the territorially defined bargaining units; otherwise industrial unions would be deprived of the opportunity to increase their bargaining power in small firms by enlisting as their ally the willingness to settle and the ability to pay of large firms. In the absence of supra-national employers' associations and facilitating state intervention, however, all that unions can hope to accomplish in building what the Commission has euphemistically called a 'European industrial relations system' (Commission of the European Communities, 1988) are consultations and, perhaps, negotiations with the headquarters of large multi-national firms (Campbell, 1989). But while this would be compatible with national industrial relations systems based on enterprise bargaining, European enterprise agreements would over time inevitably tend to exempt the national subsidiaries of the respective enterprises from the domain of sectoral-territorial bargaining. The result would be a weakening of existing national multi-employer bargaining regimes. Since sectoral-territorial bargaining is used by unions to reduce regional and inter-firm wage differentials, unions would have not just organizational but also political reasons for objecting to European enterprise-level bargaining – even if this is likely to be the only form of supra-national collective bargaining on offer.

Also, there is no reason to believe that an increase in political opportunities for labor at the European level, assuming that it will ever come to pass, will make consensus-building in European labor organizations less difficult. In fact, if outcomes matter more, interest differences assume more weight. Organizational, political and ideological divergence may be even less crippling in this respect than different national labor market structures training systems or living standards.[26] Trade unions from rich countries traditionally offer their poorer counterparts assistance in the pursuit of aggressive demands for wages, holidays, social security benefits etc. But what to them may appear to be internationalist concern for their fellow-workers' rights and well-being, the latter may eventually perceive as designed to protect their richer brothers from capital outflow and subsequent job loss (Streeck, 1991). As long as calls for Community-wide labor standards have no practical consequences, they are likely not to be opposed by unions in weaker economies. When confederal policies may have a real impact, their formulation could become more contested.[27]

European-level relations between capital and labor, instead of constituting the core of the European political economy, will for the foreseeable future remain compartmentalized in the private sphere of large multi-national enterprises, and will thus be essentially non-political and voluntaristic in character.[28] Where labor–capital relations enter the political arena, they will mainly take the form of a set of discrete 'labor' and 'social policy' issues. As such, they will have to lend themselves to being dealt with by bureaucrats, experts and intergovernmental committees in the same way as, for example, labeling rules regarding the cholesterol content of palm oil, or regulations for the recycling of mineral water containers.[29] Rather than driving the constitutional bargain that underlies the political system, the traditional class issues of industrial society will have to compete on an equal plane with 'post-industrial' themes like environmental protection, consumer rights, equality between men and women, etc. – issues that by their nature defy integration in an encompassing framework of 'class' politics.[30]

The evolutionary alternative to neo-liberalism as a model for the European political economy is clearly not (German or Scandinavian) neo-corporatism. More likely appears an American-style pattern of 'disjointed pluralism' or 'competitive federalism', organized over no less than three levels – regions, nation-states and 'Brussels'. As in the United States, and perhaps more so, this system would be characterized by a profound *absence of hierarchy and monopoly* among a *wide variety of players of different but uncertain status*. Interest associations, and quite a few of them, will certainly be among those. But they will have to compete for attention with national states, subnational regions, large firms, and specialized lobbyists, leaving their constituents with a wide range of choices among different paths of access to the Community's political center and enabling them to use threats of exit to coerce their representatives into pluralist responsiveness. Just as fundamental constitutional questions of sovereignty and hierarchy inside the Community's quasi-state – concerning, for example, the relative status of regions, nations and supra-national bodies – will remain unsettled and uncertain, so will the hierarchical relations between firms, sectoral associations and peak associations in its system of functional representation.

Given the constitutional bargain that underlay the relaunching of the European Community in the 1980s, no mechanism is in sight that could rationalize its political system, help crystallize its melange of actors and processes, and establish corporatist monopolies of representation, inter-associational hierarchies or, for that matter, a predominant position for the Commission's bureaucracy and technocracy. Whatever turn the European Community may take after 1992, it will not reverse the tide and reorganize European capitalism in the neo-corporatist cast.

Notes

1 The authors are grateful to Catherine Farry for research assistance.

2 Which was, of course, the core concept of Haas' (1958) seminal, 'neo-functionalist' theory of European and regional integration.

3 The exceptions seem to be CIC (professional association of executive workers, founded in 1951); FIPMEC (small business associations for artisanal and craft trades, 1951); CEA (business association for the insurance industry, 1953); CIF (association for public service employees, 1955); COCCEE (trade and commerce, 1957); and EUROCOOP (association of consumer cooperatives, 1957).

4 It should be noted that many of these associations affiliated national associations

from countries that are, or were at the time, not members of the European
Community. For example, UNICE had 27 affiliates in 1980 of which 14 were from
(then) non-EC countries. The ETUC has, in addition to most union confederations
from the 12 member nations, representatives from all EFTA countries and from
Malta, Cyprus and Turkey. For by now more or less outdated descriptive surveys of
European-level interest organizations, see Butt Philips (1985), Economic and Social
Committee of the European Communities (1980), Kirchner and Schwaiger (1981),
and Meynaud and Sidjanski (1971).

5 For example, Sicco Mansholt seems to have played a major role in the founding
of COPA (Lindberg and Scheingold, 1970: 173). In the extreme case of EUROFER,
the Community sponsored the creation of a Europe-wide cartel (Butt Philips, 1985:
45).

6 Not all access to these committees was, however, restricted to functional
representatives. Many involve 'experts' – which admittedly may often be difficult to
distinguish from lobbyists. For a description of 46 of these consultative bodies, see
Economic and Social Committee of the European Communities (1980: 23–52).

7 As of 1989, there were 3,277 officials assisted by 9,202 staff personnel in the
employ of the Commission.

8 Even the Committee's own propaganda literature admits that 'it was regarded as
the most unobtrusive of Community institutions' (Economic and Social Committee
of the European Communities 1986: 13–14).

9 Where, in addition, the principal lines of cleavage were not between capital and
labor but between 'Gaullists' and 'Atlanticists', and between the proponents of
supra-nationalism and of national sovereignty. As these conflicts began to dominate
and eventually block the Community's agenda in the 1960s, introducing social
questions in addition was a hopeless endeavor from the outset.

10 The formal foundation of the ETUC took place during this time, in reaction, as
Sargent points out, to 'the strength of European representatives of employers and
aspects of Community policy, in particular the Common Agricultural Policy and the
Community's policy on the free movement of labor' (1985: 236).

11 Not that Haas would have predicted, or approved, the substance of those
initiatives which, to a large extent, was clearly outside the spectrum of the 'pluralist
industrialism' of the 1950s and, in the eyes of many observers, signalled a return to
'class conflict' and 'ideology'. See Haas (1976).

12 'The high point of unity in the ETUC was probably reached in the campaign for
the Vredeling proposal in the early 1980's. All its member national labor confederations were in agreement on the need for an European policy on the rights of
employees to information and consultation in the multinational corporations. When
that battle was not won, the attention of most labor unions turned to the struggle
against unemployment and that struggle was carried out more at the national level
than at the level of the EC' (Springer, 1989: 9).

13 In that sense, the inclusiveness of labor's organizational structure at European
level, as indicated by the low number of unions compared to business associations, is
illusory. If the internal policy-making capacities of European union confederations
are taken into account, the picture changes dramatically.

14 On the difference between class and producer interests, and its reflection in the
organizational structures and strategies of business, see Chapter 3, this volume.

15 This continues until the present day. For example, Teague (1989b: 318)
emphasizes that when in 1985 the incoming President of the Commission, Jacques
Delors, proposed to revitalize the 'Social Dialogue', UNICE would participate only

if the Commission promised not to produce proposals for legislation from any agreement that might emerge.

16 This relationship is thoroughly misunderstood by authors like Northrup et al. who base their optimism for a broad 'Social Dimension' on their observation that unions 'are better organized than employers at the EC level, and the link between social policy formulation by the Commission and the European Trade Union Confederation (ETUC) is bolstered by an active and respected research arm, the European Trade Union Institute (ETUI), funded in part by the EC. The Union of Industries of the European Community (UNICE), on the other hand, which in the first place does not speak for all employers, is further hampered by [employers'] reluctance to cede authority to an organization that may draw employers into unwanted arrangements or even collective bargaining agreements at the EC level.' Also, after the experience with the Vredeling proposal, UNICE is said to be 'restrained by the hostility of its constituents towards the Commission's social policy intentions and by the vigour with which Commissioner Vredeling sided with the ETUC' (Northrup et al., 1988: 529).

17 Arguably, then, the Thatcher government in the 1980s was doing the 'dirty work' on behalf of two constituencies at the same time: European business and European nation-states. Since Thatcher could always be counted upon to enjoy playing the 'odd man out' and use her country's veto single-handedly to block both European social policy and European federalism, others could afford to be less outspoken. With Thatcher's resignation, rather than clearing the way towards a social-democratic United States of Europe, her role may now be taken by a variety of actors in varying combinations and coalitions, some of which may during the 1980s have felt free to pay lip service to 'socialist' and 'federalist' proposals which they could be sure would never be realized.

18 Of course, as has been pointed out, the period in question was also notable for attempts by unions and social-democratic governments to move the European Community to the left. With hindsight, this may be seen as another manifestation of the general confusion and indecision of the time, when the Left was still benefiting from the momentum of 1968 while the Right was beginning to launch its counter-attack with the support of, as it were, 1973. Moves towards a 'Social Europe' may in this situation have been an important reason for business and its political allies to hold back on European integration. Having not been able to escape national corporatism after 1968, it made little sense for them to accept supra-national corporatism in addition at a time when the tide was already beginning to turn in their favor.

19 For more detail, see Sandholtz and Zysman (1989), Streeck (forthcoming)

20 This is, in essence, why there is no reference to a social dimension in the Single European Act (Northrup et al., 1988); why the social dimension was always regarded as secondary to the 'economic dimension' of the Internal Market; and why the Single European Act introduces qualified majority voting on the Council exclusively on matters that are *essential* to the completion of the Internal Market (Springer, 1989: 12).

21 The exception being the 'federalist' tradition of thinking about the European Community, with its strongholds in Italy (the tradition of Spinelli) and, remarkably, in the United Kingdom (cf. Burgess, 1989).

22 Disregarding the 'Social Charter', which in its core is no more than an exercise in comparative labor law, extracting the lowest common denominator from the Community's national legal systems. In this sense, the Charter is empirical rather

than normative in character. It is also voluntary in that, as far as the European Community is concerned, no legislation will emerge from it, and its implementation at the national level will be left exclusively to national governments and will take place in line with a country's existing custom and practice. Even so, the Charter was vigorously opposed by the British government.

23 For a strong statement to this effect, see Majone (1989).

24 The following discussion owes much to a set of unpublished papers by Gary Marks.

25 'The style of interests intermediation that has emerged at European level is essentially a pluralist one which has developed a few, immature corporatist features as a result of initiatives by European labour and certain EEC bodies' (Sargent, 1985: 236).

26 While this condition has existed for a long time, it was exacerbated in the mid-1980s by the accession to membership of the three mediterranean countries, Spain, Portugal and Greece. Today regional disparities in Europe are much wider than in the United States. According to *Eurostat Review 1977–1986*, hourly labor costs in Portugal for manual and non-manual workers in 1984, expressed in ECU, amounted to 16 percent of German labor costs. The respective figure for Greece was 28 percent (UK: 63; France: 86). Later data or more exact measures are not at present available.

27 We owe this point to Peter Lange.

28 On voluntarism, see Campbell (1989: 10), who notes that 'employers resist, in particular, the legal imposition' of institutionalized labor relations 'on multinational companies'. That resistance pertains in part even to private, non-legislated arrangements: 'Based on recent discussion of the concept of labor relations at the multinational level with employers from nine European countries, the author remains convinced of the absence of much enthusiasm on the employer side for multinational labor–management relations' (Campbell, 1989: 10–11) – probably since these may set a precedent for legislative intiatives.

29 To this extent, they would become subject to a 'policy style' that is specifically 'European' – that is, community-European. The Brussels policy process seems to encourage de-contextualization and de-politicization of issues – 'pragmatically' isolating them from 'ideological' meanings and as much as possible avoiding their incorporation in any coherent political symbolism. Didactically helpful for this kind of exercise is the recurrent discovery in European Community bodies that apparently identical political arrangements and outcomes can sometimes be of completely contrary significance in different national, political and ideological environments – for example, legally based co-determination rights at the workplace in Britain and Germany. After policy 'issues' have been divested of their emotional and ideological aura, and fragmented and individualized, their treatment can be assigned to 'experts' – specialists, that is, in comparative inventories of de-contextualized and de-politicized problems, positions and compromises, and in the extraction of the smallest common denominator from such inventories.

30 This would suggest that the modus operandi labor has been developing in recent years at the European level as a temporary and provisional response to unfavorable conjunctural circumstances may be all there will be for a long time to come. Today organized European labor places its hopes on basically two tactics: (1) *making explicit the common floor* of worker and union rights in member countries, by getting employers and governments to agree to joint declarations like the Charter – in the hope of thereby confirming and reinforcing that floor; demonstrating that joint

regulations already exist and that they are not harmful; perhaps later being able to draw attention to 'implementation deficits'; and setting a baseline from which it may in future be possible gradually to raise the floor upwards; and (2) *setting precedents through voluntary agreements* with individual firms or employers' associations at the European level – hoping thus to create a situation in which employers will be unable to argue at some later time against legislative generalization of the respective provisions, for example on European-level works councils. With a significant increase in the Community's state capacity being as questionable as it is, it may well be that keeping the various European labor law inventories undated and talking employers into agreements and arrangements to which they find it impossible to make a reasonable objection will remain the principal activity of European organized labor well into the next century.

Bibliography

Abegglen, J.C., 1958: *The Japanese Factory: Aspects of its Social Organization*. Glencoe, Ill.: Free Press.

Abernathy, W.J., 1978: *The Productivity Dilemma: Roadblock to Innovation in the Automobile Industry*. Baltimore and London: Johns Hopkins University Press.

Adams, R.J. and Rummel, C.H., 1977: 'Workers' Participation in Management in West Germany: Impact on the Worker, the Enterprise and the Trade Union', *Industrial Relations Journal*, 8: 4–22.

Adler, P.S., 1987: 'Automation and Skill: New Directions', *International Journal for Technology Management*, 2: 761–72.

Alexander, J., 1989: 'Divergent European Community Unionism: a Threat to Single Market Unification?'. Ms.

Altshuler, A. et al., 1984: *The Future of the Automobile: the Report of MIT's International Automobile Program*. Cambridge, Mass.: MIT Press.

Batstone, E., Ferner, A. and Terry, M., 1984: *Consent and Efficiency: Labour Relations and Management in the State Enterprise*. Oxford: Basil Blackwell.

Baun, M., 1990: 'Europe 1992 and Trade Union Politics: towards a European "Industrial Relations Space?"', Ms.

Bayer, H., Streeck, W. and Treu, E., 1981: *Die westdeutsche Gewerkschaftsbewegung in Zahlen: Ein Datenhandbuch zur organisatorischen Entwicklung ausgewählter Industrie- und Berufsverbände 1960–1975*. Meisenheim: Anton Hain.

Bieber, R., Dehousse, R., Pinder, J. and Weiler, J.H.H., 1988: 'Introduction. Back to the Future: Policy, Strategy and Tactics of the White Paper on the Creation of a Single European Market', in R.R. Bieber, R. Denhousse, J. Pinder and J.H.H. Weiler (eds), *1992: One European Market?*. Baden-Baden: Nomos Verlagsgesellschaft, pp. 13–31.

Blau, P.M., 1964: *Exchange and Power in Social Life*. New York: John Wiley & Sons.

Brittan, S., 1978: 'Inflation and Democracy', in F. Hirsch and J.H. Goldthorpe, (eds), *The Political Economy of Inflation*. Cambridge, Mass.: Harvard University Press. pp. 161-85.

Britze, Hans-Henning, 1964: *Die Rechtskriterien des Handwerksbetriebs nach neuerer Lehre und Rechtsprechung in gewerberechtlicher Hinsicht*, 2nd unrevised edition. Münster: Handwerkswissenschaftliches Institut.

Brumlop, E., 1986: *Arbeitsbewertung bei flexiblem Personaleinsatz: Das Beispiel Volkswagen AG*. Frankfurt am Main: Campus.

Brumlop, E. and Jürgens, U., 1986: 'Rationalization and Technical Change: a Case Study of Volkswagen', in O. Jacobi et al. (eds), *Technological Change, Rationalization and Industrial Relations*. London: Croom Helm. pp. 73–94.

Brusco, S., 1982: 'The Emilian Model: Production Decentralization and Social Integration', *Cambridge Journal of Economics*, 6: 167–84.

Bundesminister für Arbeit und Sozialordnung, 1978: *Co-determination in the Federal Republic of Germany*, Bonn: Selbstverlag.

Bundesminister für Arbeit und Sozialordnung, 1979: *Mitbestimmung*. Bonn: Selbst-verlag.

Burgess, Michael, 1989: 'Federalism and European Union: Past, Present and Future in the European Community'. Ms.

Butt Philips, A., 1985: 'Pressure Groups in the European Community', *UACES Occasional Essay* 2, London: University Association for Contemporary European Studies.

Calingaert, M., 1988: *The 1992 Challenge from Europe: Development of the European Community's Internal Market*. Washington, DC: National Planning Association.

Cameron, D.R., 1984: 'Social Democracy, Corporatism, Labor Quiescence and the Representation of Economic Interest in Advanced Capitalist Society', in J.H. Goldthorpe (ed.), *Order and Conflict in Contemporary Capitalism*. Oxford: Clarendon Press. pp. 143–78.

Campbell, D.C., 1989: 'Multinational Labor Relations in the European Community', *ILR Report*, 27: 7–14.

Caporaso, J.A., 1974: *The Structure and Function of European Integration*. Pacific Palisades: Goodyear.

Castles, F.G., 1987: 'Neo-corporatism and the "Happiness Index", or What Trade Unions Get for their Cooperation', *European Journal of Political Research*, 15: 381–93.

Cawson, A., (ed), 1985: *Organized Interests and the State: Studies in Meso-Corporatism*. London: Sage.

Chesi, V., 1968: *Struktur und Funktionen der Handwerksorganisationen in Deutschland seit 1933*. Berlin: Humblot und Duncker.

Child, J., 1988: 'Managerial Strategies, New Technology and the Labour Process', in R.E. Pahl (ed.), *On Work: Historical, Comparative and Theoretical Approaches*. Oxford: Basil Blackwell. pp. 229–57.

Child, J., Loveridge, R. and Warner, M., 1973: 'Towards an Organizational Study of Trade Unions', *Sociology*, 7: 71–91.

Clegg, H.A., 1975: 'Pluralism in Industrial Relations', *British Journal of Industrial Relations*, 13: 309–16.

Commission of the European Communities, 1988: *The Social Dimension of the Internal Market: Interim Report of the Intergovernmental Working Party*. Special Edition of *Social Europe*.

Commons, J.R., 1924: *Legal Foundations of Capitalism*. New York: Macmillan.

Cox, J. and Kriegbaum, H., 1980: *Growth, Innovation and Employment: an Anglo-German Comparison*. London: Anglo-German Foundation for the Study of Industrial Society.

Cressey, P., 1989: 'Trade Unions and the Social Dialogue'. Paper presented at the IRRU conference on '*Industrial Relations and the European Community*', University of Warwick, 17–19 March.

Crouch, C., 1985: 'Conditions for Trade Union Wage Restraint', in L.N. Lindberg and C.S. Maier, (eds), *The Politics of Inflation and Economic Stagnation*. Washington, DC: Brookings Institution. pp. 105–39.

Crouch, C., 1988: 'Trade Unions in the Exposed Sector: their Influence on Neo-corporatist Behavior'. Paper prepared for a conference on 'Markets, Institutions and Co-operation: Labour Relations and Economic Performance', Venice, October.

Crouch, C., and Pizzorno, A. (eds), 1978: *The Resurgence of Class Conflict in Western Europe since 1968*, 2 vols. London: Macmillan.

Deakin, S., 1985: 'Labour Law and the Employment Relationship: Regulation of Marginal Employment in the UK'. University of Cambridge, ms.

Delors Committee (Committee for the Study of Economic and Monetary Union), 1989: Report on Economic and Monetary Union in the European Community.

Demes, H., and Jürgens, U., 1989: 'Skill Formation in the Automobile Industry: a Comparison between West German, British, American and Japanese Enterprises', in T. Blumenthal, (ed), *Employer and Employee in Japan and Europe*. Beer Sheva: Humphrey Institute for Social Ecology. pp. 59–85.

Deutsch, K., 1963: *The Nerves of Government: Models of Political Communication and Control*. New York: Free Press.

Deutschmann, C., 1987: 'Economic Restructuring and Company Unionism: the Japanese Model', *Economic and Industrial Democracy*, 8: 463–88.

Doran, A., 1984: *Craft Enterprises in Britain and Germany: a Sectoral Study*. London: Anglo-German Foundation for the Study of Industrial Society.

Dore, R., 1983: 'Goodwill and the Spirit of Market Capitalism', *The British Journal of Sociology* 34: 459–82.

Dore, R., 1987: *Taking Japan Seriously: a Confucian Perspective on Leading Economic Issues*. Stanford, Calf.: Stanford University Press.

Dore, R., 1988: 'Rigidities in the Labour Market: the Andrew Shonfield Lectures (II)', *Government and Opposition*, 23: 393–412.

Dunlop, J., 1958: *Industrial Relations Systems*. Carbondale and Edwardsville: Southern Illinois University Press.

Durkheim, E., 1964: *The Division of Labor in Society*. New York: Free Press.

Economic and Social Committee of the European Communities, 1980: *European Interest Groups and their Relations to the Economic and Social Committee*. Farnborough: Saxon House.

Economic and Social Committee of the European Communities, 1986: *The Other European Assembly*. Brussels: ESC Press, Information and Publications Division.

European Conference of Ministers of Transport, 1987: *Statistical Report on Road Accidents in 1984*. Paris: OECD Publications Service.

Föhr, H., 1977: 'Mitbestimmung und Satzungsautonomie', *Das Mitbestimmungsgespräch*: 131–4.

Fox, A., 1971: *A Sociology of Work in Industry*. London: Collier-Macmillan.

Fox, A., 1974: *Beyond Contract: Work, Power and Trust Relations*. London: Faber & Faber.

Fox, A., 1977: 'Corporatism and Industrial Democracy: the Social Origins of Present Forms and Methods in Britain and Germany', in SSRC Industrial Relations Research Unit (ed.), *Industrial Democracy: International Views*. Coventry: University of Warwick. pp. 3–54.

Fox, A., 1985: *History and Heritage: the Social Origins of the British Industrial Relations System*. London: George Allen & Unwin.

Fox, A. and Flanders, A., 1969: 'Collective Bargaining: from Donovan to Durkheim', in A. Flanders (1975), *Management and Unions: the Theory and Reform of Industrial Relations*. London: Faber & Faber.

Friedeburg, L. v. et al., 1955: *Betriebsklima: Eine industriesoziologische Untersuchung aus dem Ruhrgebiet*. Frankfurt am Main: Europäische Verlagsanstalt.

Friedman, W., 1972: *Law in a Changing Society*. Harmondsworth: Penguin.

Fröhler, L., 1965: *Zur Abgrenzung von Handwerk und Industrie: Der dynamische*

Handwerksbegriff in der deutschen Rechtsprechung. Munich: Handwerksrechts-institut München e.V.

Fröhler, L., 1971: *Das Berufszulassungsrecht der Handwerksordnung, dargestellt anhand der Rechtsprechung.* Munich: Handwerksrechtsinstitut München e.V.

Garbarino, J.W., 1984: 'Unionism Without Unions: the New Industrial Relations', *Industrial Relations*, 23: 40–51.

Gaugler, E., 1981: 'Fragen zur mitbestimmten Unternehmensverfassung', in K. Bohr et al., (eds), *Unternehmensverfassung als Problem der Beitriebswirtschafts-lehre.* Berlin: Erich Schmidt Verlag, pp. 829–38.

Geisler, G., 1981: 'Personalplanung, Personalentwicklung und Bildung', in A. Ostertag (ed.), *Arbeitsdirektoren berichten aus der Praxis.* Cologne: Bund Verlag. pp. 159–80.

Gewerkschaftliche Monatshefte, 1978: *Dokumentation*: 749–67.

Goldthorpe, J.H., 1974a: 'Social Inequality and Social Integration in Modern Britain', in D. Wedderburn, (ed.), *Poverty, Inequality and Class Structure.* Cambridge: Cambridge University Press.

Goldthorpe, J.H., 1974b: 'Industrial Relations in Great Britain: a Critique of Reformism', *Politics and Society*, 4: 419–52.

Goldthorpe, J.H., 1978: 'The Current Inflation: towards a Sociological Account', in F. Hirsch and J.H. Goldthorpe (eds), *The Political Economy of Inflation.* Cambridge, Mass.: Harvard University Press. pp. 186–214.

Goldthorpe, J.H., 1984: 'The End of Convergence: Corporatist and Dualist Tendencies in Modern Societies', in J.H. Goldthorpe (ed.), *Order and Conflict in Contemporary Capitalism.* Oxford: Clarendon Press. pp. 315–43.

Gourevitch, P., 1986: *Politics in Hard Times.* Ithaca, New York, and London: Cornell University Press.

Granovetter, M., 1985: 'Economic Action and Social Structure: the Problem of Embeddedness', *American Journal of Sociology*, 91: 481–510.

Grant, W. (ed.), 1985: *The Political Economy of Corporatism.* London: Macmillan.

Grote, J., 1989: 'Guidance and Control in Transnational Committee Networks: the Associational Basis of Policy Cycles at the EC Level'. Ms. Florence: European University Institute.

Gustavsen, B., 1986: 'Evolving Patterns of Enterprise Organization: the Move towards Greater Flexibility', *International Labour Review*, 125: 367–82.

Gutchess, J.F., 1985: *Employment Security in Action: Strategies that Work.* New York: Pergamon Press.

Haas, E.B., 1958: *The Uniting of Europe: Political, Social and Economic Forces 1950–1957.* London: Stevens & Son.

Haas, E.B., 1970: 'The Study of Regional Integration: Reflections on the Joy and Anguish of Pretheorizing', in L.N. Lindberg and S. Scheingold (eds), *Regional Integration: Theory and Research.* Englewood Cliffs, NY: Prentice Hall. pp. 3–42.

Haas, E.B., 1975: *The Obsolescence of Regional Integration Theory.* Institute of International Studies, University of California, Berkeley.

Haas, E.B., 1976: 'Turbulent Fields and the Theory of Regional Integration', *International Organization*, 30: 173–212.

Hartmann, H., 1975: 'Co-determination Today and Tomorrow', *British Journal of Industrial Relations*, 13: 54–64.

HBV (Gewerkschaft Handel, Banken und Versicherungen), 1978: 'Aufsichtsrats-wahlen', *Gewerkschaftliche Monatshefte*, 29: 701–6.

Heckscher, C.C., 1988: *The New Unionism: Employee Involvement in the Changing Corporation*. New York: Basic Books.

Heese, A. et al., 1981: 'Arbeitnehmerbezogene Personalplanung bei den Hoesch Hüttenwerken', in A. Ostertag (ed.), *Arbeitsdirektoren berichten aus der Praxis*. Cologne: Bund-Verlag. pp. 139–58.

Herrigel, G., forthcoming: 'Industrial Order in the Machine Tool Industry: a Comparison of the United States and Germany', in J.R. Hollingsworth, P.C. Schmitter and Wolfgang Streeck (eds), *Comparing Capitalist Economies: Variations in the Governance of Sectors*. New York: Oxford University Press.

Higgins, W., 1985: 'Ernst Wigforss: the Renewal of Social Democratic Theory and Practice', *Political Power and Social Theory*, 5: 207–50.

Hilbert, J., Südmersen, H. and Weber, H., 1986: 'Selbstordnung der Berufsbildung: Eine Fallstudie über die Evolution, Organisation und Funktion privater Regierungen', *Arbeitsberichte und Forschungsmaterialien*, Nr 18, Forschungsschwerpunkt Zukunft der Arbeit, Universität Bielefeld.

Hirschhorn, L., 1984: *Beyond Mechanization: Work and Technology in a Post-Industrial Age*. Cambridge, Mass.: MIT Press.

Hirschman, A.O., 1982: 'Rival Interpretations of Market Society: Civilizing, Destructive, or Feeble?', *Journal of Economic Literature*, 20: 1463–84.

Hoff, A., 1984: 'Assessing Investment-Related Medium-Term Manpower Needs: a Case Study from the German Automobile Industry', *Discussion Paper* IIM/LMP 84–3, Wissenschaftszentrum Berlin.

Hoffmann, S., 1989: 'The European Community and 1992', *Foreign Affairs*, 4: 26–47.

Holm, E., forthcoming: 'The Politics of Europe's Money', in B. Crawford and P. Schulze (eds), *European Self-Assertion: a New Role for Europe in International Affairs*.

Hotz, B., 1982: 'Productivity Differences and Industrial Relations Structures: Engineering Companies in the United Kingdom and the Federal Republic of Germany', *Labour and Society*, 7: 333–54.

IGCPK (Gewerkschaft Chemie, Papier, Keramik), 1978: 'Aufsichtsratswahlen', *Gewerkschaftliche Monatshefte*, 29: 682–9.

IG Metall, 1984: 'Beschäftigungsrisiken in der Autoindustrie. Vorschläge der IG Metall zur Beschäftigungssicherung und zur Strukturpolitik in diesem Industriebereich'. Frankfurt am Main, November.

IG Metall, 1985: 'Beschäftigungsrisiken in der Autoindustrie: Eine aktualisierte Berichterstattung zur Entwicklung der Beschäftigung in der Autoindustrie unter Einbeziehung der Arbeitsplatzeffekte aus der Verkürzung der Arbeitszeit. Vorgelegt vom Vorstand der IG Metall'. Frankfurt am Main, 11 September.

Jacobs, E., Orwell, S., Paterson P. and Weltz, F., 1978: *The Approach to Industrial Change in Britain and Germany*. London: Anglo-German Foundation for the Study of Industrial Society.

Jaikumar, R., 1986: 'Postindustrial Manufacturing', *Harvard Business Review*, November–December: 69–76.

John, P., 1979: *Handwerkskammern im Zwielicht: 700 Jahre Unternehmerinteressen im Gewande der Zunftidylle*. Frankfurt am Main: Europäische Verlagsanstalt.

Jürgens, J. and Unterhinninghofen, H., 1978: 'Unternehmertaktiken und -strategien zur Entmachtung des Aufsichtsrats', *Das Mitbestimmungsgespräch*: 88–95.

Kahn-Freund, O., 1967: 'A Note on Status and Contract in British Labor Law', *Modern Law Review*, 30: 635–44.

Kendall, W., 1975: *The Labour Movement in Europe*. London: Allen Lane.

Keohane, R.O. and Hoffmann, S. 1989: 'European Integration and Neo-functional Theory: Community Politics and Institutional Change', Ms. Cambridge, Mass.: Harvard University.

Kern, H. and Schumann, M., 1984: *Das Ende der Arbeitsteilung? Rationalisierung in der industriellen Produktion*. Munich: C.H. Beck.

Kerr, C., 1954: 'The Trade Union Movement and the Redistribution of Power in Postwar Germany', *The Quarterly Journal of Economics*, LXVII: 535–64.

Kerr, C., Dunlop, J.T., Harbison, F.H. and Myers, C.A., 1960: *Industrialism and Industrial Man: the Problems of Labor and Management in Economic Growth*. Cambridge, Mass.: Harvard University Press.

Kirchner, E.J. and Schwaiger, K., 1981: *The Role of Interest Groups in the European Community*. Farnborough: Gower.

Korpi, W., 1978: *The Working Class under Welfare Capitalism: Work, Unions and Politics in Sweden*. London: Routledge & Kegan Paul.

Koshiro, K., 1979: 'Japan's Labor Unions: the Meeting of White and Blue Collar', in Japan Culture Institute, *Politics and Economics in Contemporary Japan*. Tokyo: Japan Culture Institute. pp. 143–56.

Krupp, H.-J., 1984: 'Herausforderungen des Strukturwandels für die Wirtschaftspolitik', *Schriftenreihe über Arbeit und Arbeitsbeziehungen* 5/1985. Vienna: Bundesministerium für soziale Verwaltung. pp. 28–38.

Lehmbruch, G., 1979a: 'Liberal Corporatism and Party Government', in P.C. Schmitter and G. Lehmbruch (eds), *Trends towards Corporatist Intermediation*. London and Beverly Hills: Sage. pp. 147–83.

Lehmbruch, G., 1979b: 'Concluding Remarks: Problems for Future Research on Corporatist Intermediation and Policy-Making', in P.C. Schmitter and G. Lehmbruch (eds), *Trends towards Corporatist Intermediation*. Beverly Hills and London: Sage. pp. 299–309.

Lehmbruch, G., 1984: 'Concertation and the Structure of Corporatist Networks', in J.H. Goldthorpe (ed.), *Order and Conflict in Contemporary Capitalism*. Oxford: Clarendon Press. pp. 60–80.

Lindberg, L. and Scheingold, N. and S.A., 1970: *Europe's Would-Be Polity: Patterns of Change in the European Community*. Englewood Cliffs, New Jersey: Prentice Hall.

Lipietz, A., 1980: 'The Structuration of Space: the Problem of Land and Spatial Policy', in J. Carney, R. Hudson and J. Lewis (eds), *Regions in Crisis: New Perspectives in European Regional Theory*. London: Croom Helm.

Lodge, J. and Herman, V., 1990: 'The Economic and Social Committee in EEC Decision-Making', *International Organization*, 34: 265–284.

McCracken, P. et al., 1977: *Towards Full Employment and Price Stability: a Report to the OECD by a Group of Independent Experts*. Paris: Organisation for Economic Co-operation and Development.

MacNeil, I., 1974: 'The Many Futures of Contracts', *Southern California Law Review*, 47: 691–816.

Mahon, R., 1987: 'From Fordism to ?: New Technology, Labour Markets and Unions', *Economic and Industrial Democracy*, 8: 5–60.

Maier, H.E., 1987: Das Modell Baden-Württemberg: Über institutionelle Voraussetzungen differenzierter Qualitätsproduktion', *Discussion Paper* IIM/LMP 87–10a, Wissenschaftszentrum Berlin.

Maine, H.S., 1960: *Ancient Law: its Connection with the Early History of Society, and its Relations to Modern Ideas*. New York: Dutton.

Maitland, I., 1983: *The Causes of Industrial Disorder: a Comparison between a British and a German Factory*. London: Routledge & Kegan Paul.

Majone, G., 1989: 'Preservation of Cultural Diversity in a Federal System: the Role of the Regions'. Ms. Florence: European University Institute.

Marks, G., 1989: *Unions in Politics: Britain, Germany and the United States in the Nineteenth and Early Twetieth Centuries*. Princeton, New Jersey: Princeton University Press.

Marsden, D., 1981: 'Collective Bargaining and Positive Adjustment Policies', Working Party on Industrial Relations, MAS/WP3(81)4. Paris: Organization for Economic Co-operation and Development.

Marshall, T.H., 1964: *Class, Citizenship, and Social Development*. Garden City, New York: Doubleday & Company.

Marx, K. and Engels, F., 1964: 'Manifest der kommunistischen Partei', in Siegfried Landshut (ed.), *Karl Marx, Die Frühschriften*. Stuttgart: Alfred Kröner Verlag.

MBK (Mitbestimmungskommission), 1970: *Mitbestimmung im Unternehmen*. Stuttgart: W. Kohlhammer.

Meynaud, J. and Sidjanski, D., 1971: *Les groupes de pression dans la Communauté Européenne*. Brussels: Institut de Sociologie.

Mitbestimmung, 1982: 'Verlautbarung der Pressestelle des Bundesgerichtshofs': 121.

Mitbestimmungsgespräch, Das, 1979: 'Für ungehinderte Information und Zusammenarbeit. Eine Stellungnahme zu den BDA-Arbeitspapieren "Mitbestimmungsgesetz 1976"'.

Nagel, B., 1981: 'Beschaffung und Weitergabe von Informationen durch Mitbestimmungsträger im Aufsichtsrat', in H. Diefenbacher and H.G. Nutzinger (eds), *Mitbestimmung*. Frankfurt am Main: Campus. pp. 249–58.

Naphtali, F., 1928: *Wirtschaftsdemokratie: Ir Wesen, Weg und Ziel*. Berlin: Verlag des ADGB.

Neuloh, O., 1960: *Der neue Betriebsstil*. Tübingen: J.C.B. Mohr.

Niedenhoff, H.U., 1979: *Mitbestimmung in der Bundesrepublik Deutschland*. 3rd edn, Cologne: Deutscher Institutsverlag.

Nisbet, R.A., 1967: *The Sociological Tradition*. London: Heinemann.

Northrup, H.R., Campbell, D.C., Slowinski, B.J., 1988: 'Multinational Union–Management Consultation in Europe: Resurgence in the 1980s?', *International Labour Review*, 127: 525–43.

Nugent, N., 1989: *The Government and Politics of the European Community*. Durham, NC: Duke University Press.

Offe, C. and Wiesenthal, H., 1980: 'Two Logics of Collective Action: Theoretical Notes on Social Class and Organizational Form', *Political Power and Social Theory*, Vol. 1. Greenwich, Conn.: JAI Press Inc. pp. 67–115.

O'Higgins, M., 1985: 'Inequality, Redistribution and Recession: the British Experience, 1976–1982', *Journal of Social Policy*, 14: 279–307.

Olson, M., 1965: *The Logic of Collective Action: Public Goods and the Theory of Groups*. Cambridge, Mass.: Harvard University Press.

Olson, M., 1982: *The Rise and Decline of Nations*. Cambridge, Mass.: Harvard University Press.

Olson, M., 1983a: 'Beyond Keynesianism and Monetarism', *Discussion Paper* IIM/LMP 83–24, Wissenschaftszentrum Berlin.

Olson, M., 1983b: 'The Political Economy of Comparative Growth Rates', in D. Mueller, *The Political Economy of Growth*. New Haven, Conn., and London: Yale University Press. pp. 7–52.

Olson, M., 1986: 'A Theory of the Incentives Facing Political Organizations: Neo-corporatism and the Hegemonic State', *International Political Science Review*, 7: 165–89.

Ouchi, W.G., 1981: *Theory Z: How American Business can Meet the Japanese Challenge*. Reading, Mass.: Addison-Wesley.

Padoa-Schioppa, T., 1988: 'Questions about Creating a European Capital Market', in R. Bieber, R. Dehousse, J. Pinder and J.H.H. Weiler (eds), *1992: One European Market?* Baden-Baden: Nomos Verlagsgesellschaft. pp. 283–92.

Parsons, T., 1951: *The Social System*. New York: Free Press.

Parsons, T., 1968: *The Structure of Social Action*. New York: Free Press.

Perner, D., 1983: *Mitbestimmung im Handwerk? Die politische und soziale Funktion der Handwerkskammern im Geflecht der Unternehmerorganisationen*. Cologne: Bund-Verlag.

Peters, T.J. and Waterman, R.H., 1982: *In Search of Excellence: Lessons from America's Best-Run Companies*. New York: Harper & Row.

Piore, M.J. and Sabel, C.F., 1984: *The Second Industrial Divide: Possibilities for Prosperity*. New York: Basic Books.

Pirker, T. et al., 1955: *Arbeiter – Management – Mitbestimmung*. Stuttgart and Düsseldorf: Ring.

Platzer, H.-W., 1988: 'Transnational Politics of Interest Groups in Western Europe'. Ms. Tübingen.

Popitz, H. et al., 1957: *Das Gesellschaftsbild des Arbeiters*. Tübingen: J.C. Mohr Paul Siebeck.

Przeworski, A. and Wallerstein, M., 1982: 'Democratic Capitalism at the Cross-roads', *Democracy* (July): 52–68.

Puchala, D., 1972: 'Of Blind Men, Elephants and International Integration', *Journal of Common Market Studies*: 267–84.

Redfield, R., 1955: *The Little Community: Viewpoint for the Study of a Human Whole*. Chicago, Ill.: University of Chicago Press.

Regini, M., 1986: 'Political Bargaining in Western Europe during the Economic Crisis of the 1980s', in O. Jacobi et al. (eds), *Economic Crisis, Trade Unions and the State*. London: Croom Helm. pp. 61–76.

Repertoire des Organisations Professionelles crées dans le cadre des Communautés Européennes. Several editions. Brussels: Edition Delta.

Sabel, C.F., 1989: 'Flexible Specialization and the Re-emergence of Regional Economies', in P. Hirst and J. Zeitlin (eds), *Reversing Industrial Decline? Industrial Structure and Policy in Britain and her Competitors*. New York: St Martin's Press. pp. 17–70.

Sabel, C.F., Herrigel, G.B., Deeg, R. and Kazis, R., 1987: 'Regional Prosperities Compared: Massachusetts and Baden-Württemberg in the 1980s', *Discussion Paper* IIM/LMP 87–10b, Wissenschaftszentrum Berlin.

Sabel, C. and Kern, H., 1990: 'Trade Unions and Decentralized Production: a Sketch of Strategic Problems. Ms. Cambridge, Mass.: MIT.

Sandholtz, J. and Zysman, J., 1989: '1992: Recasting the European Bargain', *World Politics*, 23: 95–128.

Sargent, J., 1985: 'Corporatism and the European Community', in Wyn Grant (ed.), *The Political Economy of Corporatism*. London: Macmillan. pp. 229–53.

Scharpf, F.W., 1987: 'Inflation und Arbeitslosigkeit in Westeuropa: Eine spieltheoretische Interpretation'. Cologne: Max-Planck-Institut für Gesellschaftsforschung, ms.

Schmitter, P.C., 1974: 'Still the Century of Corporatism?', *The Review of Politics*, 36: 85–131.

Schmitter, P.C., 1988a: *Corporatism (Corporativism)*. Ms.

Schmitter, P.C., 1988b: '"Corporatism is Dead! Long Live Corporatism!" Reflections on Andrew Shonfield's "Modern Capitalism"', *Government and Opposition*. 24: 54–73.

Schmitter, P.C., 1989: 'A Sketch of an Eventual Article on the European Community as an Extreme Example of a Newly Emergent Form of Political Domination', Ms. Stanford, Calif.: Stanford University.

Schmitter, P.C. and Streeck, W., 1981: 'The Organization of Business Interests: a Research Design to Study the Associative Action of Business in the Advanced Industrial Societies of Western Europe', *Discussion Paper* IIM/LMP 81–13, Wissenschaftszentrum Berlin.

Selznick, P., 1969: *Law, Society, and Industrial Justice*. New York: Russell Sage Foundation.

Shell, 1985: *Deutsche Shell-Aktiengesellschaft, Hamburg: Verunsicherung hinterläßt Bremsspuren: Shell-Prognose des PKW-Bestandes bis zum Jahr 2000*. September.

Skidelsky, R., 1979: 'The Decline of Keynesian Politics', in C. Crouch, (ed.), *State and Economy in Contemporary Capitalism*. London: Croom Helm. pp. 55–87.

Sorge, A., 1985: *Informationstechnik und Arbeit im sozialen Prozess: Arbeitsorganization, Qualifikation und Produktivkraftentwicklung*. Frankfurt am Main: Campus.

Sorge, A. and Streeck, W., 1988: 'Industrial Relations and Technical Change: the Case for an Extended Perspective', in R. Hyman and W. Streeck (eds), *New Technology and Industrial Relations*. Oxford: Basil Blackwell. pp. 19–47.

Sorge, A. and Warner, M., 1986: *Comparative Factory Organization: an Anglo-German Comparison of Manufacturing, Management and Manpower*. Aldershot: Gower.

Spencer, H., 1961: *The Study of Sociology*. Ann Arbor: University of Michigan Press.

Spie, U. and Bahlmann, W., 1978: 'Arbeitsdirektoren in der Eisen- und Stahlindustrie', *Das Mitbestimmungsgespräch*: 245–50, 272–8, 301–8.

Spieker, W., 1977: 'Gewerkschaftliche Grundfragen der Mitbestimmung auf Unternehmensebene', in U. Borsdorf et al. (eds), *Gewerkschaftliche Politik: Reform und Solidarität*. Cologne: Bund-Verlag. pp. 353–72.

Springer, B., 1989: *The Social Dimension: Progress or Retreat* Ms.

Strauss, G., 1984: 'Industrial Relations: Time of Change', *Industrial Relations*, 23: 1–15.

Streeck, W., 1978: 'Staatliche Ordungspolitik und industrielle Beziehungen: Zum Verhältnis von Integration und Institutionalisierung gewerkschaftlicher Interessenverbände am Beispiel des britischen Industrial Relations Act von 1971', *Politische Vierteljahresschrift*, Special Issue 9: 106–39.

Streeck, W., 1979: 'Gewerkschaftsorganisation und industrielle Beziehungen. Einige Stabilitätsprobleme industriegewerkschaftlicher Interessenvertretung und ihre Lösung im System der industriellen Beziehungen der Bundesrepublik Deutschland', in Joachim Matthes (ed.), *Sozialer Wandel in Westeuropa: Verhandlungen des 19. Deutschen Soziologentags*. Frankfurt am Main: Campus. pp. 206–26.

Streeck, W., 1981a: *Gewerkschaftliche Organisationsprobleme in der sozialstaatlichen Demokratie*. Königstein/Ts.: Athenäum.

Streeck, W., 1981b: 'Qualitative Demands and the Neo-corporatist Manageability of Industrial Relations: Trade Unions and Industrial Relations in West Germany at the Beginning of the Eighties', *British Journal of Industrial Relations*, 14: 149–69.

Streeck, W., 1982: 'Organizational Consequences of Corporatist Cooperation in West German Labor Unions: a Case Study', in Gerhard Lehmbruch and P.C. Schmitter, (eds), *Patterns of Corporatist Policy-making*. Beverly Hills, Calif., and London: Sage. pp. 29–81.

Streeck, W., 1983: 'Die Reform der beruflichen Bildung in der westdeutschen Bauwirtschaft 1969–1982: Eine Fallstudie über Verbände als Träger öffentlicher Politik', *Discussion Paper* IIM/LMP 83–23, Wissenschaftszentrum Berlin.

Streeck, W., 1984a: *Industrial Relations in West Germany: the Case of the Car Industry*. London: Heinemann/New York: St Martin's Press.

Streeck, W., 1984b: 'Neo-corporatist Industrial Relations and the Economic Crisis in West Germany', in John Goldthorpe (ed.), *Order and Conflict in Contemporary Capitalism: Studies in the Political Economy of West European Nations*. Oxford: Clarendon Press. pp. 291–314.

Streeck, W., 1987a: 'Industrial Relations and Industrial Change: the Restructuring of the World Automobile Industry in the 1970s', *Economic and Industrial Democracy*, 8: 437–62.

Streeck, W., 1987b: 'The Uncertainties of Management in the Management of Uncertainty: Employers, Labor Relations and Industrial Adjustment in the 1980s', *Work, Employment and Society* 1: 281–308, and *International Journal of Political Economy*, 17: 57–87.

Streeck, W., 1989: 'Skills and the Limits of Neo-liberalism: the Enterprise of the Future as a Place of Learning', *Work, Employment and Society*, 3: 90–104.

Streeck, W., 1991: 'More Uncertainties: West German Unions Facing 1992', *Industrial Relations*, 30: 317–49.

Streeck, W., forthcoming: 'The Social Dimension of the European Economy', in W. Hager, D. Mayes and W. Streeck, *Public Interest and Market Pressures: Problems Posed by Europe 1992*. London: Macmillan.

Streeck, W., Hilbert, J., van Kevelaer, K.-H., Maier, F. and Weber, H., 1987: *The Role of the Social Partners in Vocational Training and Further Training in the Federal Republic of Germany*. Berlin: European Centre for the Development of Vocational Training (CEDEFOP).

Streeck, W. and Hoff, A., 1983: 'Manpower Management and Industrial Relations in the Restructuring of the World Automobile Industry', *Discussion Paper* IIM/LMP 83–35, Wissenschaftszentrum Berlin.

Streeck, W. and Rampelt, J., 1982: 'Einstellungen und Erwartungen von Unternehmern gegenüber Wirtschaftsverbänden: Ergebnisse einer Befragung von Unternehmern in der Berliner Bauwirtschaft', *Discussion Paper* IIM/LMP 82–12, Wissenschaftszentrum Berlin.

Streeck, W. and Schmitter, P.C., 1985: 'Community, Market, State – and Associations? The Prospective Contribution of Interest Governance to Social Order', *European Sociological Review*, 1: 119–38.

Stütz, G., 1969: *Das Handwerk als Leitbild der deutschen Berufserziehung*. Göttingen: Vandenhoeck und Ruprecht.

Swenson, P., 1989: *Fair Shares: Unions, Pay and Politics in Sweden and West*

Germany. Cornell Studies in Political Economy. Ithaca, New York: Cornell University Press.

Tannenbaum, F., 1964: *The True Society: a Philosophy of Labour*. London: Jonathan Cape.

Teague, P., 1989a: 'Trade Unions and Extra-National Industrial Policies: a Case Study of the Response of the British NUM and ISTC to Membership in the European Coal and Steel Community', *Economic and Industrial Democracy*, 10: 211–37.

Teague, P., 1989b: 'Constitution or Regime? The Social Dimension to the 1992 Project', *British Journal of Industrial Relations*, 27: 310–29.

Teague, P. and Grahl, J., 1989: 'European Community Labour Market Policy: Present Scope and Future Direction', *Journal of European Integration*, 13: 55–73.

Tegtmeier, W., 1973: *Wirkungen der Mitbestimmung der Arbeitnehmer*. Göttingen: Vandenhoeck und Ruprecht.

Teubner, G., 1980: '§ 242 (Grundsatz von Treu und Glauben)', in: G. Brüggemeier et al., *Kommentar zum Bürgerlichen Gesetzbuch*. Vol. 2, Allgemeines Schuldrecht. Neuwied: Luchterhand. pp. 32–91.

Thompson, J.D., 1967: *Organizations in Action*. New York: McGraw-Hill.

Titmuss, R.M., 1970: *The Gift Relationship: from Human Blood to Social Policy*. London: Allen & Unwin.

Tolliday, S. and Zeitlin, J., (eds), 1986: *The Automobile Industry and its Workers: between Fordism and Flexibility*. Oxford: Polity Press.

Treu, H.-E., 1979: *Stabilität und Wandel in der organisatorischen Entwicklung der Gewerkschaften: Eine Studie über die organisatorische Entwicklung der Industriegewerkschaft Bergbau und Energie*. Frankfurt am Main: Rita G. Fischer.

Unterhinninghofen, H., 1978: 'Aufsichtsratswahlen 1978: Erfolge und Probleme', *Gewerkschaftliche Monatshefte*, 29: 654–65.

VdTÜV (Vereinigung der Technischen Überwachungsvereine im Auftrage des Bundesministers für Verkehr) (ed.), 1986: 'Untersuchung der Auswirkungen einer Geschwindigkeitsbegrenzung auf das Abgas-Emissionsverhalten von Personenkraftwagen auf Autobahnen: Abgas-Großversuch'. Cologne and Bonn.

Vidich, A.J., 1982: 'The Moral, Economic and Political Status of Labor in American Society', *Social Research*, 49: 753–90.

Visser, J., 1989: 'Trade Union Diversity in Western Europe: Dimensions, Origins, and Consequences'. Paper presented at the IRRU conference on 'Industrial Relations and the European Community', University of Warwick, 17–19 March.

Visser, J., 1990: *In Search of Inclusive Unionism*. Bulletin of Comparative Labor Relations 18. Deventer and Boston, Mass.: Kluwer.

Wallyn, L., 1988: 'The Social Policy of the Community and Participation of the Social Partners in Decision-Making at European Level', *Social Europe*, 1: 13–20.

Webber, D., 1986: 'The Framework of Government–Industry Relations and Industrial Policy Making in the Federal Republic of Germany'. *University of Sussex Working Papers Series on Government-Industry Relations* No. 1. Brighton: University of Sussex.

Weber, M., 1978: *Economy and Society* (eds Günther Roth and Claus Wittich). Berkeley, Calif., Los Angeles and London: University of California Press.

Weekes, B. et al., 1975: *Industrial Relations and the Limits of Law: the Industrial Effects of the Industrial Relations Act*. Oxford: Basil Blackwell.

Wernet, Wilhelm, 1965: *Zur Frage der Abgrenzung von Handwerk und Industrie:*

Die wirtschaftlichen Zusammenhänge in ihrer Bedeutung für die Beurteilung von Abgrenzungsfragen. Münster: Handwerkswissenschaftliches Institut.

Wilks, S., 1984: *Industrial Policy and the Motor Industry*. Manchester and Dover: Manchester University Press.

Williamson, O.E., 1975: *Markets and Hierarchies: Analysis and Antitrust Implications*. New York: The Free Press.

Williamson, O.E., 1979: 'Transaction Cost Economics: the Governance of Contractual Relations', *Journal of Law and Economics*, 22: 233–61.

Williamson, O.E., 1980: 'The Organization of Work: a Comparative Institutional Assessment', *Journal of Economic Behavior and Organization*, 1: 5–38.

Williamson, O.E., Wachter, M.L. and Harris, J., 1975: 'Understanding the Employment Relation: The Analysis of Idiosyncratic Exchange', *The Bell Journal of Economics*, 6: 250–78.

Willman, P., 1986: 'New Technology and Industrial Relations: a Review of the Literature'. Department of Employment Research Papers. London: HMSO.

Wilpert, B., 1975: 'Research on Industrial Democracy: the German Case', *Industrial Relations Journal*, 5: 53–64.

Witte, E., 1980: 'Der Einfluß der Arbeitnehmer auf die Unternehmenspolitik', *Die Betriebswirtschaft*, 40: 541–59.

Witte, E., 1981: 'Die Unabhängigkeit des Vorstandes im Einflußsystem der Unternehmung', *Zeitschrift für betriebswirtschaftliche Forschung*, 33: 273–96.

Witte, E., 1982a: 'Klassenkampf und Gruppenkampf im Unternehmen: Abschied von der Konfliktideologie', in H.-D. Ortlieb et al., (eds), *Hamburger Jahrbuch für Wirtschafts- und Gesellschaftspolitik*, 27: 167–82.

Witte, E., 1982b: 'Das Einflußsystem der Unternehmung in den Jahren 1976 und 1981: Empirische Befunde im Vergleich', *Zeitschrift für betriebswirtschaftliche Forschung*, 34: 416–34.

Wood, S. and Elliott, R., 1977: 'A Critical Evaluation of Fox's Radicalization of Industrial Relations Theory', *Sociology*, 2: 105–25.

WSI-Mitteilungen, 1981: 'Die mitbestimmten Unternehmen gemäß MitbestG 1976 bis zum 30. Juni 1981', *WSI-Mitteilungen*: 569–73.

Zander, E., 1981: 'Personalwirtschaftliche Konsequenzen der unternehmensverfassungsrechtlichen Mitbestimmung', in K. Bohr et al., (eds), *Unternehmensverfassung als Problem der Betriebswirtschaftslehre*. Berlin: Erich Schmidt Verlag, pp. 309–28.

Zelditch, M. Jr., 1968: 'Status, Social', in D. L. Sills (ed.), *International Encyclopedia of the Social Sciences*, Vol. 15. London: Macmillan. pp. 250–73.

Index